We Are in This Together!

by Dr. Donald Salem

RoseDog Books
PITTSBURGH, PENNSYLVANIA 15238

RoseDog Books
585 Alpha Drive
Suite 103
Pittsburgh, PA 15238
Visit our website at www.rosedogbookstore.com

ISBN: 978-1-6442-6712-7
eISBN: 978-1-6442-6735-6

This book and these herculean volumes are dedicated to the patience of my wife, Roen, the encouragement of my children and inspiration of friends, like Moti and Harvey. I am monumentally grateful, but take full responsibility for these volumes!

Introduction

I was astounded at what I had come across over the years: thousands of linked events and facts veering into oblivion. It was obvious to me that we faced clear and abundant threats to our culture of freedom, democracy and tolerance. Even more so, it was a giant mystery that our leadership could leave us at such risk. I kept asking myself, how dumb can we be?

I saw a way to shine some light on the problems that our democracy faces. I merged a satirical parable of a painful, surprisingly destructive environmental cataclysm, with the broad reality of a magnified 9/11.

To explain this, I created five characters, survivors of that catastrophe, who do tremendous research to light the apparent darkness. They attempt to answer the mystery of "how dumb can we be?"

I called them the Fiery Five. With their pain and losses, they had a fierce determination to learn how this disaster happened and how to prevent the next. They worked like Sherlock Holmes times five.

In the real world, some of us already grasped those serious dangers, but it required a super team and a magnificent electronic media resource to share how close these threats are. The "Fiery Five" reviewed over 40 years of my reading and research, over 40,000 articles, and over a hundred books. To make sense of all the research, they connected the dots for us and created the clearest of pictures from which conclusions and decisions could be made. But would our clergy, elected officials and those who shape public awareness be willing to read and act before it was too late?

Narrated by the "Fiery Five", these findings were shared in 22 chapters. An important discovery occurred when they realized that Israel is not only a valuable ally to the USA, but our miner's canary. We can learn from Israel's challenges and triumphs how to protect our way of life. The Five exposed the costly mistakes of self-serving government officials, the failures of condescending academics, the coddled entitled attitudes and haughty entertainment moguls. There were many toplofty clergy and outspoken arrogant actors spouting political solutions.

They discovered an "incidentism" forced on the military.

But they were most appalled by failures of the main stream media to report balanced news, maintain objectivity and to avoid advocacy. A propagandized media is the surest way to erode our exceptional way of life.

My belief is that if citizens are educated, motivated, steadfast and proactively move to deal with the perils that face us, we can assure our future won't fall again into the inferno of some of our past nightmares. I learned the essential value that allies need real allies.

After reading this, readers will be able to lift the shroud surrounding what and who is attacking our exceptional way of life. They will have clarity of how our current misperceptions, especially of the Middle East, are undermining our way of life. Leaders will be able to proactively protect what we have held dear.

With that hurdle in mind, I recalled the English political theorist Lord Acton saying: ***"It is difficult to prophesy, especially about the future."***

The mystery we must solve is, CnWeGtSmrtFstEnf?

Sincerely,

Ploni Almoni

***Caveat Lector: Quotes and sources can be verified online if not listed.

Book 1 We Are in This Together!

#1 The American Dream: Can We Regain it?

Why is it that in the lushest of times, only few imagine how bad this could become?

Overindulged, Simon Callwell lounged in his body conforming, leather surround-sound chair, with his second latte of the day, dreaming of new ways to enjoy himself.

At the same time, unnamed government sources, those without their first latte, said that "alarmist" weathermen, volcanologists and seismologists had exaggerated the threats of unusually concentrated cloud formations and lightning bolts that were knocking down power lines in many different countries.

They did not deny the ominously dark sky and swirling, howling winds creating tornadoes. They did not want a picture of floating inverted volcanos cremating small towns on television. But the government told everyone not to worry. Those who double-checked the YouTube videos saw the devastation and did worry.

Who could believe this?

Photoshop for sure!

Why did governments declare it was too risky for airplanes to fly?

Certain volcanologists blamed this on the Ring of Fire Volcanoes in the Pacific that were shooting lava thousands of feet into the air.

Could that supervolcano in Yellowstone National Park erupt again?

The President supplied that these people were scare mongers using photoshop.

Not in our lifetime, harrumphed Simon as he dittoed the President.

Government sources marginalized the reports as being fake news and hysterical. But no one in government even mentioned a supervolcano eruption about 70,000 years ago at the site of Lake Toba in Sumatra, Indonesia. It caused a volcanic winter that blocked out the sun for between six to eight years and resulted in a period of global cooling lasting a thousand years.

Scare tactics wouldn't work with Simon Callwell. At 26 he already had a graduate degree from Harvard in the economics of climate anthropology. Everyone who was anyone knew that the Earth's weather pattern of warming and cooling followed cycles over the millennia. He had learned that major solar flares, heated water from leaks in the planet's core, and eruption of a super-volcano could totally change the planet's climate.

At the end of the day, government sources assured the public, that the dark skies from the volcanoes could not affect us. They guaranteed that our leaders would be on the right side of history.

Some of Simon's friends wagged their politically correct fingers at him reminding him that only U.S. reduction of fossil fuels could create a sustainable world environment. Then the skies would be clear again.

But reasonable people knew that fossil fuel excesses were far greater half way around the world where growing economies were exploding. Like there was no Russia, China, or India that could impact the world more than the U.S.?

The government now put out the word that the alarmists were divisive to our pluralistic thinking and to ignore them.

Offended, Simon wondered. "Divisive to pluralism? Isn't that just a contradiction in terms?"

Journalists rhapsodized that one man's weather map is another man's divining rod. One man's volcanologist was another man's fire happy geologist.

It would get better if government would just appease the self-proclaimed weather experts.

Reflective Simon was aware of his immigrant, grandfather's poverty and how he had established the beginnings of an exceptional business. His grandfather had not experienced this equal opportunity in the "old country" as he did in the USA. He heard stories of how his grandfather volunteered to go off to war to fight the Nazis, leaving one of his arms in Europe.

Simon's father had taken advantage of what his father had done and used those opportunities to grow the business into a worldwide conglomerate. Simon knew that exceptionalism in the USA was tied to upward mobility for those who strived. That was the American Dream!

On rare occasions, Simon wondered if he was entitled to any of this wealth.

No wondering right now. The big game was on and his team was in the playoffs! That was important.

Chunky Simon just nuzzled in between the plush cushions in his glove-soft, red Italian leather chair. His hair was marvelously done for only $400. A smile played upon his face as he washed down warm French pastries with his non-fat, cinnamon topped cappuccino latte. His 120" OE-LED/ Plasma, 3D 4KTV was focused on the last game of his team's basketball playoffs.

Now this was the fun he was entitled to!

Some said that all teams were equal, but his team had created an exceptional record this year. They weren't perfect but as an exceptional team they had earned first place.

Doesn't get better than this!

During a commercial he looked outside - eerie darkness.

Selfish Simon had surround sound to block the surging outdoor noises. It was better than being at the overcrowded playoff, the backed-up bathroom lines and horrible waits at over-priced food stands. And they did not even have his favorite, Fettuccini Alfredo adorned with mellow French truffles.

The ugly weather was the government's problem. The public was told they would be on the right side of history if they did not question the government's fiat that volcano debris could not create that much excessive force.

Simon's progressive government insisted that we must be fair and give the sun a chance to come out. They declared that tolerance was what the country believed in and not a rush to judgment.

Rigid Simon believed in fairness and tolerance for all. Those who disagreed with his position should keep quiet.

He ignored bullet-like torrents of rain, quivering in waves against his case-hardened windows.

Not comforting right now.

He was entitled to more important things, like the Finals.

No question, at the end of the day, he and those who thought like him would be on the right side of history.

No need to take extreme measures.

To others, that view of "be happy, don't worry" sounded like paralysis or a concealed indecisiveness, not progressiveness.

Happy Simon was smugly confident. He already had it all, including an exceptionally strong, termite resistant, earthquake reinforced house his father had willed to him.

His computerized heating unit would always keep him toasty despite rapidly dropping temperatures.

Sometime after the first quarter, his fiancé', Yael, thought that she heard dripping of water somewhere.

He scoffed and discounted it. Couldn't take time away from the big game.

Several commercials later, he heard what sounded like a train roaring outside his house.

Just wind.

The game got more exciting in the second quarter. Simon knew he could deal with the nuisance drip later. With a phone call, he would outsource, just like the government.

Overreacting was not his style. We should wait and see how this works out.

Alarmists over react.

Over reaction was the way of the extremists, not good people.

Surely the damaging weather would moderate if we gave it time. He began to hum, "The sun will come out tomorrow."

The "alarmists" responding narrative was that Simon should just look out his oversized picture window and connect the dots.

Why believe what you see when you can see what you believe?

Others could deal with it.

A news special interrupted the game. There was looting in several cities and the police were unprepared. Looters claimed they had been victimized by inadequate housing, small welfare checks, poor schools, inadequate medical care, and proper protection.

Progressives explained that these were just competing narratives of the alarmists and the government.

But alarmism was not for Simon. His people would not use disproportionate measures. People, like him required a "smoking gun", the undeniable, substantiated, tested proofs first.

Nonetheless his mansion, far from the beaten road, was protected by walls

10 feet high and a steep slope down to the river.

The walls made him confident. And Simon knew that police would protect him so he felt no need for weapons.

At half time, Simon looked up and saw that the dripping actually was coming from a ceiling tile. He asked his fiancé, Yael, if there might be an open window upstairs. Maybe one of the maids left the sliding door open on the sun deck.

Affluent Simon opened his brand new 10G video-cell phone to get the latest weather report. Then he changed his mind and decided to call other friends and neighbors to ask if they wanted to come over to watch the big game on the life size TV. He would treat to pizza, popcorn and beer.

Yael was now sitting in her comfort chair amused at Simon working his calls.

She was not happy that he was trying to talk friends into coming over in this dangerous weather by offering food and fun.

"People love treats," reasoned Simon. These treats would bring confidence building measures to make sure his friends would stand with him in this horrible weather.

When his buddies arrived, some were soaked. Some had umbrellas turned inside out.

Whoa, did they have narratives, tales and stories about their problems.

Salo, an old friend from school, swore it was raining dirt or ash and he hadn't seen the sun for days. This was not predicted.

Just another narrative.

Bill's story was that he had survived violent, baseball sized hail and swirling winds that had dented his car and cracked his windshield.

Ha, probably the size of marbles.

An old-time friend, Tom the techy geek, had found some small termite droppings and holes in the woodwork at home, but he sealed the borders of his windows because rain was muscling in.

Not Simon's job to interpret the weather.

No time to listen to offbeat narratives. Besides, he heard the government say the weather was worse in other countries but would never get that bad here.

"Get over it", Simon thought, "My government knows what it is talking about."

The government assured the TV viewers that the intensity of the weather would moderate. Volcanoes come and volcanoes blow on the surface of the planet and that was just temporary.

Despite his hopes, the dripping, dirty water and drumming of the hail were not stilled. It could not be as extreme as a small handful of scare-mongers said.

But it was sure dark and weird out there.

Strange high-pitched noises from whiny wind outside were distracting but life was good inside his home.

Those were other people's problems.

During the fourth quarter the guys were jumping and cheering for their team. One friend noticed that a ceiling tile was bulging like muscles on a steroid weight lifter but was afraid to say anything that might upset his friends. You got to go along to get along.

Simon turned up the surround sound volume on the TV and settled in for victory.

They all knew that this was their last window of opportunity to see their team win. What was more important, really?

They could ignore the weather for a while longer.

The tile would not break.

Less than five minutes before the game was to end, the stretched ceiling tile gave way. A chilling shower of grey, murky water and plaster chunks poured onto Simon's head and chair.

Yuck…

He could easily have it replaced tomorrow.

What was more important was to get back to the good times. His team was winning!

Simple Simon was confident that he would not have to make any painful choices.

He grabbed a big towel and stumbled over the mess and joined his friends on the big couch.

Enjoy yourself!

Many academics still said this weather would moderate if we would do our part. They insisted that it was important to change our ways to appease these angry conditions outside. All we had to do was make some concessions.

Back to the finals.

The guys were screaming for their team to score when a deep crackling noise interrupted the game.

There was a loud crunch as though the roof was hit by a meteor.

Several drenched ceiling tiles burst open.

Icy waterfalls, filled with chunks of the roof, wood and wires cascaded down on everyone.

Smoke billowed from the cracked TV set.

No picture.

Room dark.

Ear splitting, unnerving squall, inside and out.

Friends panicked and scattered. Andy lay motionless on the floor next to a brick sized chunk of hard brown roof tile.

Warmth fled.

An apple sized hail stone hammered the side of Simon's head and he toppled off the couch onto the slimy floor grasping his head in pain.

Blood.

Dazed Simon looked up. An angry grey sky, like the evil eyes of TerVol glared at him. He had heard of that chimera and now it had become painfully real!

Where was his fiancé?

Fear, paralyzing fear.

Everyone was bleeding from flying shards of glass and falling ceiling parts.

Some were hemorrhaging into connecting lakes on the floor.

A roof air conditioner crushed Bill and he drowned in the red, murky swamp that had been an elegant TV room, moments before.

Simon had never imagined that his survival was in question until now.

These things only happen to others.

Days later the nightmare began to fade from their puny memories and some sun was visible.

Wet, cold and hungry, Simon and Yael realized that his self-centered wealth had been decimated, but fortunately not eliminated.

Bandaged Simon, still in pain, had time to think, to connect some dots and begin to adjust his attitude.

He and Yael talked.

The citizens of the country should not tolerate this lack of preparation, the concealed information, the incompetence, and brutal demonization of any who disagreed with the politically correct position!

This was existential and to lose was to lose everything.

Trembling Simon recalled his college days and the warning from Thomas Mann, "Tolerance is a crime when applied to evil." Tolerance to negligence was also a crime.

Karl Popper, the well-known sociologist who expanded that "Unlimited tolerance must lead to the disappearance of tolerance. If we extend unlimited tolerance even to those who are intolerant, if we are not prepared to defend a tolerant society against the onslaught of the intolerant, then the tolerant will be destroyed, and tolerance with them." On the Paradox of Tolerance, in The Open Society and Its Enemies, 1945.

Days later the super storm had completely subsided, paramedics had come and gone, windows were boarded up and those friends who hadn't been hospitalized returned to their damaged homes.

Simon began connecting the dots. Why didn't he notice that the government appeared to be tolerating these conditions and not preparing the people? It now seemed obvious the people had been misled.

There were many examples of tolerating risk in history that had become the proverbial Trojan horses. His government had let those destructors of their exceptional country ride in the same way the democratic society of ancient Greece was destroyed.

Gaining clarity, Simon began shaking off the cold as he wondered, "How Dumb Can We Be?"

What a Mystery! He had not experienced this much confusion or pain in his life. What motivation!

The average person in our exceptional country has potential answers from the World Wide Web. People can be informed.

Simon decided that most Americans had become lazy, lushly affluent, unquestioningly mislead and many were dependent on entitlements and government handouts.

It was now obvious that the presumed boogeyman, TerVol, was the sum of silent, pacifying, selfish germ-carrying *ter*mite colonies and .the catastrophic capacities of violent *vol*canoes, tornados and earthquakes. That is how TerVol got its name.

• •

"The world is a dangerous place to live, not because of the people who are evil, but because of the people who don't do anything about it," said Albert Einstein.

There were times when Simon's fiancé would burst into tears if clouds became dark. Simon would sometimes jump at the sound of a light switch going on. These painful feelings caused them to resolve to never again be put in that position of vulnerability that those violent storms and governmental rot had created.

People in pain don't change until the pain becomes too great not to change.

How the suffering that they had experienced had come about was a big mystery to most people across the land.

Simon needed to get out of his house and go for a walk in the shell-shocked neighborhood.

In a local, boarded up but functioning coffee shop, Simon connected with some acquaintances who were also overwhelmed with hundreds of questions. Most were angry that the government had let them down. They needed clarity. They needed someone to solve the mystery of TerVol's sudden power.

Yael, a deeper thinker, added some questions:

Why not start by trash-canning the "silly solutions" that clutter our minds with ambiguity, confusion and disunity?

Simon laughed when someone said that suicide was always a "solution."

Where was the information from our allies who had other resources? Why wasn't it shared?

Simon puffed out his chest because he knew his job would be to find out how to identify and conquer this evil, TerVol.

Was this really a violent external threat or a silent internal implosion of forgotten responsibilities and greed for entitlements?

Was this the beginning of the end of the American Dream?

Why are so many countries ignoring the deathly failure of that tolerance seen as (unreciprocated) multiculturalism?

Had political conformity smothered debate by demonizing the other?

Why should we deny our exceptionalism and core values to appease those who are jealous?

Are we being made victims of the termite colonies, those of personal self-indulgence, aggressive demands for entitlement and national self-flagellation?

What could prevent another jet liner from flying into a sky scraper, poisoning a water supply, frying our electrical grid or destroying our communications system?

Without the availability of the "American Dream", how can we sustain our exceptionalism?

Would these events surely and seamlessly merge into the next major tragedy if we did not discover our errors and change our ways before we lose it all?

Simon says: I got it. We are giving up on our exceptionalism. We have lost the work ethic and replaced it with easily accepted entitlements. Public servants have become self-serving bureaucrats. Our government won't acknowledge that! How dumb can we be, and can we get smart fast enough and become proactive pursuing the American Dream?

Look, we are all benefiting, one way or another, in the ongoing American Dream. It was gifted to us by the Founding Fathers, the Declaration of Independence, the Constitution and the fallen, wounded soldiers. The gifts included freedom of opportunity, the ability to serve, the potential for personal prosperity, upward mobility, the right to pursue happiness with responsibility, free public exchange of ideas, personal security, a fair legal system and freedom of religion. To those who will work hard for as long as it takes, accept the risks and save wisely, the American Dream is at their fingertips. But the Founding Fathers never guaranteed a perfectly groomed, thorn-free rose garden.

Let's see what Simon says once he discovered the value of teamwork and that meant international teamwork, too. Simon scanned the planet. Most European countries had given up on free speech and upward mobility. He found another democratic society also facing the challenges of maintaining exceptionalism in tiny Israel.

Simon had some initial clarity about having a base of thought to solve a problem. He realized what all great philosophers had taught, that one needs to understand one's own values to provide a basis for success in any big endeavor, business, political, economic, or military. It is the only thing which gives consistency to one's efforts. A democratic society's survival must be based on reality, not projection of one's values and feelings onto others.

Simon had read Aristotle's seminal discussion in Politics: A Treatise on Government. Aristotle stressed the necessity of active and committed citizens if the state is to flourish and remain strong; where such commitment is absent, the state invariably grows weak and decays into anarchy or absolutism. Those who are on the hand out, get hung out. A government that gives you things can take away things. There is no escaping these signs of a civilization in decline.

Simon had no choice. He knew that he had to start with a bedrock base, learning about human behavior from philosophy, history and politics. He would need intense focus and energy.

After we find the dots (called facts), connect them, and erase ambiguity, then we can create a clear picture. With a clear picture, applying sound principles (he would call that ***authentic hindsight***) to current, real time situations we build a superstructure for foresight and proactive movements.

Even with his academic background, and plunging into the web, it took weeks of staring at the computer screens to recognize the obvious: that this mystery was very, very big and complex. The dots were at his fingertips. There were just too many of them. As he discovered more, his cockiness shrunk more.

Bleary eyed and feeling overwhelmed, he finally admitted to himself that he was incapable of handling all the research on his own, let alone drawing proper conclusions. He was pressured because there was no time to waste.

The dark pressure almost caused him to quit. He found a spark and decided to give this mystery one more chance. He thought about his connections from school and business. And in a last gasp frenzy, he began calling whoever he thought would join him to solve this mystery. The spark was teamwork.

A new Simon emerged.

Simon Callwell loved games like Clue or figuring out solutions to his

Rubik's Cubes and puzzles while sipping chocolate milk and eating bags of chocolate chip cookies. That was how he got his nickname, "Chip." This mystery was like a dozen interconnected giant Rubik's Cubes. His graduate work at Harvard reinforced the idea that he had a good mind, but his inherited wealth made him a bit of a self-indulgent, lazy narcissist.

He was determined to understand what had happened and the new Simon appeared. He had to create a team.

He went out and bought four large Sony HD computer screens, a magnificent server, a box of chocolate covered croissants, a little refrigerator and a microwave to decorate his enormous wood paneled study. Now he had his mansion rebuilt with extra caution such as double backup electrical power, independent plumbing, and special locking entries with eye-scanner coding. Even he had to laugh at this paranoid approach.

He placed his chunky fingers on his ivory keyboard to ask "Uncle Google" some questions! He still kidded himself that he could do it.

He fell asleep that night wondering what his resources could be?

About a week later, many dead-end phone calls, dozens of cups of cappuccino and five more belly-pounds worth of chocolate chip cookies and croissants, Simon was ready to quit again.

He slumped down in his chair and slid onto his plush carpet. His cocky self-confidence was evaporating even more rapidly. There were just too many uncertain constructive and destructive dots for him to connect from too many different areas.

He felt the urgency. He was losing his temper. He kept bumping into the reality that to solve this problem he had to set aside some of his ego. He needed more than his energy, money, or knowledge to solve the mystery. Before he pulled out what was left of his hair, he realized that he needed help!

A few days later, dismayed Simon walked into that semi boarded up local coffee shop and noticed some acquaintances. He looked around as they jabbered and joked. What was happening in their heads? Why did they appear oblivious as to how the horrendous damage that had occurred? Someone had to be as upset as he!

Sipping a cappuccino his first thought turned to the person to whom he was closest, his beautiful, all too independent, fiancé, **Yael Marrano.** They did love basketball. They really enjoyed a good argument and each other's intellect. She even laughed at his jokes. Aside from the other attributes they shared together, he knew that the training her Ph.D. in Middle Eastern Religions and History held an area that he could not fathom. Besides, she had spent years living in the Middle East and was fluent in Hebrew, Arabic and Farsi. She could read resources that no one else could. He figured that nothing is like that type of experience. Simon, like most, had no insight into these cultures, religions or languages. He needed her more than ever.

Comfortably perched in a chair, like the Cheshire Cat, Simon smirked because he knew he could use his charm and their relationship to excite her into joining this ultra-marathon.

At first Yael thought he was nuts. The job was too big. Let the government do it. Simon convinced her why they had to do it, why they could no longer have the same trust in the government or the mainstream media. He was imagining that this was how Rand Corporation came into being.

Yael had more common sense and positivity than Simon and convinced him that by using his wealth and superb salesmanship, they could get three or four other qualified, determined people as a team. This time, Simon set aside enough ego and decided to listen to his fiancé. Well, maybe he did some begging, too. But it wasn't that easy for an egotist to deal with a very bright maverick.

During another trip to the bandaged coffee shop, Simon happened to glance around and his eyes and mind fell on **Tom Konvertere,** a dispassionate, often boring, computer geek. He had been at the basketball final playoffs when the house gave way to the attack by the environment.

He knew that Tom's parents had fled Denmark at the start of WW II and he figured Tom would be more sensitive than he appeared because of his proximity to that tragedy. Tom's poker face hid the depths Tom's upset. Inside, his wounds were still throbbing.

For some reason Tom wanted to hide his Danish background. He always wore faded denim shirts, tired blue jeans, and scruffy cowboy boots. Tom could be mistaken for a forgettable ranch hand who always had one hand on a cup of black coffee, but no cigarette. He had a dark handle bar mustache, long side burns and loved to wear that cowboy hat with the hidden video camera; real, blend-in Americana. What time zone was he from, thought Simon?

Simon assessed Tom as an important blessing to the team. He was now sure he had to increase his network.

Simon ambled over to Tom and grabbed a chair and a smile.

Ordinarily, Tom sat in the corner of the room with his overloaded laptop, expensive headphones and his personal metal cup of coffee. Simon had trouble getting Tom's attention until he lifted one of the headphones. Tom had a reputation of technical expertise. Not long into the conversation, Simon was shocked that tranquil Tom seemed to hold a similar fury about what had happened. This quiet guy betrayed his internal anger when he slammed his mug, coffee flying, onto the table. Simon was laying his trap. Tom's response suggested that he believed that what had happened was more than a chance occurrence.

Simon smiled to himself. The bait was fresh and delicious. Simon already knew the open secret that Tom was a hacker extraordinaire, no matter how much Tom had denied any knowledge of hacking. As bribery, he would buy Tom special computer hook ups and government level software to harness Tom's anger. Simon began weaving his web around Tom. It wasn't long before Simon's charm worked its magic around Tom's adrenaline overflow. Tom signed on.

That evening Simon and Yael began to search their minds for other people they could recruit. They needed personally wounded ones who felt the public's pain, but they had to be knowledgeable, creative thinkers.

Simon was a naturally gifted salesman yet had a very big challenge to sell. Many of his bright college friends walked away from his request because there was no money in it for them, claimed that he was a conspiracy nut, or they were still unquestioning believers, whose egos prevented them from admitting they had voted for the wrong office holders. Yael found others who still believed that the government would take care of them. Others said there was no solution. Of course, they could be right.

Finally, Simon struck gold with his brainiac friend, ***Solomon, "Salo" Neo-***

fiti. Yael knew him but was not a fan of this arrogant social moron. Salo was a high functioning luftmensch. Salo's social IQ was the opposite of his academic capabilities. He chose to be a loner because he said he did not deal well with fools. To him, almost everyone was a fool. He appeared to be only attracted to enormous intellectual challenges that others could not handle. He reminded Simon of Alan Turing and learned that this social outcast had also been hurt by the storms. It did not take Simon long to lure him in with the goal of being on a team that could solve this dizzying mystery and perhaps a Ferrari. After all, this challenge was about them personally and was about life and death.

Salo had always been obsessed over big intellectual challenges. This did not include combing his curly red hair, eating with his mouth closed, brushing his teeth, or changing his clothes. Simon knew Salo from Harvard where Salo had gotten his first Ph.D. on Appeasement and International Diplomacy: Failure Twins. People, those illogical and irrational ones, confounded him. He had a Star Trek, Spock-like personality, yet liked materialistic possessions.

He still wanted to know what moved people. With an IQ like Mount Everest, Salo attracted many universities and chose a post grad scholarship to Stanford University. They wanted him for research. But he wanted a second Ph.D. and cash. That was workable.

Still interested in the irrational ones, his thesis was on Terrorism as a Form of Propaganda. Salo's genius attracted "friends" in high places so he had access to mega computers. Professors wanted their department to show off a big star and potentially a Nobel Prize winner, especially because he had been mentored by Prof. Aumann, Nobel Prize winner in Game Theory. Stanford made the money available. It was a fair trade as far as all were concerned.

As Simon discussed what he planned, Salo too, admitted that he was bothered by the seemingly free-floating pixels, although he preferred the term "voxels", that surely could be made into dots, and dots into clear pictures using the right algorithms. There were too many dark holes. He, too, would not trust any government or political figures any more. That was his style anyway.

Simon, Yael, Tom, and Salo wanted to know what moved people and what caused so many to act as submissive Stepford Wives, brainwashed into submission by the "Men's Club." They were determined to puncture condescending Politically Correct Elites, or "Politically Corrosive" hot-air balloons who only cared about getting paid and re-elected.

They wrestled and decided that the highly variable human component was beyond their scope. Humans were predictable only based on gaining pleasure avoiding pain, but many described their pleasure and pain in bizarre ways. On top of it, there was constant thug, called inertia, dead footing the human mindset. Simon's team knew they had to bring in an extraordinary person who understood human nature, particularly corrupt, narcissistic politicians.

Dozens of web interviews, their search ended up with a forensic psychiatrist, **Dr. Kelsey Landmark**. She was actually another acquaintance from the past. She was a descendent of famous psychiatrist, Victor E. Frankl. They invited her to come in for a face to face interview with the team.

For such a bookish lady, her auburn hair in a high pony tail, smooth complexion, lean frame and dark framed, oversized glasses, made her appear much younger than she actually was. Even though Dr. Landmark dressed in a business-like way, including her leather attaché, she had that look of someone that you could talk to. Certainly, she did not appear threatening despite her prior work with the CIA.

She entered Simon's most comfortable dining room because he wanted to impress her. He offered her a prized cappuccino and even some of his chocolate covered croissants which she politely declined. In the center of the room, an extravagant looking chandelier hung over a large inlaid wooden table sculpted to seat twelve that now acted as a board room. Simon wanted to impress people with his wealth and what it could do for them. Even the lighting had been mood designed with the computer-controlled music system playing some light classical music. It had the feel of a stable calm environment despite Simon's overdone attempts to decorate.

Yael never said anything but silently wondered how Simon could be so smart and so mismatch on decorating.

Dr. Landmark wondered what this extravagance revealed about Simon. Perhaps he liked to bribe people.

Simon figured that if he could get her onto the team, she would also be useful in controlling tempers. Competing, self-confidant researchers always had tempers. Because of her serious position, quiet charm and athletic good looks, the team felt a resonance with her. There was an additional plus to her being on the team. They knew she had made many friends in FBI and CIA. She could count on them for some straight information.

She listened to Simon's bait while Yael, Tom, and Salo sat there nodding their yeses. Simon offered her many inducements that were more than reasonable. After all, she would be the glue that held the team together when the squabbling began. She recognized that solving this most serious of mysteries was an existential challenge. She could be part of the team that could "Save Our Society." Even psychiatrists have egos. Kelsey wanted in.

Simon had plenty of rooms restored in his mansion. He offered each of them their own temperature-controlled bedrooms, on suite bathroom and kitchenettes in anticipation of long stays.

This talented, Fiery Five (Simon, Tom, Yael, Salo and Kelsey) had all been traumatized by the unpredicted, bizarre weather. This was more than a team bond. All were orphans in their own way and were to become family in many other ways.

Yael had lost two siblings during the storms.

Salo never saw his mother again, even with Tom's help.

It had been Kelsey's day to take the kids to school, but she had to rush to the hospital due to the overload of hysterical people. Her husband volunteered to take the kids in Kelsey's car. The car was pounded by rocks, violent blinding rain and whipping tree branches with visibility worse than a hurricane. Confused by the noise and swirling mud, he drove off the road into a rampaging gully. No one could get out of the crushed car. She was in the hospital when the body bags were brought in.

And each of them was also haunted not knowing why they were lucky enough not to be at any of the "ground zeros" when so many of their friends and family were gone forever.

Additionally, they were bound together by the fear and the anger that they had been abandoned or deceived by the government and the main stream media.

The five were so overwhelmed at how close they came to dying that they all suffered varying levels of PTSD.

They could no longer request to know why. They had to demand it. This was the beginning of an angry all-star, focused research team. Could they do it alone? Probably not, but they were driven never to be victims again, never again.

The common lesson they had learned growing up was how they had to deal with schoolyard bully. They all observed that the bully who seeks to torment or subjugate, naturally goes to soft targets such as smaller individuals, those who try to appease the bully and loners.

At a larger level, international bullies picked on smaller ethnic groups and smaller countries first. Historically, voxels (Salo preferred this to pixels) and dots confirmed this.

Their beginning findings found that dots did need voxels to create four-dimensional definition, size, color and clarity just like the best holograms. Some dots may seem trivial by themselves, but as they connect, the puzzle becomes clearer.

The team referred to these as connecting the dots by authentic hindsight. Kelsey reminded them that human nature had not changed and was only modified by culture. From this they could broadly project future consequences by past behavior especially from the ideologically committed.

The team first went to the history books looking at disintegrated, decomposed or decayed societies that had disappeared throughout history like the Mongols, Huns, Gauls and Macedonians; the Jebusites, Hittites, Amorites, Canaanites, Perizzites, Hivites and Girgashites of the Jewish Bible. They read about the downfall of the Roman Empire, the English Empire and the Spanish Empires. Dots were connected to clarify what they had in common. The lessons were now clearer, and the answers were no longer so ambiguous.

They tried to get help from the government, but kept bumping into doublespeak. When they asked for information which raised their suspicions about the government's integrity and the newly realized enemy, TerVol, they were stonewalled. The question arose, was TerVol amongst them?

So far, they had worked together arguing only when they were tired. Salo would never give in, but he found that he was not always right, even with his extraordinary mind and the vocabulary he regularly used to distract them.

So many of our leaders had not learned the keys as to why other societies have suffered from declinism to death. Scholars offered answers.

One scholar, *Victor Davis Hanson,* wrote "Why do societies give up?" (Jewish World Review Feb. 14, 2013). The theme throughout history appeared to be the ugly quadruplets of consistent self-indulgence, forced entitlements without responsibility, media control and a government that would pinch the prosperous and give it to those who would vote for those politicians. Those were the societies who no longer could guard themselves against external enemies because the citizens were focused on their personal desires. They were slobbering as they ate the Golden Goose they had killed.

In other words, they were living in a society where too many asked not what they can do for their country but what their country can do for them. This double duo destroyed the incentive of those who worked hard, took risks to earn rewards, created new products, while creating jobs and services. Political casuistry (that is a big word for p.c.) conflicted with independent thinking. These faults, like termites in a building, undermined the resources to survive. One key observation was that whoever robs Peter to pay Paul will always get Paul's vote.

Sir Edward Gibbon (1737-1794), author of <u>The Decline and Fall of the Roman Empire</u>, wrote tellingly of the collapse of Athens, which was the birthplace of democracy. He judged that, in the end they wanted security more than freedom. This was because they did not want to give to society, but for society to give to them. The freedom they were seeking was freedom from responsibility.

State paternalism was one of TerVol's termite colonies quietly eating the substructure of freedom. Humans soon learned that when some of them can get benefits from the government for free and not have to work for them, they should pursue that course and claim it as an entitlement. They did not learn until it was too late, that the more government gives, the more it controls and the more it can take away.

Salo mumbled, "It appears that we haven't learned the lessons of history either."

For example, the once powerful Ottoman-Turkish Empire was following the dictates of Islam, fueled by personal avaricious and merciless leadership. They conquered vast lands, they rapaciously deforested, drained economies, murdered with impunity, conscripted children to fight for them (the Janissaries), brutally burdened those who could not flee, and taxed a broad area from modern day Turkey to the tip of the Hejaz (later called the Arabian Peninsula) for four centuries. They had taken much of it by war from the preceding conquerors, the Egyptians.

To amass more wealth Ottoman Turks brutally seized property and land from the successful Armenians. To do it, as many as two million Christian Armenians were robbed, slaughtered or displaced. Their greed, literally, had no boundaries.

Democracies did not learn the proper lesson, but Hitler did. He saw that no one besides Armenians cared about their genocide by the Turks. He saw what the Turks got away with by simply denying the atrocities ever occurred. He saw that the League of Nations became a bag of waste wind.

In other failed history lessons, Simon recalled the Barbary Pirates extortions, the Spanish American War, the Civil War, WWI, WW II and the Holocaust.

Looking back on WW I, Simon could point out, greedy European, imperialist winners had created new nation states (from recently discovered oil wealth) from previously occupied Turkish land. Based on that history, he discovered that the tiny country of Israel could have not occupied "Arab" land because it was ruled by Turkey or rigidly controlled by absentee Turks for 400 years. How many knew that the Turks are not Arabs?

The group uncovered that modern political leaders really had not learned the proper moral lessons or the longer term, practical consequences of ignoring the facts of history. The team agreed that this was not a proud reflection on Homo Sapiens.

The lessons required a clear, accurate description of the problem. Often it is valuable and instructive to describe a problem with a paradigm or model.

For models, the team chose to examine two countries whose chief identity and connection was Exceptionalism and Democracy. The U.S. was huge and Israel quite small. Why had so few countries earned the exceptionalism that the United States or Israel had demonstrated?

A large majority of U.S. voters still subscribe to the view that there is something very special about America.

Rasmussen Reports (reported 9-15-13) that a national telephone survey finds that 59% of likely U.S. Voters believe the United States is more exceptional than other nations. Just 27% disagree, with 14% more were not sure.

Exceptionalism is always a work in progress. Exceptionalism never claims to create perfect societies unlike Communism or Islam have claimed. Exceptionalism is cultivated by a spirit of free enterprise bound by laws. It is always envied.

The identity of a society or individual can be perceived the same way we look at ourselves in a mirror. In a good light that gives clarity, we can connect the dots. Together, they give a feeling (only) of dimension to the dots reflecting who we are at that time, in that light.

Some in a society get their identity looking through a window when it is a two-way mirror. They think they are looking out when they are looking at themselves. As they look at what they thought was a window, they believe that everyone looks just like they do because as they are looking at the reflective side. The do not realize that the rest of the world, looking from the other side, see us with different identities from them.

Digging deeper, Simon found that there were two types of dots, not just one type of dot. He called them Destructive and Constructive Dots.

Destructive Dots are made by multiple pixels. Connected, they represented the signs of decline of a human or a society. Ignoring or denying the destructive dots threatened one's existence.

Constructive Dots are made by those multiple pixels necessary for security, stability, freedoms, upward mobility, civility, wealth and health. Acknowledging this was the easy part.

The hard part would be in keeping the team together. They were all extraordinary individuals with ample self-confidence bordering on narcissism.

Simon realized that the team would get deeply involved in their existential assignments and it would be easy to create hostility and turf wars. To keep communication more or less friendly, creative and constructive, the team agreed upon six rules guided by Dr. Landmark.

The first rule was never to criticize the other person when they brought information that someone didn't like. Challenge the information, not the person.

Second rule: There would be no yelling, humiliating, throwing of objects or silent treatment.

Third rule: At meetings where they pooled information and brainstormed, they had to agree that they would be well rested, well documented even to the point of boring, and should be willing to stay as many hours or days as was necessary to define a piece or pieces of the puzzle to create clarity of the picture. All food, drinks, showers, etc. would be supplied by Simon (as they requested) who secretly hoped that everyone loved pizza and chocolate chip cookies as much as he did. Bathroom breaks could not be used as a hideout.

Fourth rule: They must start by defining terms and assert specific values and the personal power that a value had. All needed to agree these existed before dialoguing.

Fifth rule: Accept only what is verifiable and move on from there.

Sixth rule: Kelsey, as a psychiatrist, would be the one to mediate any heated sessions.

They started and agreed with these terms:

Constructive Dots are bonding and strengthening elements of a society. Generally, these builders are seen as an acceptance of common values, common goals, respect, caring about the other and fellowship. The Constructive Dots were the antidotes to debilitating Destructive Dots, such as self-indulgence and ambiguity.

Destructive Dots can be analogous to inaudible avaricious Termite colonies and exploding fiery Volcanoes (hence the name, TerVol).

Planet Earth offered an analogy from where the human Destructive Dots come. Volcanoes start at the center of our planet. The center of the Earth is filled with superheated magma. The 2,000 degree Fahrenheit lava shoots up and out when there are shifts in tectonic plates (like during earthquakes) on the surface or the bottom ocean floor of the planet. This magma from the earth's raging core can be compared to the passionate hatred that has always lain deep in humanity since Cain and Abel.

Cultural upbringing has the potential of deep earthquakes and shifting tectonic plates from which volcanoes and wars explode. Cultural upbringing or "civilizing" a child can be the healing, too.

A nuclear world war could be compared to a series of large volcanoes spewing lava and rocks, leaving ash to blacken the sky for tens of thousands of square miles, smothering enormous areas, and dropping planet temperature radically.

Salo did what he did best and dropped some trivia on Simon: "There are actually about 1900 active volcanoes on our planet, today. There is a supervolcano in Yellowstone National Park. We also know that a supervolcano, about 75,000 years ago, almost extinguished the entire human race with a volcanic winter and catastrophic famines."

Simon couldn't stop Salo. "In two and a half days in 1562, Catholic hatred of Huguenots erupted with volcanic force and close to 30,000 Huguenots were killed. It was called the St. Bartholomew's Day massacre. I had to read that twice."

"Hate has destroyed tens of millions under Nazism, 20 million under Stalin in Russia, at least 65 million under Mao Tsedong in China. During centuries of Islamic conquests tens of millions perished. I won't bother you with more…for now."

There are also quiet Destructive Dots: the inaudible, internal rot of termites. One example is the concept of moral equivalence based on ambiguity by pseudo intellectual academics and their acolyte journalists.

For our society, the termites represent a combination of convenient amnesia of history, losing our values and ambiguity towards right and wrong. They destroy "off the radar." Social scientists have observed that the social termites quietly tear and eat holes into the fabric that is the safety net of a society. Graffiti and destruction of public and private property have been called art or venting feelings. The strength of the social fabric depends on clarity and respect of common values. Termite damage is often undetected until severe structural weakening appears.

There is always a destructive class in a culture that cares less for the society's well-being, freedom and security than their personal agenda.

These clever purveyors of possibilities act to convince fellow citizens that the accusations of the country's adversaries are entirely possible and reasonable. This initiates a feeling of guilt for those who stand up to the demands. This would be a form of moral equivalence. They tend to ignore their adversaries past behavior and threats. These paternalistic purveyors posture themselves as having the moral high road proclaiming that they know this is either for the greater good of all, or "we know what is good for you." Throughout the centuries, the majority of cultures have disappeared primarily because of internal rot and a cataclysmic event.

Admittedly, "ambiguity" in a philosophical, classroom or religious discussion, can be civilized and creative.

"Ambiguity" in living a life is a form of paralysis and the basis for personal, social and national rot. It hides behind relativity. Ambiguity is the opposite of clarity. Politically, it is a national poison. A Constitution can protect a society from that rot if it is obeyed by all.

When government leaders do not present a clear picture of what a country stands for or defies its Constitution and laws, people lose trust in their government.

Humans need clarity for direction, reliability, and resources to take the proper action. This is like looking at a current, thorough map (more thorough than Waze) to see how to get to a clearly chosen destination or goal. Without those, ambiguity causes humans to wander and flounder.

Ambiguous about their identity, countries wander into new alliances for economic, political and military reasons. The team knew they needed greater clarity on this issue.

How does ambiguity affect human behavior?

The team had to be focused on how ambiguity could be dangerous.

There are examples that answer that question.

On a personal level, ambiguity can be critical: It should be obvious to any thinking human that to mistake a rabid Rottweiler for a drooling Saint Bernard or a shark for a dolphin, is a one-time mistake.

It should seem obvious that there are other areas in which we need absolute clarity.

Is the water safe to drink? How much sun exposure does it take to cause skin cancer? How many cigarettes will it take to cause cancer? How much alcohol can I drink and still drive? Where am I going? What am I clearly willing to preserve at all costs, like my life?

Ambiguity is risky especially when it comes to holding on to that which we truly value, beginning with the morals that guide our society.

Thomas Sowell, www.tsowell.com 5-8-12, reflected that there is a (common) moral infrastructure, one of the intangibles, without which the tangibles don't work. Like the physical infrastructure, its neglect (termites?) in the short run invites disaster in the long run.

On a national level, if we are ambiguous about who we thought was a trusted ally or who is a mortal enemy, we will inevitably betray our allies and aid our enemies.

Indecisiveness is the paralysis that results from ambiguity. Ambiguity, then is an inability to respond appropriately to a concern because one is indecisive. It robs clarity. Clarity can be seduced by directed ambiguity (also known as propaganda) through:

1. Misinformation and disinformation (like prejudice, divisiveness, lies, faulty assumptions);
2. Information underload (forgetfulness, media and government under-reporting, mainstream media withholding information);
3. Information overload ("TMI") in quantity, repetition or in rapidity of delivery.
4. Value replacement seduction (George Orwell wrote on this).

Yael and Kelsey were chilled while reviewing historians' observations of failing democracies. Failing societies were identified when citizens had no concern beyond protecting their immediate pleasures and their perceived entitlements without responsibilities. Well to do citizens (the protected class) were in extreme denial of unpleasant facts, unaware of their own hypocrisy, and self-absorbed in their indulgences. This was where the rot began. People discarded the work ethic and forgot the sacrifices that built the country. The feeling of kinship with fellow citizens was numbed and divided; the shared vision of the future had disintegrated. In other words, they were ambiguous about what their values were.

Ambiguity erases the values that connect citizens of a country to one another. When the people's leaders bow to foreign values by denying their civilization values, the rot begins.

Ambiguity amplifies such issues as excessive tolerance and hypocrisy. By every new social position for which we become tolerant, we must be intolerant of that social environment that preceded it.

In a democracy, we enjoyed the profits of pluralism, but pluralism is not the same as unreciprocated multiculturalism. Pluralism meant the co-mingling of different ethnicities and races in one place and sharing a far greater number of similar values than dissimilar ones. Pluralism does not support invading or controlling another's ethnicity or a country's laws.

The "Multis"

Multiculturalism is currently a toplofty proposition dealing in comforting ambiguity. It can be called a "universalist" urge at the expense of a country or culture's particular qualities, convictions and identities.

Multiculturalism seemed like a noble experiment. Currently, reality proved it had become an unreciprocated multiculturalism, a nation dividing universalism.

They asked Dr. Landmark what she thought. First, she said, that this was a team and she wanted to be called by her first name. Then she said that unreciprocated multiculturalism, was a new name, but was also a continuing aspect of humanity rather than something new. Multiculturalism often morphs into the failure to stand by one's own values if it is contradicted by another's. In that "melting pot" of real multiculturalism, one flavor predominates and then dominates.

"Am I being ambiguous about that?" she smiled.

Abraham Kuyper long ago wisely observed that when the principles that run against our deepest convictions begin to win the day, then the battle is our calling, yet fighting for peace appears a sin. You must fight the price of denying exceptionalism with all the fire of your faith.

Was the ambiguity of multiculturalism that bad?

Tom had been searching the internet for practical examples about those places that tried to put multiculturalism in place. "It is really about the failure of respectful integration of certain new cultures into the host society. Look at the examples I just dug out."

The Canadian Multiculturalism Act states that all are equal under the law regardless of their race, national or ethnic origin, color, or religion. Canada was the first country in the world to legislate national multiculturalism. Under this policy, all citizens "can keep their identities, can take pride in their ancestry and have a sense of belonging."

Citizens also "have the freedom to preserve, enhance, and share their cultural heritage," and "full and equitable participation of individuals and communities of all origins in all aspects of Canadian society" is promoted. Diversity in Canada is deemed a national asset. Its constitution offers all citizens equal rights and freedoms. Yet it also requires "equal responsibilities."

In multicultural Canada, diversity incentives are embraced as the answer to combat racism. One cannot exclude the unfortunate consequences of racism as a societal scourge with harmful social and psychological repercussions that require attention as a human rights issue. But a Constitution and laws must be adhered to by all its citizens.

Far too many interfaith cultural dialogue sessions have focused on appeasement of those claiming an aggrieved narrative, rather than true dialogue with immigrant or minority groups. These dialogues often ignore human rights abuses from their foreign countries of origin; abuses which many immigrants have accepted as the norm and often seek to maintain in an effort to sustain the dignity of their group identity.

The reason for the self-destructive failure of this "multiculturalism" was that tolerant societies were confronted with immigrant minorities who sought to undermine the open society, refused to integrate, claimed their communities as their own land, defied the host values, employed violence to further that minorities aims and even bred indigenous second-generation lawlessness.

German Chancellor Angela Merkel declared that in Germany, multiculturalism has "utterly failed."

Jose Maria Aznar, Spain s ex-prime minister reached the same conclusion about multiculturalism in their countries.

Australian Prime Minister John Howard (2006), and ***British Prime***

Minister David Cameron (2011) referred to this when, speaking of Muslim immigration, that multiculturalism had failed. Cameron went so far as to say it was time to stop being tolerant of intolerance. He also warned that multiculturalism is fostering extremist ideology and directly contributing to home-grown Islamic terrorism.

Nigel Farage, UK Independence Party leader stated that the United Kingdom s push for multiculturalism has not united Britons but pushed them apart.

The proof of the failure of unreciprocated multiculturalism is becoming painfully overwhelming as documented by the scholar, *Soeren Kern,* in his 2015 piece on "European No-Go Zones: Fact or Fiction?" http://www.gatestoneinstitute.org/5177/no-go-zones-britain

Lebanon was another model of failed multiculturalism. Today, Lebanon has been brutally balkanized by continuing religious and ethnic fighting and disruptive foreign involvement. The people do not share common national values or mutual respect. They are coming unglued as a society under the gun. What was exceptional, no longer is.

Professor Bat Yeor (in "Eurabia", Oct 10, 2012) observed that the vision of the European Union is part of the globalist agenda to replace the nation-states with a world government that would be the United Nations, an international center that would promulgate laws for the entire planet.

This is very clear from the speeches of *Javier Solana*, from his desire to strengthen the U.N. by weakening the European States.

This is also part of a messianic humanist aspect of Communism: They propose to recreate a fraternal humanity, without borders, without divisions, subject to the same laws, in which everyone is equal, everyone is kind and gentle, and in which the differences between the peoples would disappear. It's like what the Soviet Union and Communist China initially planned to do, but utterly and brutally failed in the human rights domain.

John Fonte, in a new book, <u>Sovereignty or Submission</u>, makes clear how this ideology of anti-exceptionalism was "widely embraced by the privileged in Europe and, increasingly, among untouchable elites in the U.S. This ideology was undermining liberal democracy, self-government, constitutionalism, individual freedom and even traditional internationalism of sovereign states."

The salacious, slippery slope of Moral Relativism merges with Multiculturalism

Moral relativism is based on a refusal to call "evil", "evil", and a concomitant willingness to denigrate truth if truth requires you to call it evil.

"Relativity" slathers oil on the slippery, steep marble slope of ambiguity and dissolves any concept of morality.

Political ambiguity also gives rise to relativism considered by many historians as a nation-killing doctrine. Albert Einstein was pulling his hair out worrying that people would take his mathematical theory of relativity and distort it into a social science.

In daily life, relativism renders life meaningless ("meaning" itself, demanding a goal beyond personal satisfaction, requires clarity), undermines the desire to have more children at the expense of fun, promotes hedonism and idealizes pacifism. That is because nothing interests those other than their own pleasures and personal security. Relativism therefore saps a nation's will and its stamina to confront evil or defend itself against external threats.

If everything in life is relative, how can there be right or wrong, moral or immoral, truth or lies, facts or fictions? And who will be the judge?

Here is where the base from which moral relativism mendaciously merges into multiculturalism.

Frederic Bastiat, the 19th century French economist and philosopher once warned against this creed. He questioned those who, "though they are made of the same human clay as the rest of us, think they can take away all our freedoms and exercise them on our behalf."

Yael found ample resources that there are problems today in many European countries with waves of unreciprocated Islamic migrants. England, Belgium, France, Norway, Denmark, Sweden and Holland are experiencing growing threats to their way of life from Jihad, Sharia and, what some of the misguided call, "radical" Islam.

Yael offered an example of why Israel is our miner's canary, hopefully not a Cassandra. Here is one example of how failed multiculturalism has become divisive to a society. "In Britain, most Muslims are descended from the Indian sub-continent, particularly Pakistan and they are not Arabs. What is 'Palestine' to them that they would be out in the streets fuming at Israel about a war in Gaza, nowhere near their country of origin? Those Muslims have not integrated into British society." Yet, it was Hamas's double war crime of both shooting and sending rockets at Israeli civilians while hiding behind civilians. That should be infuriating the entire civilized world.

Once unreciprocated multiculturalism eventually gains force, it tends to grow into multilateralism. This means turning many of our own national interests (free speech, defense, economy) into the hands of others, such as the U.N. The U.S government narrowly voted not to give up our Second Amendment rights to the U.N. in 2014.

The current ivory tower concept of multiculturalism demands respecting other cultures and subcultures but does not demand respect for their own culture. In this sense, multiculturalism is then, a divisive failure.

In the U.S., multiculturalism focuses not on the unity of Americans, but the divisions that exist between Americans in terms of race, gender, religion, culture, and economic class.

Without moral conviction, how could we ever be willing to pay the heavy price required to protect and nurture such rights as we enjoy in the U.S.?

When all is relative, "What's the difference?" is the favorite phrase of the relativist. How can there be right or wrong, fact or fiction? Who gets to be the judge…the powerful?

Moral relativism proposes that truth is just a "narrative." If truth is relative and narratives are truths, does that not make all narratives merely continuously negating truths? Then each competing narrative invalidates the other narrative.

Watch out for those who add the word, "narratives", into our conversation. Their credo is negated. "What's mine is mine and what's yours is negotiable. We cannot negotiate with those who say this." –President **John Fitzgerald Kennedy.**

The many non-democracies, theocracies, communist states, and dictatorships in the U.N. dominate the U.N. voting. They are often antagonistic to our interests, values and exceptionalism. Our Constitution is our mainstay.

Multilateralism, the UN, Sharia, and "Agenda 21" can redefine for us, without our consent, our identity, who is an ally or an enemy, politically, militarily and economically. This is not in our self-interest.

Another way to anticipate what multilateralism can do is to imagination how it shifts political and economic power away from the citizens of successful democratic nation-states and their elected representatives to unelected bureaucrats, judges, religious leaders, lawyers and Non- Governmental Organizations (NGO's) which are supposed to work independent of government influence.

The more unelected bureaucrats there are, in a giant governing authority, the less responsive it will be to those they oversee. With multilateralism in play, foreign individuals and institutions can wield transnational authority "beyond" nations, and "supranational authority", "over" nations.

There are those who espouse "world citizen" as their gift. Their claim is that a citizen has a primary allegiance to all the community of human beings around the world, not to their own communities. It is contrary to the health of our national security, exceptionalism and, of course, patriotism. There is no force in existence that can make people from any society, give up their identity and give away their material benefits to worship "world citizenry", hence the failure of the concept before the gift wrapping is removed from the "gift."

For Americans to embrace "the brave new world of global governance," we will have to give up the structure of our Constitution, voluntarily agree to share our wealth, remove our sovereignty, dissolve our borders, change our values, and eliminate national security for the benefit of others everywhere on the planet.

Many other countries and cultures passionately envy, even hate the exceptionalism seen in the U.S. and in Israel in terms of wealth, standard of living, personal upward mobility, liberal democracy, our legal rights, our freedom of speech, a free (?) press, our separation of "church and state," our powerful military and our voluminous scientific and medical research contributions.

Let's be clear, in the USA, our "poor" have it better than most people over most of the planet.

Our successes and our exceptionalism are greatly admired, envied, and coveted.

Autocratic leaders of other countries know that our successes make them look bad. There are some supercilious leaders in our country who want to see our prosperity and strength ended, thinking that some can benefit by taking what we have earned, giving it to others without our permission and then boldly call that equality.

Kurt Vonnegut's science fiction novel, **<u>Harrison Bergeron</u>** shows most clearly what is before us. He lays out what happens in a society (he picks 2081) when the government keeps everyone equal. The job is assigned to the Handi-capper General whose team of agents ensure that all laws of equality are strictly enforced in everything from good looks (wear a mask) to intelligence (con-tinuous deafening noise from a full-time earpiece) to physical abilities (wearing weights for the quick or agile, etc.), to speech impediments (given to those who are pleasant sounding), to distorting glasses for those with good vision, to wealth… Can we strengthen the weak, by weakening the strong?

Simon joked: "In golf we should redistribute the strokes amongst all the players so that there is equality in all final scores. No one will be better than another!"

Tom's technical side kicked in and he drawled, "Ain't it crystal clear that the world would be a horrible place, but for USA's (and the young state of Is-rael) exceptional contributions to health, food, technology, water usage, farm-ing, preserving human rights and policing, never exhibiting colonialism? Hell! We do not have to be ashamed of our exceptionalism.

We have nothing to apologize for. We earned our successes…o.k. not all in a saintly way, but we should still be proud! What is the shame in our successes?"

"But there are those who voice disapproval of our exceptionalism, as being decadent, unfair, selfish, colonial, greedy, salacious and imperfect," replied Yael.

Tom shot back. "Who is perfect? Being imperfect does not mean we have not shared our advances in every area, that we are not generous and excep-tional, nor that we have to give up what we have earned. Let's get out our bull whips out."

"The thermometer of success is merely the jealousy of the malcontents."

Salvador Dali

We need more clarity, not less, as in the following examples:

Outspoken Islamic jihadists, Iranian Mullahs and others call for "Death to America, Death to Israel!" At the same time, our transnational progressives are offering invitations to the cloaked Jihadists and the Muslim Brotherhood to enter our country and enter the ranks of our government and Homeland Security. This is despite common knowledge that the Muslim Brotherhood's Charter calls for the removal our constitution, our democracy and our freedoms.

Clarity is the antidote to the debilitating, aimless ambiguity that results in the denial of who our enemies are. Of course, this clarity has a price for calling an enemy a mortal enemy. But there is a far greater price to be paid for failing to do so.

The clarity of values (linked constructive pixels and dots) are evidenced by the common bonds of the people of a nation. These bonds define its distinct national values, its social cohesion, its common future vision, its moral infrastructure, its past heroes, its social pleasures and the perception of identity as seen contrasted to other countries. This is by no means a rigid view.

Many long term constructive dots were connected by the concept of exceptionalism between individuals and countries. Exceptionalism is an energizing antidote to the rot of mediocrity, decline, and indifference. Might (strength) can only gained with clarity.

Exceptionalism comes from hard work, teamwork, postponing gratification and an environment that nurtures creativity. Both the U.S. and Israel can point to an infrastructure that has been built by the generally mutual values, hard work, fighting enemies, sacrifice and delayed gratification. And neither country is perfect. To discredit those two countries accomplishments by decrying the imperfections is to negate their reason for existence.

Ibn Warraq, in "Why the West is Best," urges us to "defend these rights without compromise and without fear of hurting the feelings" of potentially friendly Muslim countries or of angry Islamic terrorists. Westerners must not self-censor or censor and must not allow "barbaric laws from 7th century Arabia" to supersede Western freedoms. He urges us to end our failed policies dealing with multicultural relativism, anti-Americanism, and anti-Westernism which have led to a most profound, possibly suicidal crisis. Indeed, this is the best way we can strengthen our like-minded allies who are trapped in theologically fundamentalist Muslim countries."

If we are ambiguous (that is to fail to be clear between risks and rewards) about recognizing differences between the criminal and the policeman; the arsonist and the fireman; the terrorist and the freedom fighter; the aggressor and the defender; the bully and the tormented, totalitarian rule and democratic rule, how can we deal with crime, arson, terrorism, land theft, bullying, or enslavement?

For clarity, let's find an example to connect some sobering dots that defined a peace treaty that goes beyond the absence of war and terrorism.

There is a major difference of the peace between Democracies (with the restraining influence of the electorate) and stained toilet paper peace with non-democracies, rigid theocracies or of totalitarian regimes. Common sense and history validate this.

The absolute preconditions (Constructive dots) of peace amongst international neighbors is that they (the government and institutions) require educating each citizen in each generation not to hate the other; to not dishonestly delegitimize each other or fabricate their own contending history to negate the others' rights. They must refrain from violence or threats thereof and honor the treaties and contracts ("Pacta Sunt Servanda" in international legal terms). This is embodied in the preamble of the United Nations Charter.

We know from history, that the hate sermons which used to be preached in Churches and Mosques throughout Europe, the Middle East and Nazi Germany preceded violence. The hate sermons and rallies plant the seeds of future conflict and murder! Just as the past was pregnant with the present, the present is pregnant with the future.

Yael used the Gaza District, brutally dominated by totalitarian Hamas, next to democratic Israel.

Here is how it happened. In 2005, Israel completely uprooted generations of Jews living in Gaza and relinquished all claims to that land mass. Under international law Israel had no residual responsibility.

A few benighted individuals predicted that Gaza would be "democratically" ruled by the Hamas. With this "freedom," Hamas was able to terrify its own people and terrorize Israeli citizens with thousands of rockets. It was a good example of a military-political party shutting down social media, disallowing conferences, repressing women, torturing dissidents, using summary executions and arrests journalists. Logic implores one to accept that there is scant hope for constructive steps toward regional peace with that type of enemy constantly calling for another country's annihilation.

Nations that disregard the freedoms of their own people are not likely to care much about maintaining peace with their view of historic competitors. Peace begins internally with a commitment to protecting the human rights of its own citizens, allowing people to speak out and avoiding coercion through lies or violence.

The threat of violence is simply an extortion agenda.

It holds a country hostage to a potentially damaging force. For instance, the PLO (Arafat) told the U.S. that it will stop murdering American citizens abroad, if the U.S. will just recognize them as a legitimate organization. This followed the documented, Arafat ordered, murder of the U.S. Ambassador to the Sudan. ***President Nixon*** did as Arafat ordered. Extortion worked.

Thomas Jefferson decided to study the Koran to see what Muslims believed in and what the Barbary Pirates goals were. Jefferson put a copy of the Koran by his bed for more information. At that time there was no more British protection of the high seas. Jefferson had to struggle with his own patriots, like John Adams who was advocating costly appeasement. For over 15 years the American government paid the Muslims millions of dollars for safe passage and return of American hostages. In 1805 Jefferson sent a strong military force instead of ransom. He prevailed and ended the extortions. The total defeat of the Barbary Pirates did not end until 1815.

It was Tom's turn to protest. "Isn't appeasement, like compromise, fair? We compromise in our society all the time. What about those who are loudly griping that they are not getting 'fair' treatment that they are entitled to?

Shouldn't we compromise with them?"

Dr. Landmark came up with the answer: "We all know that children whine about what is 'fair.' We can be sure of what it is not. 'Fair' is not forcibly taking from children the toys they own, just because other children whine loudly enough. The Founding Fathers of this country extolled equality of opportunity in the pursuit of happiness, not by taking away the fruits of one's labor by force and giving it to those not desirous of being in the labor force."

The following are some of the groups that complained that life wasn't fair to them, and what they did was terrorize:

The Underground Weathermen, the Bader-Meinhoff gang, the Jesse James Gang, the Ku Klux Klan, the Black Panthers, Posse Comatatus, Aryan Nations, the Sendero Luminoso (in South America), Jamaat Ul Furquan, al-Mourabitoun, al Qaeda, the FARC in Columbia, the Muslim Brotherhood, al Shabaab in Somalia, Boko Haram in Nigeria, Aum Shinrikyo in Japan, the Communist Party of the Philippines, the ETA in Spain, the Tanziim in Israeli territory, Kurdistan Worker's Party, Muslim brotherhood, Darfur Liberation Front in the Sudan, Hamas, Egyptian Islamic Jihad, the I.R.A. in Ireland, the Quds Force from Iran, Gamaa Islamiya, Hezbollah, Jaish-e-Mohammed, Kurdistan Workers Party (PKK), ISIS (Daesh), the Taliban, Palestinian Islamic Jihad, Abu Nidal and the Liberation Tigers of Tamil Eelam.

"Enough? Why don't we try and connect those dots?" challenged Salo. He was having fun as he could see where this was going.

Salo smirked as he belched a challenge to all of them. "Where is the supposed moral high ground claimed by those refusing to struggle their utmost to hold on to our precious life style and freedoms instead of bowing down to others claims and demands?

"Answer me a simple mathematic equation. How much more is the price of war compared to the cost of peace? Is slavery a price worthy of giving away your freedom and accepting someone else's definition of peace?

"Can we buy peace by giving up our possessions, our power and our freedoms any more than we can buy love by giving up our money, our strengths or our identity?

"Historically, peace has been consistently achieved through the perception of one's strength by their enemies that aggression would be very painful and costly."

As usual, Salo had one parting shot. "Plato's ancient wisdom advised, 'Si Vis Pacem, Para Bellum: If you want peace, prepare for war.'"

He turned to Tom, "Now give me a bite of your salami sandwich."

Totalitarian movements and aggressive despots are the natural enemies of democracies.

The freedom and independence we have are dangerous to the rule of tyrannical regimes. The inhabitants want to have what is seen in exceptional countries. Television, Facebook and other electronic social media carry pictures of the gifts from democracies around the planet.

So Totalitarian states must be the natural enemies of Democracies, at least when it comes to basic human rights and quality of life.

Simon, Tom, Yael, Kelsey and Salo now had an historically sound, philosophical basis to identify what was wrong and the decisions that created this horrible mess. Now they needed to find and organize more facts so that healthy, sustainable conclusions could be reached for our civilization.

Simon says:

This is not a joke! Resolving these challenges will determine the fate of humanity.

Our freedoms are not sustainable without the same efforts and sacrifices that previous generations had won for us.

First, we must identify what our most important values are. Then we must sort out that which could destroy our way of life. It appears that global TerVol is it. To expose TerVol will bring clarity.

We have to define the parts of this mystery and share what we learn. If it is global, we have to find allies to combat it.

With all the sub-national groups' enormous fire power, cyberwarfare, enormous explosives, poisons and today's technology we need real allies and certainly not frenemies.

With some work we can identify the real allies and enemies of the U.S.

Defining who is who will give us clarity. We can define what makes those allies special to us; who will stick with us and who will try to divide us both internally and externally. We must be smart enough to absorb the wisdom of great thinkers and con-

nect the dots.

Our children's future depends on our immediate pro-active changes. Step one is that we must work hard to clarify the qualifications of real allies. The Democracies of America and Israel appear to be natural interdependent allies.

There is much to be learned. Let's push forward and find out what and who are critical to our national interests and our children's future.

They had no idea how much work they had ahead of them.

Chapter 2 ALLIES NEED REAL ALLIES

America and Israel are Natural and Interdependent Allies

Simon Says:

"We are starting to identify previously unknown destructive dots. There are those peoples and nations who don't hold our most cherished values. Could there be other constructive and destructive dots on that scale of doublespeak that ran from ally to mortal enemy? Put in proper order, the dots will create the philosophical lens through which we can connect the constructive dots and separate out the destructive dots. This improves clarity. Why not start by mining the great minds of history? We must be able to define our true allies."

Sir Edmund Burke, using Judeo-Christian morality, is quoted to have warned that, "The only thing necessary for the triumph of evil is for good men to do nothing."

He is also reported to have expanded on this saying, "When bad men combine, the good must associate; else they will fall, one by one, an unpitied sacrifice in a contemptible struggle."

Although one might presume that the term "ally" could apply to other allies of the U.S., it will be clear that Israel is an essential ally for America for many reasons that other allies can't be.

"This finally makes sense to me," Salo said. "In today's world where distance and oceans seem like safety cushions, they can create insouciance."

"Darn it, Salo," cried out Tom. What does your big word, "insouciance" mean?"

"It simply means nonchalance, indifferent carelessness about our security," smiled Salo.

The team found that there was a deeper understanding of the reciprocal alliance between Israel and the U.S. At first glance, one could see that both allies have very similar (never identical), voting records in the U.N. because they stand for similar creeds and values. Allies support friends and deter foes. An ally respects and supports another ally's sovereignty. America's enemies deeply and intuitively understand that no U.S. goals or resources in the Middle East are remotely as imposing, important, and calming as Israel. One reason is that neither Israel nor the U.S. have imperialistic visions.

Those who wish to undermine U.S. interests will first try to isolate Israel from the U.S.

The link between democracies is a critical component of true allies. Salo wanted to share just five reasons from the thirteen he'd found on "Democracy for All." http://www.streetlaw.org/democlesson.html.

The clarity of these points explains why it is necessary for any totalitarian conquest to separate Israel from the United States. Putting "daylight" between two democracies weakens both.

Salo put on his red white and blue Constitutional hat and listed five of the reasons:

1. Whereas, freedom, including freedom of speech, is one of the two cardinal principles of democracy, Arab-Islamic culture is strictly authoritarian, which is why its media is overtly or covertly state-controlled. Democracy demands citizen participation based on a free and independent media and press.

2. Whereas democracy's cardinal principle is equality and authority given from the bottom up, Arab-Islamic culture is hierarchical and dual. Top-down leadership is a fundamental principle of Islamic theology. Authority runs down from Allah to Muhammad and from Muhammad to the ruler of the regime and his religious scholars.

3. Whereas democracy is based on the primacy of consent, Arab-Islamic culture is based on the primacy of coercion. Historically and routinely, agreements between rival Muslim factions do not really terminate animosities, which is why such agreements are short-lived. The primacy of consent adorns democratic societies with a certain easy-going civility. Not only are past grievances swept aside, but political oppo-

nents can be friends despite their differences. Differences are resolved by mutual concessions, and agreements are usually lasting. In contrast, killing opponents is not uncommon in countries controlled with a warlord culture.

4. Whereas democracy is based on the primacy of consent, the pursuit of peace is the norm of democratic states. The foreign policy norm of Arab-Islamic states is intimidation and conquest. The basis is in the Arab-Islamic warlord culture. The primary reason why Muslim violence is found throughout the world today is simply this: Jihad (holy war) is a basic principle of Islamic theology, evident in Islamic scriptures on which Muslims are weaned. It is this theology which Israeli and American powder puff peace prevaricators chose to ignore. It has been seen in 1400 years of intra-Muslim fighting.

5. Whereas contemporary or normative Jeffersonian democracy is inclined toward moral diversity and respect of the other, within a constant legal system, Islam is based on absolutism and dualism.

"Do I sound like Thomas Jefferson or what?" He concluded with a smile showing the gap between his two upper front teeth.

Trying to disconnect Israel from the United States can't be done, only tried. For instance, even those who call themselves "jihadist" – Shi'a and Sunni alike - are right about one thing: Israel is the Middle East's lone outpost of Judeo-Christian values. Israelis demonstrate, under the most difficult of circumstances, democracy, freedom, pluralism, tolerance, human rights and minority rights. At least right now, 17% of Israel's citizens are Muslims. All of their citizens enjoy rights not available to Muslims in any Muslim-majority lands.

One grand example is that with the full backing of the United States, Israel's existence and strength have prevented Russian intrusion and leverage into the Arab oil market that would have crippled the U.S. economy and given Russia a toehold into African riches. In the UN, only Israel consistently voted with the US, better than any other ally. Our allies reflect our values. Despite the voting record in the UN, some still errantly project our own values onto our adversaries. By doing so, we assume "they are like us" so we can reason with them. This sets up faulty assumptions, faulty communications, faulty assessments and faulty conclusions leading to failures.

For some of the kingpins in the State Department, it is gospel that the United States has paid a terrible price to support Israel. There are over 50 Muslim State Desks in the State Department and only one for the Jewish State. Which chorus can scream louder?

Former Qatar Ambassador, **Andrew Kilgore**, now on the Arab Lobby payroll, was a State Department desk officer for Syria, Jordan, Lebanon and Iraqi affairs. He gets paid handsomely to spread much of the canard that Israel is bad for the U.S.

It was strangely short sided that **Henry Kissinger** would say (1975) "We don't need Israel for influence in the Arab world. On the contrary, Israel does us more harm than good in the Arab world. We can't negotiate about the existence of Israel, but we can reduce its size to historical proportions."

American enemies of Israel, like **Prof. Michael Scheuer** of Georgetown U. said that Israel is not only an unnecessary and self-made liability for the US but is an untreated and spreading cancer on our U.S. policies.

And from the ivory towers, a fault-laden conspiracy theory emerged in 2007 from the book, <u>The Israel Lobby and US Foreign Policy</u>, by **Prof. Stephen Walt** (Harvard's Kennedy School of Government), **Prof. John Mearsheimer** (University of Chicago) stating that Israel has been a damaging weighty, albatross around the neck of the U.S.

They did not bother to balance the extraordinary, wealthy lobbyists for foreign interest on the Arab States or the massive "donations" to U.S. upscale universities like Harvard or even the Clinton Foundation. They seem to be the perfect examples that paranoid people are often intelligent and act reasonably until we uncover their specific paranoia.

Not content with inexact symbols, Salo researched the term "albatross." It is sometimes used metaphorically to mean a psychological burden and weight that feels like a curse. It is an allusion to Samuel Taylor Coleridge's poem "The Rime of the Ancient Mariner" (1798). In the poem, an albatross starts to follow a ship going out to sea — ironically, being followed by an albatross was generally considered an omen of good luck. Killing it was bad luck.

Walt & Mearsheimer never bothered to balance the extraordinary number of lobbyists for the foreign interests of the Arab States and massive "donations" to U.S. politicians and upscale Universities, like Harvard. Those professors reportedly got $750,000.00 advance for their book.

Who paid?

American citizens of all backgrounds are entitled to speak out against perceived grievances that go against our American way of life. Yet these professors painted a picture of Israel as dead—a stinky albatross strangling the necks of the U.S. citizens.

The Arab Lobby, an excellent resource book by **Mitchell Bard, PhD.,** has hundreds of dots debunking the Walt and Mearsheimer, anti-Israel, anti-Jewish attack.

Simon found another booklet with a more concise assessment, published by the Washington Institute for Near East Policy, Israel, a Strategic Asset for the United States. It was written by **Robert Blackwill**, (who served in four White Houses, most recently as George W. Bush's deputy national security adviser), and **Walter Slocombe**, (a senior Pentagon official in the Carter and Clinton administrations who worked as a defense adviser in Iraq in 2003). They concluded that America's close ties to Israel have advanced, not jeopardized, its national security interests. Since 1973, "We can't find a single example of tangible actions by Arab governments for which the U.S. paid a price for its relationship with Israel. Israel is a friend of the U.S."

The concept of a "chain" holding the two countries together is no longer a good analogy to describe the relationship between the U.S. and Israel (and its corollary, the weakest link). A zipper is a better analogy, with many teeth.

If a single tooth in a zipper breaks, the zipper still holds, unlike the analogy of the weakest link of a chain. Zippers are far easier to repair than chains. There are two main factors that make for healthy or unhealthy decisions. Clarity creates the ability to differentiate and decide while ambiguity creates ambivalence and indecision.

If a country does not have clarity (ability to discriminate) of who their allies and enemies are, then inevitably that country will betray its allies and aid its enemies. There are many facets and we can only see half of them at any one time, like a spinning mirrored disco ball. Each mirror represents a meaningful and different facet.

The team wanted to share 12 important linkages. "Zipper teeth, if you will. Each of these is independently binding in its own way," emphasized Salo.

They called them the **"Five Epiphanies"** and **"The Seven Connectors."** **What are the Five Epiphanies?**

1. **Size, economy, geography, and topography count:** Israel is small (8,019 square miles), smaller than Vancouver Island in Canada, about the size of New Jersey and is less than 1/800 the size of the Arab/Muslim land mass.

The United States is 3.79 million square miles. Israel could be dropped into Lake Michigan and would disappear! Two of Israel can fit in one San Bernardino County, California! Forty-six of the United States are larger than Israel at this time.

Israel is surrounded and infiltrated by nations and sub-national groups that want to see it destroyed. The United States is surrounded by water on the east and west and friendly countries to the north and the south. Dependable allies make you stronger. Mountain ranges separate countries and afford protection from invading troops. Geography provides wealthy resources to some and arid land to others. The U.S. GNP is 57 times the Israeli GNP, even with the Israeli discovery of 8 big gas fields and some oil fields.

2. **Might Makes Right:** "One person with a belief is equal to a force of ninety-nine who have only interests," said **John Stuart Mill.**

The might can come from several different sources and one can dominate.

   a) personality.
   b) religious.
   c) military.

d) economic.

e) political.

f) intellectual (computers, creativity, etc)

g) tenacity or endurance.

h) propaganda.

i) elasticity of inertia.

k) leadership and organizational

l) the perception of the opponent

3. **Trust** is essential and comes from a history of a country's stability, reliability, capability and dependability. Democracies exemplify this.

4. **The natural enemies of Democracy are Totalitarian movements**, regardless of the current cover name. It is a way to distinguish an enemy even if quiescent or not threatening at the time. Here are some pixels that make up the dots.

   a) Enemies use propaganda against us, first with their own people and then internationally, linked with "fourth and fifth columns." That is why we must know what they say amongst themselves. Sometimes they are actually the fourth estate (the main stream media).

   b) An enemy will NOT support our best interests but will seek to undermine and weaken our way of life.

   c) Our enemies do not have the same values as we do, like freedom of speech, freedom of religion, equality before the law, and respect for individual rights.

   d) Enemies do not to honor agreements, memorandums of understanding or treaties for long.

Often, they re-interpret international laws so that they can deny their responsibility to those.

Joseph Heller cleverly summarized it. "The enemy is anybody who's going to get you killed, no matter which side he's on."

It's critical that the most powerful country in the world today, America, demonstrates it is a trustworthy ally of other democracies and allies. Power is demonstrated through loyalty of allies. America must advocate for its allies in the international arena. Allies are not opportunists.

The Brainiac interjected, "It's easy to foresee the consequences to the people of the 'free world' if America faltered in her obligation to take action against those who have declared war on any of our allies or our values here in the U.S. Here is how:

1. America would lose her identity as the most important active advocate for the advancement of freedom and human rights in this world.
2. Allies of America would wonder if she could be trusted to keep her word.
3. Once the leaders of a democracy push or urge an ally to endanger its people, it weakens the relationship. The smaller ally at risk, looks to other countries it feels can strengthen its ability to protect its people.
4. Losing America's reputation will encourage and radicalize her enemies. We would see the re-emergence of the evil we have fought against since the birth of our nation.

Eli Wiesel once said, "We must always take sides. Neutrality helps the oppressor, never the victim. Silence encourages the tormentor, never the tormented."

Salo became really picky, but as usual clarified how politicians and journalists fool and confuse us. "We must listen closely. This is what clarity is all about. Using the term 'Ally' as an example of diplomatic doubletalk and journalistic jingo should suffice as an example of why we must listen closely and read carefully.".

Simon asked, "What if two countries are involved in an existential fight? Can an ally act as a mediator or even an honest broker, rather than as a protector of their ally? What if one is a true ally and the other is an asset? Sometimes leaders don't lead their country to act as an ally."

Our government and our press called Russia an "ally" in WWII. But they were only an asset. Where was our commonality of values other than a temporary common enemy? History can be illuminating:

During World War II there was a tragic story of the Russians and Warsaw, Poland in 1943. Russia was, at best, a big asset, but not an ally. The last major Polish uprising in August 1944 was to be launched in concert with the liberating Soviet Red Army. But the advancing Red juggernaut suddenly and inexplicably halted. Advised by General Georgi Zhukov, Stalin rejected the appeals of the Western allies to assist the insurgents. For two months the courageous Poles fought the Nazis in urban warfare without any assistance. Stalin had simply halted the advance of the giant Red Army to allow the Germans to destroy the non-communist freedom fighters: 200,000 Poles perished and 800,000 were deported to the death camps. The city of Warsaw was erased by orders of Adolf Hitler; and the Soviets, at the outskirts of the city, did nothing. This is not the work of an ally.

The team needed time to imbibe in these dots so they could now listen to diplomats more accurately and have productive discussions.

The bottom line is that naming an ally as an ally is always self-serving. Allies can rely on getting something from each other.

Kelsey used her resources. They came back with small dots buried in the pages of disparate papers in corners of government storehouses. It was shocking to learn that for two decades since Israel's birth, Israel had been without military support from the U.S. government. It did not make sense if the word "ally" was to be bantered about. They could see that during this period the USA was not really an ally of Israel despite the common connections. Dots created clarity.

5. **"Exceptionalism"** was a phenomenal epiphany upon the team as a whole. It links the two countries. These are truly constructive dots. For clarity's sake, we need to describe exceptionalism by some of its components.

Joseph Sisco, a former Assistant Secretary of State for Near Eastern and South Asian affairs, once told Israeli author **Shmuel Katz**, "I want to assure you, Mr. Katz, that if we were not getting full value for our money, you would not get a cent from us." American foreign policy-makers often try to act like pragmatists, not moralists. U.S. aid to and dependence on Israel is animated by national self-interest.

It should be clear that Israel is an extension of democracy and everything America stands for.

If Israel is strong, the United States and other countries will value and respect it. If Israel appears militarily or politically weak, aggression against it will occur. The U.S. will lose the value of its most trusted democratic Middle East ally.

It is in U.S. interests not to have another war and expose American troops to danger. A big part of losing our values, is the failure of communal institutions and government to convey a strong enough public message that our exceptionalism is not only o.k. but is something to be very proud of. Currently, to some, it is unpatriotic. Those who value the exceptional achievements and generosity have esteem and admiration for Israel and the US. Exceptionalism prevents Decline.

Decline previews a society that will disappear from the pages of history. Studies Simon shared with Salo and Yael indicated that the strongest bridge linking people in these two democracies might be argued "Exceptionalism" based on similar values. This bridge was held up by arches and beams, like free enterprise, equality of opportunity (not equality of outcome as a social goal), a parallel to the American dream, free speech, freedom of religion, respectfully (mostly) competing philosophies, trust in the police, equality in the legal system and government.

Yael reminded them that the bridge between the USA and Israel goes back to the Founding Fathers of the United States. The Fathers described themselves as a parallel to the Exodus of the Hebrew slaves from Egypt.

Many countries envy, even hate the exceptional benefits that the U.S. and Israel offer their citizens. They witness the material progress, military power, educational advances, technological advances, comforts, and medical strides the U.S. and Israel have made.

These two countries have accepted and aided millions of immigrants from many countries who want to accept our way of life peacefully. These are the two countries that offer hope of a better future for people fleeing unbearable conditions. We should be proud.

The people of Israel and the people of the United States are economically rewarded for their accomplishments and offer a Judeo-Christian concept of sharing.

Those are just some of the reasons the American people remain fundamentally committed to the Israeli people.

We have witnessed that all U.S. and Israeli international apologies gain no allies, no respect and serve to strengthen our enemies resolve. Apologies for our exceptionalism smack of defeat, negativity, abnegation, loss of values, political weakness or perhaps submission to other powers.

We must start with the Judeo-Christian/Western definitions of peace, love, freedom, health, equal opportunity before the law, upward mobility, and prosperity—the measurements of our exceptionalism.

By those standards, we have learned that the failures of Islam and Communism for a "perfect" society reflect distinct values and definitions different from ours. We must have clarity about those differences.

Studies Tom shared with Salo and Yael, supported the idea that Exceptionalism was the strongest bridge linking people in these two democracies. Many historians today are in awe of the millennial Jewish survival defying all odds and theories of history. Some call it a miracle or series of miracles.

Jewish existence, despite the millions murdered for only being thought Jewish or of Jewish ancestry is a miracle unto itself, or at least exceptional.

The resurrection of the Hebrew language after 2,000 years in exile is an exceptional miracle, never seen before in all of history.

The rebirth return and reinvigoration to their land of origin, the country of Israel, is a re-flowering of a national liberation movement. Jews entered the abused land and found sparsely inhabited areas because of deserts, swamps, rampant malaria, massive deforestation and a hostile human environment.

In the US Revolutionary War, it seemed the U.S. was fighting against horrible odds. During Israel's early struggle for survival and Independence (1947-1949) every pundit and General was expecting the Jews to be annihilated, slaughtered in short order. It did not happen.

Salo, with need for definition, pointed out that the opposite of Exceptionalism was decline ("declinism"). Exceptionalism often requires fences to prevent trespassers and enemies from sneaking in. In decline the fences fail.

Decline is mediocrity, apathy, indifference, dependence, irresponsibility, no desire to procreate if it interferes with pleasures and ultimately servitude.

Decline is the first telltale mega-destructive dot in the history of so many civilizations that have disappeared.

The team agreed that the bonds of the U.S.-Israel relationship could easily fall under one word: Exceptionalism. This clarity gave them direction in the same way that ambiguity concealed direction.

When did this Exceptionalism begin?

This was Yael's zone of knowledge and she asked Kelsey to help her out with the human response aspects. She did not want to bore them, so she shared a broad review of history related to growth and decline.

For the last 400 years, the West has demonstrated a surge in an aggressive, intellectually questioning attitude and desire to gain freedom from the tyrannies of a harsh environment, totalitarianism, disease and ignorance. It began as the Age of Enlightenment, using reason, challenges and individualism.

This led to political ideals (such as the Declaration of Independence and the U.S. Bill of Rights) and the Scientific Revolution in the Western World. It led to the release of the grip on power that the Church had used to control people for centuries. The ideas, values and institutions embodied in the Declaration of Independence and Constitution are based directly on our Judeo-Christian civilization. This civilization is the only one that sanctifies and legalizes our rights to Life, Liberty, and the Pursuit of Happiness and is derived in great part from the Hebrew Bible. These ideas and values have continued in the spirit of the American People.

On December 24, 1968 - during the first manned mission to the moon, aboard Apollo 8 – **Commander Frank Borman, Lunar Module Pilot William Anders** and **Module Pilot Jim Lovell**, recited to the American people the first ten verses of Genesis Chapter 1: "In the beginning God created the heaven and the earth... and God saw that it was good."

The profound influence of Jewish tradition on the American Founding Fathers can be seen in the Constitution.

President John Adams' view expressed in a letter to **Thomas Jefferson**: "I will insist that the Hebrews have done more to civilize man than any other nation."

Matthew Arnold, the British critic of the mid-19th Century wrote, "As long as the world lasts, all who want to make progress in righteousness will come to Israel for inspiration as to the people who had the sense for righteousness most glowing and strongest."

Many of the founders of the U.S. felt that Hebrew was a prerequisite for early American scholars. Many universities required it in their curriculum. Hebrew was compulsory at Harvard until 1787. To this day, Yale's insignia bears the Hebrew phrase, Urim V'Tummim (roughly meaning Oracle Learning).

Simon smacked down his last Twinkie when one of those papers by **Prof. Paul Eidelberg,** caught his eye. The professor queried the Israeli governments' failures to highlight America's economic as well as strategic and technological interdependence with Israel even with the threat of oil boycotts.

The U.S. (and much of the world) has been dependent on foreign oil from Middle East countries. Meanwhile, Saudi Arabia, a Sunni Muslim kingdom, has supported the Sunni dominated terrorist gangs, like Al Qaeda and the PLO for several decades, brought the extremist brand of Wahabbi Islam to the U.S. by building hundreds of Mosques and funding universities and Presidential museums with millions of dollars.

At this time, there seems to be a wavering of U.S. dependence on Saudi oil and US economic profits by selling American arms to the Saudis. If there is an economic meltdown in the United States, the availability of this oil from OPEC could become more important.

If the U.S. becomes "oil independent", that political leverage on the U.S. is dramatically diminished. Oil resources can be used as a weapon against Israel and the U.S. There has been an intense Saudi Plan to pressure Washington to view the Israel-Arab/Palestinian conflict as the core of the Middle East problem, and that the solution of this problem requires the U.S. with its military supplier power to induce Israel to return to her pre-1967 borders as a starter. http://www.americanthinker.com/2011/11/israel_and_the_two-state_delusion.html#ixzz1dQ18SuSP

Saudi and **Qatari** oil silently lubricate the repeatedly failed narrative of "land for peace," that Israel is an illegitimate state, and the other hallucination, called a "two state solution."

The intense enmity of the Saudis to Israel was seen in this headline: "Saudi Royal Ups Bounty For Israeli Soldier To $1 million" posted by the Associated Press; RIYADH, Saudi Arabia October 30, 2011.

What does history show about the foundations of relationships:

In World War II, the Arabs were slow to enter the war against Hitler. Some actually aided Hitler like the Mufti of Jerusalem. Iraq was taken over by pro-Nazis in 1941 and joined the Axis powers.

Most of the Arab states sat on the fence, waiting until 1945 to see who would win. By then, Germany was doomed. Since it was necessary to join the war effort on the Allies side to qualify for membership in the nascent United Nations, the Arabs belatedly began to declare war against Germany in 1945: Egypt, on February 25; Syria, on February 27; Lebanon, on February 28; and Saudi Arabia, on March 2. And yet many of these same countries harbored Nazi war criminals for years.

The land for peace is a two-fold fallacy that many American politicians have fallen for. Two states had already been created from the original boundaries given to the Jewish People for a homeland in International Law.

It is true that one country can trade land that is legally owned for land legally owned with another country. Land not owned cannot be traded for owned land. Only a tangible can be traded for a tangible. Promises from an autocracy are unreliable. That is why land cannot be traded for promises.

The second part of the fallacy is that "Palestinian" is only an abbreviation for the "British Mandate of Palestine" held as a trust, by the British specifically for a Jewish Homeland. Anyone born in the thirty year-long British Mandate of Palestine, be they Christian, Muslim or Jewish had their birth certificate stamped with the Mandate of Palestine on it.

Therefore, some were Christian Palestinians, some were Muslim Palestinians and some were Jewish Palestinians.

Many of those who were Arabs (often called nomads) had relatively recently emigrated from many different countries because they were looking for a better life and the work that Jewish enterprises had created. Some were fellahin, impoverished land workers, who did not own property and had no attachment to it. Some had been forcibly mass transferred from countries like Egypt. Many were wandering. Some didn't even have the common language of Arabic considered central to being an Arab.

There is/was no State of Palestine to exchange land with. The land was a territory carved out of the defeated Turkish (not Arab) empire. Even the Turkish Empire did not have boundaries or borders as we know them.

There is another American parallel. When the U.S. "conquered the West", there were tribes of Indians but no demarcated boundaries or borders because of the nomadic quality of their existence.

For historical balance, we need to measure this against nearly a million Jewish Arabs who had lived in and prospered in Arab countries for centuries. They were forced to flee for their lives due to hostile government decrees. These Jews were of the Arabic culture at the time of fleeing. They were known as either Sephardic or Mizrahi Jews. They brought with them a great brain trust but left enormous wealth, property and possessions behind.

Soviet Jews who fled their homeland under duress also brought great talent and education. They were harnessed into the Israeli society's exceptionalism in medical, technological, business, agrarian and humanitarian areas. They're also known as Ashkenazi Jews from Europe and America. The Sephardic and Mizrachi Jews make up half Israel's population. This parallels what has happened in the United States. **President Kennedy** wrote a book about this, A Nation of Immigrants.

Yael learned that Israel has been America's biggest strategic bargain despite malignant media distortions and what Israel bashers have mendaciously spouted. Together with Tom's computer hacking and Salo's big view, they were now ready to lay out their research for a hidden story.

Natural Interdependent Allies

Salo led the way. "We must be aware that while exceptionalism can cause animosity and hatred but also respect and gratitude. Israel has shown in 67 years how an underdeveloped, barren, deforested desert of a country can modernize, whereas many of the former European colonies and even some European countries are collapsing. This makes Israel's exceptional successes an embarrassment to many European leaders.

I am ready to give you thirteen examples at this time about the connector of exceptionalism:

1. U.S. aid and dependence on Israel is animated by national self-interest. What does the U.S. get from Israel? Israel must spend all of the U.S. military aid in the United States, where it provides jobs for over 50,000 American workingmen and women.

2. For FY2007, U.S. military grants to Israel was $2.34 billion and was scheduled to increase to $3.00BN in FY2008.

3. U.S. military aid to Israel stimulates a demand for, and the purchase of, tens of billions of dollars of U.S. weaponry by Saudi Arabia and other Arab states like Libya, Jordan, Turkey and Iraq. This is very profitable for the U.S.

4. Total exports from the U.S. to Israel, between 2004 and 2008, were $58.6BN, almost five times the $12BN Israel received in U.S. aid during this period.

5. The annual average of U.S. exports to Israel during this period was $11.7BN, almost 4 times the average American aid package. So, Israel not only enriches the American economy but saves unimaginable amounts of money for the U.S.

6. We recall that in 1970 the U.S. was tied down in Vietnam. At Washington's request, Israel prevented a Soviet backed Syrian invasion of Jordan. By protecting Jordan from that client of the Soviet Union, Israel thwarted Moscow's ambitions in the Middle East at that time.

7. Let us paraphrase a report of Yoram Ettinger, former Israeli liaison to the U.S. Congress: Israel constantly relays to the U.S. lessons of battle and counter-terrorism, which reduce American losses in Iraq and Afghanistan, prevents attacks on U.S. soil, upgrades American weapons, and contributes to the U.S. economy.

8. Innovative Israeli technologies boost U.S. industries.

9. Without Israel, the U.S. would have to deploy tens of thousands of American troops and a fleet of ships in the eastern Mediterranean

Basin, at a cost of hundreds of billions of dollars a year.

10. In 1981, Israel bombed the Iraqi nuclear reactor, thus providing the U.S. with the option of engaging in conventional wars with Iraq in 1991 and 2003, thereby preventing a possible nuclear war and its horrendous consequences.

11. In 2005, Israel provided America with the world's most extensive experience in homeland defense and warfare against suicide bombers and car bombs.

12. American soldiers train in IDF facilities and Israeli-made drones fly above the Sunni Triangle in Iraq, as well as in Afghanistan, providing U.S. Marines with vital intelligence that saved many American lives.

13. Israel provides America with 25,000 high tech workers, over 300 scientists, and over 900 doctors who studied medicine in Israel, 1,800 Israeli professors and lecturers, 171 high ranking military officers, and thousands of other professional people whose contribution to the American economy is priceless.

Looking at exceptionalism, **Dror Eydor** wrote in 2015 that "Israel is Nothing Short of a Miracle." http://www.israelhayom.com/site/newsletter_article.php?id=25183&r=1

He began measuring in 1984, when the population of Israel was 4.1 million. Thirty years later, the population doubled to stand at 8.2 million.

In 1984, the GNP per capita was $7,000, and in 2014 it climbed to $36,000 — an increase of more than 400%.

In 1984, Israel's foreign currency reserves amounted to $3 billion. Thirty years later, our reserves skyrocketed to $90 billion — an indication of financial stability.

In 1984 high-tech exports were valued at $1 billion, and at $37 billion in 2014 — a 3,600% increase.

According to the Wall Street Journal, Israel is the second most educated country in the world, placing behind Canada and ahead of Japan.

Of the 148 countries analyzed, Israel ranks first in innovative capability, second in entrepreneurship, and third in global innovation.

Thomas Cahill, Irish author of <u>Gifts of the Jews: How a Tribe of Desert</u>

<u>Nomads Changed the Way Everyone Thinks and Feels (Hinges of History...)</u> poetically explained, "The Jew gave us the Outside and the Inside - our outlook and our inner life. We can hardly get up in the morning or cross the street without being Jewish. We dream Jewish dreams and hope Jewish hopes. Most of our best words, in fact - new, adventure, surprise, unique, individual, person, vocation, time, history, future, freedom, progress, spirit, faith, hope, justice - are the gifts of the Jews." This is part of the American Dream.

The <u>Start Up Nation</u> by **Dan Senor** and **Saul Singer** and The Israel Test by **George Gilder**, both written in 2009, are two more books with hundreds of pages and statistics to support more proof of exceptionalism.

Beyond the obvious, Yael pointed out, was an exceptional bridge connecting the American People and Israeli People. The thousands of Israeli and American soldiers who come together at military schools, training facilities, joint exercises, and military industrial plants, in both countries, create a personal human bridge.

Thousands of Israelis study in American universities.

Fedayeen (Arab commandos or guerillas who sacrifice themselves to murder Jews) and terrorist attacks from Arab areas were common occurrences for the Jewish pioneers and Jewish civilians. This is similar to the American westward advancement which required surviving Indian attacks.

Kelsey interrupted with a psychoanalytic insight. "You see, many bright people believed that it is difficult for some nations of the world to live in the presence of the Jews. To them, the Jews represented a conscience. A conscience, of course, can be limiting, irritating and uncomfortable. This miniscule nation of peoples' standards and accomplishments were beyond the imaginable, even if only measured by the exceptional number of Nobel prizes."

The average American sees Israel's independence as a mirror of their independence. American ideals are seen as Israeli ideals.

From the Hebrew Bible, the Christian world derived their Bible and even their Saviour.

Europe during the past centuries teaches us a curious lesson: nations which received and in any way dealt fairly and mercifully with the Jew have prospered, and that the nations that have tortured, murdered, oppressed rejected and expelled them, have written out their own curse. They ignored their own miner's canary. http://www.americanthinker.com/2011/11/israel_and_the_two-state_delusion.html#ixzz1dQ18SuSP

The (ex) Muslim scholar, **Ibn Warraq** observed and documented in, <u>Why the West is Best</u>, that many non-western countries, including Islamic, have had long histories of racism, colonialism, imperialism, slavery, gender and religious apartheid. Much of this history has been omitted from school textbooks, in both the East and the West. The West has fought and won wars to end slavery and has withdrawn from most of its former colonies. It has also steadily granted freedom and rights to both women and minorities. Nevertheless, some Western intellectuals continue to blame only the West for the stagnation in Arab/Muslim countries. He points out that Islam uses intense, rigid dogma in madrassas (Muslim schools) all over the world to ingrain their followers' belief systems. The Muslim problem with Israel is the same problem the medieval Catholic Church had with Galileo when he was put up by an Inquisition.

One possible explanation is that the Arab-Muslim world educational programs teach children to blame the Jews and the West for their situation. Their economic plight is in no small part caused by their leaders who have stolen hundreds of billions of their dollars from international donors or kept oil profits for themselves. The average man is taught that they are victims and deserve aid, compensation and above all, revenge. Typical of this rage was seen when wealthy Jews purchased the 21st century, highly profitable, greenhouses in Gaza and gave them to the Arabs when the Jews were deracinated. The Arabs first act upon gaining autonomy in Gaza was to loot and destroy the profitable greenhouses and every building. Read more: http://www.americanthinker.com/2011/11/israel_and_the_two-state_delusion.html.#ixzz1dQ18SuSP

The total sum of exports from the greenhouses of Gush Katif, which were owned by 200 Jewish farmers was estimated to be $200,000,000.00 per year. http://en.wikipedia.org/wiki/Gush_Katif#cite_note-6

Kelsey needed to add this psychological view. "The U.S. and Israel do not see themselves as victims. That underlying attitude bonds the people in the U.S. and Israel. It shows up in and surveys continuously.

In March of 2013 a poll of Americans showed: Favorable view of Israel,

66%, Palestinian Authority, 15%; Unfavorable view, Palestinian Authority 77%, Israel 29%. by **Frank Newport** and **Igor Himelfarb,** Gallup March 7, 2013 http://www.gallup.com/poll/161159/americans-least-favorable-toward-iran.aspx"

The U.S. bonds with Israel are official, too. On March 5th, 2014 the U.S. House of Representatives adopted the United States-Israel Strategic Partnership Act by a 410-1 vote. The bill declares Israel a "major strategic partner" of the U.S.

The bill expands the U.S.-Israel relationship in a number of areas including forward-deployed U.S. weapons stockpiles in Israel, the transfer of essential military equipment to Israel, assistance for the Iron Dome missile defense system, and the promotion of cooperation in energy, water, science, homeland security, and agriculture. A President cannot override these bills. http://www.jns.org/news-briefs/2014/3/5/aipac-applauds-house-passage-of-us-israel-strategic-partnership-bill#.UxjQTU2PLnt

The uniquely well read, photographic memory of Salo reminded them there was also a "Super Poll" conducted daily on Capitol Hill, where support of Israel constitutes a rare bi-partisan common denominator. About 75% of House Members and about 80% Senators – who are sensitive to the worldview of constituents - overwhelmingly support legislation and resolutions positive to Israel, even in opposition to a President.

Kelsey added that this was natural. Most legislators and constituents identify the Jewish State with their own values: faith, religion, tradition, patriotism, education, democracy-liberty, military strength and counter-terrorism. In reality, there is no Jews-only, "Israel Lobby." What we see is a pro-Israel sentiment that pulses through the American people. Statistics show that the meaning of a "Jewish Lobby" really means most Americans, and the multitudes are not Jewish.

Simon was a little more pragmatic about political realities. To soothe Salo's technical concerns, he explained some of the nature of politics:

- Allies can be economic competitors at times.
- Allies do spy on each other at times.

- Allies can have disagreements at times.
- Allies will not always have identical or time-coincident interests and goals.
- Allies sometimes diverge or grow together, as in a democracy when a new administration takes over.
- Allies can and do compromise with each other for internal political reasons. Thus, the relationship is much like a marriage but with a more valuable certificate of life.

Yael pointed out that the most basic concept of a democracy is that the relationship to government is driven from the people up. That is why people who value life can always choose to resist sending their youth to war. We have seen this in Israel and the U.S.

For democracy to work in a nation there must be a sense of equal opportunity in commerce, education, equal treatment by the law, mutual respect, an irrational pride in their institutions that are often based on religious values, ethnicity or other forms of recognition. These create a sense of political allegiance to the nation which is not valued by the "world citizen."

They turned to the well-known **Prof. Fukuyama** to aid in their definitions and his book, <u>The End of History and the Last Man</u>, 1992. Of Greek origin, "democracy" means the "rule of the people." But what is a "people"? A people is not a polyglot as in "one-man-one-vote" America. The essence of people-hood or nation-hood is particularist and not universalist or humanist. A people must have a distinct ethnic character or way of life, whatever the differences among its individuals.

Professor Fukuyama states that "Democracy requires checks and balances, and it is largely through civil society that citizens protect their rights as individuals, force policymakers to accommodate their interests, and limit abuses of state authority. Civil society also promotes a culture of bargaining and gives future leaders the skills to articulate ideas, form coalitions and govern."

The concept of citizenship which implies rootedness, partiality and particularity, has no meaning to global citizens. If we are citizens of everywhere, we are also citizens of nowhere.

Yael used the example of what was then going on in Egypt to demonstrate what a democracy is not. The chaos in Egypt originally brought forth pious praises of democracy arising.

"So what if the Muslim Brotherhood seizes power?" the pundits asked. "As long as there are democratic elections."

Real democracy, of course, is not one man, one vote, one time. It is possible to have a democracy of cannibals deciding which member they will eat, so long as the majority agrees that's the way to go. Cannibal members have no "bill of rights."

A Constitutional Democracy is health food for its citizens. It is a means, not the end. It is a sustenance that can grow only in a certain type of terrain. The American system makes it very difficult for even democratic elections to undo Constitutional rights or even improve them.

In contrast, the immutable, the perfect Koran is Allah's direct word that can only be temporarily repressed, never undone or changed. While there are differences in some of the details, there is no significant reformation over 1400 years from any of the five major legal schools of Sunni Islamic jurisprudence. (http://www.al-islam.org/inquiries-about-shia-islam-sayyid-moustafa-al-qaz-wini/five-schools-islamic-thought).

The schools all agree that Islam promises an answer to everything. In times of turmoil, it is to Mohammed, and the Koran's hortatory about him as a perfect religious visionary to whom loyal Muslims turn for guidance. This model is profoundly embedded in Muslim culture and will always be there in their politics particularly when they have governmental and military control.

The Koran would not have aided Hitler's rise to power but strangely democracy did!

Democratically elected Hitler and his henchmen always felt reassured they could act with impunity when the international community kept silent in the face of Nazi outrages. Silence was interpreted as acquiescence. Thus, silence helped evil flourish.

Martin Luther King said: "The greatest tragedy of this generation which history will record is not the vitriolic words of those who hate, or the aggressive acts of others, but the appalling silence of the good people."

What are the Seven Constructive Connectors?

With these eye-opening epiphanies, we can now see how and why **Seven Constructive** (Dots) **Connectors** make Israel and the U.S. natural allies. The strength these connectors offer makes survival and prosperity possible as we will see later. Each connector represents a form of Exceptionalism and a form of Democracy. These connector zones also help us define who is a real ally.

1. Cultural
2. Humanitarian
3. Military
4. Reliability + Stability + Dependability = Trust
5. Economically
6. Politically
7. Democracy's Natural enemies.

1. CULTURALLY – HISTORICALLY

Simon could finally toss in his research about some US history.

Our forefather's energetic and fearless pragmatism conquered a continent, industrialized an agrarian nation, won wars and beat a depression. In two centuries, America, with its vast swaths of land, handled waves of immigrants looking for a chance at upward mobility. Americans were able turn ethnic, racial and religious groups into a single prosperous, powerful imperfect nation.

Many acknowledge that Ancient Zionism was a role model for this. Modern Zionism in Israel repeated it in 60 years.

Our nation's builders felt our Bill of Rights were "endowed by our Creator"; a biblical concept originating in the Jewish Bible.

The Founding Fathers recognized the importance of our right to freedom of speech, freedom of religion, yet separation of religion from state, and freedom of the press. They recognized not only our right to pursue wealth honestly and own property, but also to be secure in that property.

Americans have been drawn to the rightness of the Zionist story of pioneering, hearing in it the echoes of our own national narrative. Americans are impressed at the miraculous revival of Hebrew as a spoken language. In all of world history, Hebrew is the only case of a "dead national language" being revived.

Some Americans are drawn for religious reasons. Some are drawn to a democracy where Christianity can not only be practiced, but not attacked, unlike the Arab or Muslim countries.

Like the U.S., culture is important in Israel.

Despite its size, Israel has more orchestras and museums (over 200) per capita than any other nation in the world and publishes more books per capita than any other nation in the world.

Like, the U.S., hospitals are for all citizens. In Jerusalem, Israel, Hadassah Hospital was founded in 1918, long before the State of Israel existed.

Another major hospital, Sha'are Tzedek, also treats all individuals regardless of their religious backgrounds. Its opening ceremony took place on January 27, 1902.

In the Middle East, Israel alone hosts memorials, demonstrating a camaraderie for President Kennedy and Martin Luther King Jr.

Israel is the only country to honor the U.S. by displaying two replicas of the Liberty bell.

Israel built a Living Memorial Plaza and a sculpture to the 9/11 tragedy that befell the United States with melted steel from the Ground Zero Wreckage. Surrounding the monument are plaques with the names of the victims of 9/11.

The ideas and institutions embodied in the Declaration of Independence and Constitution are founded on our Judeo-Christian values.

The US Founding Fathers regarded themselves as "the modern-day People of the Covenant". This naturally connects people to people.

President Woodrow Wilson said that the ancient Jewish nation provided a model for the American colonists: Recalling the previous experiences of the colonists in applying the Mosaic Code to the order of their internal life, it is not to be wondered at that the various passages in the Bible that serve to undermine royal authority, stripping the Crown of its cloak of divinity, held up before the pioneer Americans the Hebrew Commonwealth as a model government.

Judaism and Christianity have gone through many reformations through the centuries, becoming more tolerant and attaining multiple sub-group identities. Enduring these traumas, while maintaining their identity, is exceptional.

That is why people-people connectors endure beyond transient leaders.

Gallup 2014 World Affairs poll of Americans, conducted Feb. 6-9, 2014 revealed the percent who replied that have a very favorable or mostly favorable view of the country:

- 72% Israel
- 45% Egypt
- 35% Saudi Arabia
- 19% Libya
- 19% Palestinian Authority
- 16% Iraq
- 13% Syria
- 12% Iran

http://www.gallup.com/poll/167474/americans-mideast-country-ratings-show-little-change.aspx?

1. *As a CULTURE we value individual freedom. How do we define this? Which countries are considered free?*

Salo wasn't going to let anyone outdo him. He got Tom to open his computer to the U.S. Freedom House report of 2013.

In the Freedom House ratings, a "free" country is one where there is political competition, a climate of respect for civil liberties, significant independent civic life, and independent media.

A "partly free" country is one in which there is limited respect for political rights and civil liberties. A "not free" country is one where basic political rights are absent and civil liberties widely and systematically denied.

Israel is the Middle East's only "free" state, the US-based Freedom House wrote in its annual, a ranking in stark contrast to claims by the country's critics – both domestic and international – who argue that the Jewish state's democratic values are steadily eroding "Israel remains the region's only free country". Israel's ranking is completely dissimilar to that given the West Bank and Gaza – one under the P.A. control and the other under Hamas rule – which are both classified as "not free."

At the same time, "while some areas in the Middle East experienced improvements, it also registered major declines, with a list of worsening countries that includes Iraq, Jordan, Kuwait, Lebanon, Oman, Syria, and the United Arab Emirates." This was before the Syrian Civil War erupted in 2011.

That report, which ranks the world's countries by political rights and civil liberties, characterized Jordan and Syria as "not free," and Egypt and Lebanon as "partly free."

Of the "worst of the worst" countries, the nine countries given the absolute worst ratings in the world, two were in the region: Saudi Arabia and Syria. Sudan was also rated in the bottom nine.

Turkey currently leads the world in the number of journalists behind bars," the report read.

According to the report, during his early years in power P.M. Erdogan pushed through laws toward greater minority rights. "More recently, however, his government has jailed hundreds of journalists, academics, opposition party officials, and military officers in a series of prosecutions aimed at alleged conspiracies against the state and Kurdish organizations," the report continued. Islamic religion is now on the resurgence.

http://www.freedomhouse.org/sites/default/files/FIW%202013%20Booklet.pdf

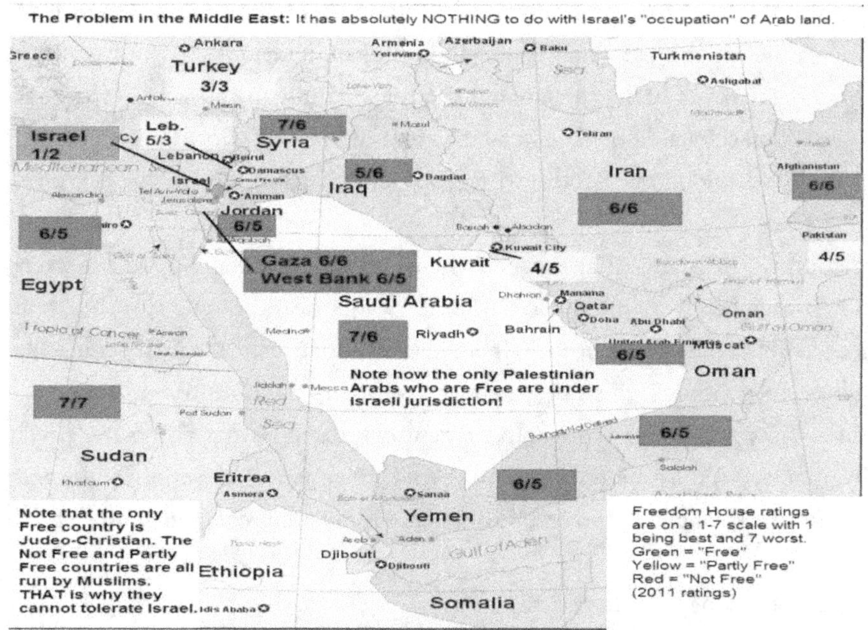

The problem is not nor has it ever been Israeli "occupation" of Arab land, noting that the Arabs attacked Israel repeatedly prior to 1967. The problem is that Israel is a LIVING DAILY REMINDER that what its neighbors call Islam can offer their people nothing but poverty, ignorance, superstition, violence, and squalor

Tom smiled. "I'm starting to get it. This makes the U.S. and Israel different from other countries in the Middle East and more similar to each other. Totalitarian, authoritarian, fascist, kingships, despotisms, communist, dictatorships, oligarchies or theocracies should probably not be considered true or reliable allies. Pure theocracies cannot accept man made laws because it would undermine or contradict their religious beliefs."

There are several types of people to people connectors embedded in our cultures between Israel and the United States. So, while the leadership of each country is important, they are elected for limited periods of time, but the people to people connectors span decades. Kelsey proposed to discuss just five in this context.

1. Common values like freedom, responsibility, Judeo-Christian morality and a sense of mutual fellowship crossing ethnic borders and religious beliefs are visible in the West.

2. Personal Locus of control: The Judeo-Christian value system leans heavily on personal responsibility for individuals behaviour – guilt is the result of poor behaviour. Removing guilt and atonement for one's unacceptable behaviour is seen as a desire and effort to correct one's behaviour, and even retribution/compensation for damage caused.

In contrast, in Islam, Allah rules all the believers and Allah's word is perfect. When non-believers intrude on Islamic "waqfs" (land they claim they conquered in the past and is now theirs in perpetuity), Muslims entitle themselves to be seen as victims which they believe gives them the right to retaliate in any way for any presumed wrongs. In that culture, shame (what others negatively say about you) must be removed no matter how many generations old it may be. If the loss of control over a waqf occurs it must be regained at all costs.

3. Personal Identity
    In the liberal, non-Islamic West, the concept of personal identity dominates over group identity in many ways. Aside from parenting, individuals derive their identity from individual aspirations. Their identities can and do change with time. This leads to creativity, progress, arguments and dissension.

In Islam, group identity dominates over personal identity, particularly with devout Muslims, immersed in that culture. The group can be the clan, the tribe or Islam. National identity subsumes to Islam, the clan or the tribe. Many devout Muslims would rather die than give up the group collective identity as that is where they attain their admission to Paradise for eternity. This dampens creativity dramatically, creates cohesion and consensus. This is a concept in sociology called "collectivism."

4. Tolerance and respect of subculture to varying degrees occurs in the Judeo-Christian value system. In Islam there is a concept that the House of Islam must eliminate the House of War. Islam considers itself superior to all other movements.

5. In the West, generally, citizens trust that the law of the land will be consistent and fairly applied to all, as a basic belief, however flawed. In Islam there is a clear dualism in applying laws.

2. HUMANITARIAN

Both the U.S. and Israel send many groups for natural disaster aid, agricultural aid, health aid, economic independence and education. We came up with sixteen easy ones, but here are the top nine.

1. According to **US Congressman Ted Poe**, Israel was the only country in the world to physically come to aid of the U.S. citizens by distributing large supplies of gas to hospitals, food, batteries, and generators who were devastated by Hurricane Sandy in Oct. 2012 while 158 countries were still busy cashing checks from America.

2. Israel is the largest immigrant-absorbing nation in the world, per capita. People from over 120 different nationalities have come to Israel. Most immigrants come in search of democracy, religious freedom, and economic opportunity. This is also part of U.S. history.

3. Israel is the only country in the Middle East where the Christian population has grown over the last 50 years. This is part of US history, too.

4. Israel is the only country in the Middle East where women enjoy full political rights. This is part of the US, too even if flawed in some ways.

5. Israel is very research oriented, like the U.S. One Israeli break through was a unique coagulating bandage, that was used to stop the life-threatening head wound during the attempted assassination of Rep. **Gabrielle Giffords.** It saved her life.

6. Every year in U.S. hospitals 7,000 patients die from treatment mistakes. An Israeli company developed a computerized system for ensuring proper administration of medications, thus removing human error from medical treatment.

7. Close coordination with the US enabled Israeli medical teams to arrive amongst the first on the scene in the earthquake-Tsunami in Japan, 2010; Hurricane in 2010 Haiti; earthquakes in 1985 in Mexico;

Armenia 1988; Argentina 1994; Greece,1999; Kosovo,1999; Kenya, 2002; Nepal in 2015.

8. Feeding the people: The Middle East has been growing date palms for centuries. The average tree is about 18-20 feet tall and yields about 38 pounds of dates a year. Israeli date trees are now yielding 400 pounds/year and are short enough to be harvested from the ground or a short ladder. Americans are also looking into ways to increase the food supply.

9. Water scarcity is a very serious issue in the Middle East. About 20,000 people seeking the Israeli know-how responsible for expanding the country's water-related exports to an estimated $1 billion to $2 billion over the last five years were shared by Israel.

Rivka Borochov's report was illuminating. http://www.mfa.gov.il/MFA/InnovativeIsrael/WATEC-Israel-Nov_2011.htm

The list grows every year.

3. **MILITARILY – Strategic**

    Simon, Tom and Salo understood the necessity of a preemptive response to a danger to a country's civilians. Anticipatory self-defense and therefore preemption with a reference to the United Nations: "In 2004, the U.N. secretary general convened the "High-level Panel on Threats, Challenges and Change." The conclusions of this panel state clearly that "any group seeking to attack civilians is guilty of terrorism; the right of self-defense includes thwarting an imminent attack, without waiting for the actual event; and that reckless regimes should not be permitted to develop weapons of mass destruction."

In 2014, **General Chuck Krulak**, former Commandant of the US Marine Corps, remarked that "the formulation of US battle tactics is based on the Israeli book."

In March, 2007, **General John Craddock**, the Supreme Commander of NATO, told the House Armed Services: "In the Middle East, Israel is the closest ally of the US, consistently supporting our interests through security cooperation."

In July, 2003, **Brig. General Michael Vane**, Deputy Chief of Staff at the US Army Training and Doctrine Command stated that Israel's counter-terrorism experience shaped the US war on terrorism. Together they uncovered a powerful bond between the Israeli military and intelligence, with the Pentagon, the CIA and the Department of Defense, that went deeper than any in the Executive Branch. Allies have similar enemies. Enemies are usually adversaries from opposing types of governance. Allies tight relations strengthen each other's security.

And Israel Provides the U.S. with 3 Early Warning systems:

Early warning system #1 The Canary in the Mine

What happens to Israel and the Jews first is a harbinger for other democracies. History has repeated that, like the miner's canary, harm to the Jews or Israel is the first warning sign of bigger destructive attacks on human rights. Current examples are Nazi Germany's final solution for the Jews; Iraq's farhuds (massacres and pogroms) and expulsion of the Jewish population; Poland's participation in the mass murders of the Jewish population; and Stalin's, murderer of approximately 18 million and murder of prominent Moscow doctors (most of whom were Jewish) in 1952.

Early Warning System #2 and The Cassandra Effect

Certain brave leaders have spoken out to be rejected and attacked by too many:

1. **Zev Jabotinsky's** warnings to Jews about Hitler before WW II.
2. **Israeli Prime Minister Begin's** elimination of Iraq's Osirak nuclear reactor in 1981.
3. **Israeli Prime Minister, Olmert's** elimination of the Syrian al-Kibar nuclear facility (aided by North Korea) under Bashar Assad in 2007.
4. **Israeli Prime minister, Netanyahu's** warnings about a nuclear Iran (aided by North Korea).

Early Warning System #3 comes from Israeli Intelligence sources that cannot be gotten by the U.S. or NATO, spy satellites or electronic intercepts alone.

The U.S. gets superb harbors and sea-lift capabilities that the U.S. can count on from Israel. Not so with Libya, Egypt, Tunisia, Iran or Turkey.

General Alexander Haig, who was the Supreme Commander of NATO and US Secretary of State was clear: "Israel is the largest, most battle-tested and cost-effective US aircraft carrier, which does not require even one American soldier, cannot be sunk and is located in a critical region for American national security and economic interests. If Israel did not exist - the US would have to deploy a few additional aircraft carriers to the Mediterranean, along with tens of thousands of military personnel, costing the US taxpayers $20BN annually and dragging the US into additional regional and international confrontations."

At 2013 figures, each American soldier costs the U.S. $200,000 a year to station abroad with the necessary military supplies. The U.S. pays for about 2.2 million soldiers. Approximately 220,000 are overseas. It pays for 160,000 private contractors out of country. You do the math. How much does Israel save the U.S. by acting as its eastern flank? (FLAME, www.factsandlogic.org, Nov. 2013)

Annual military aid to Israel, is roughly equal to one quarter the cost of building one Zumwalt-class destroyer (multi-role, surface warfare, anti-aircraft, and naval fire support).

According to **Senator Daniel Inouye**, former Chairman of the Senate Intelligence Committee and current Chairman of the full Appropriations Committee, the intelligence –shared with the USA - exceeds the scope of intelligence received by the US from all NATO countries combined.

An Israeli company, **Rafael** has developed a miniature anti-missile system that detects incoming projectiles and shoots them down before they reach the armored vehicles. If successful, the "Trophy" system could radically alter the balance of power.

State-owned **Israel Military Industries** is producing **"Iron Fist,"** an anti-missile defense that is expected to be installed on Israeli armored personnel carriers.

That system takes a different approach from **Trophy**, first using jamming technology that can make the missile veer off course, and if that fails, creating a "shock wave" to blow it up, **said Eyal Ben-Haim,** vice president of the company's land-system division. **Moriya Ben-Yosef** 12/2/2012.

The **"ManPack RJ"**, can jam the signals that trigger an IED (Improvised Explosive Device). http://www.israeldefense.com/?CategoryID=483&ArticleID=911

Plasan, an Israeli company, created-armored mine- resistant ambush-protected vehicles. In 1989, Plasan won its first contract to make body armor for the Israel Defense Forces, and then for IDF vehicles.

General George Keegan, former Chief of US Air Force Intelligence, stated that between 1974 and 1990, **"Israeli aid to America was worth between \$50-80BN in intelligence, research and development savings, Soviet weapons systems captured and transferred to the Pentagon, and testing Soviet military doctrines up to 1990 when the USSR collapsed...Equal to five CIAs."**

Israel is America's only trusted advance supply depot for the whole Middle East.

For the Pentagon, developing and deploying a major new system can take more than a decade. By contrast, the Israel Defense Ministry gave Rafael the contract for Iron Dome in 2007, and by March 2009 the system was fully ready for testing. The tenet was, the closer the Israelis were to attaining the same technical breakthrough, the more willing the United States would be to share the technology. Israel represents the deep connection to America as its front line of defense from fanatic sources originating in the Middle East.

According to **Ambassador (ret.) Yoram Ettinger** ("Israel-Hamas: the Frontier of the Clash of Civilizations" in Israel Hayom, November 23, 2012, http://bit.ly/XJCo4j), noted Israel's battle against Hamas constitutes the most recent chapter in the clash of civilizations between Western democracies and Islamic terrorism. This battle highlights the role of the Jewish State, as the national security and high-tech beachhead of the US, in a region which is critical to vital US defense and commercial interests. The role of Israel as a national security and high-tech producer, for the US, is doubly pertinent at a time when the US was experiencing a military and economic contraction.

Israel confronts Hamas, which is increasingly dominated by the intolerant, supremacist 7th century aspects of Islam. While Western democracies cherish life, Hamas and the PLO consecrate Shuhada - martyrdom and suicide bombing – and the despicable use of human shields using children and women.

This one is very important to the U.S.: Israel's power projection of the U.S. can contribute to the stability of pro-U.S. Arab regimes, threatened by anti-US rogue and terrorist regimes. In 2012, Israel's posture of deterrence bolstered Jordan's pro-US Hashemite regime. The Hashemite are currently threatened by the surging trans-national ISIS, anti-US, Muslim Brotherhood, the "parent" organization of Hamas, which is using Russian-manufactured military systems, supplied by Iran through the anti-US Sudan.

A strong Israel extends the strategic might of the U.S. in the Middle East at a time when unreliable Arab allies of the US are increasingly threatened by ISIS, al-Qaeda, Hezbollah and Hamas-terrorists some even backed by Russia.

The **Joint Helmet-Mounted Display** system for F-22 pilots leans heavily on Israeli technology.

Israel's ongoing war against Hamas terrorism highlights Israel's added-value to the US national security and economy via the **"David's Sling"**, and **"Arrow 3"**, **"Iron Dome"** and **"Iron Beam"** (laser) anti-missile air defense systems.

Ground-breaking Israeli developed "Iron Dome," (which is co-financed with the US) will eventually be deployed by the US and its allies. They will be co-manufactured by the US and Israel, expanding employment, research and development and the export base of the US.

Additionally, the US and Israel are working on **"Underground Iron Dome"** for tunnel detection capabilities. This protects a country's borders and finds enemy storage depots.

Israeli **Elbit Systems** designed the airline industry's most impenetrable flight security, **MUSIC,** (multi spectral infrared countermeasure). This can prevent commercial airliners from being shot down by missiles. The experience that Israel has had fighting terrorism and all its different tentacles has supplied valuable information to the U.S.

The list grows every year.

Salo wondered: If an Arab or Muslim country had the military power that the U.S. or Israel has, would they hesitate to use that power to destroy the only Democracy in the Middle East?

4   *RELIABILITY = STABILITY + DEPENDABILITY =TRUST*

Yael began with a bang, "This is the most important underpinning of the international Connectors. It is why the "Arab Spring," is really a horrendous haboob (a mammoth, sun-covering wall of a moving sandstorm). It is bad for all.

A weak country cannot be dependable. An unstable country can't be reliable. Reliability is paramount: Currently there is a growing fear among America's traditional Arab allies that Washington's support can no longer be relied on those they consider aggressors, specifically Iran and its proxies. Dependability is a critical part of being an ally. We must be able to TRUST an ally to be STABLE much more than those who we do not consider allies.

The relationship must be a two-way street, like a marriage. It has been historically validated that democratic governments are much more stable than autocracies, dictatorships and theocracies. Logic 101 states that when an ally is weakened militarily, economically or politically, it will not be as stable or reliable."

Can we expect stability from OPEC countries? They are all run through wealthy oligarchy systems in which are a minority in their own country. The GCC (Gulf Cooperation Council) countries cooperate with each other off and on.:

- Saudi Arabia, Kuwait, Bahrain, the UAE, Qatar and Oman, once rock-solid, have broken up into three groups.
- Arab/Muslim countries disagree on borders amongst themselves:
- Syria, does not recognize its border with Lebanon.
- Turkey's annexation of the province of Iskenderun (Alexandretta) was destabilizing.

"Is this a reliable ally?" asked Simon. "Turkey's **Recep Tayyip Erdogan** and his ruling Justice and Development Party (AKP), specifically went against the U.S. sanctions with Iran by 'the massive 'gas-for-gold' sanctions-busting scheme that yielded neighboring Iran some $13 billion in Turkish gold between 2012 and 2013. Turkey funneled precious metals into Iran and identifies the sources of metals for which Turkey served as a transit point. It specifically cites 'the UAE, Switzerland, Ghana, and South Africa" for their roles in various schemes.'" The Foundation for Defense of Democracies (FDD), 14th March 2014.

Syria also claims Arab-populated territories along Turkey's southern border and has a water conflict with Turkey while being torn apart by an internationally involved civil war.

Iraq does not recognize Kuwait and has dormant claims to its border with Iran.

The borders between the various United Arab Emirates have not been finally determined; nor has the one between Saudi Arabia and Yemen.

Egypt has longstanding border conflicts with Sudan and Ethiopia.

Libya has border claims with Chad.

There are various border conflicts between Morocco, Algeria, and Mauritania that have already sparked several rounds of war. Iran has territorial claims in the Persian Gulf, including a claim to all of Bahrain.

Jordan has claims regarding Syria.

Simon, added there were several ways to measure stability.

1. With more than 3,000 high-tech companies and startups, Israel has the highest concentration of hi-tech companies in the world — apart from the Silicon Valley in the U.S. Now it seems that the state of Texas has the most hi-tech companies. Foreign investment is a great sign of stability.

2. Outside the United States and Canada, Israel has the largest number of NASDAQ listed companies.

3. Israel is ranked #2 in the world for venture capital funds right behind the U.S. Venture capital does not take risks in unstable areas.

4. Israel's $100 billion economy is larger and more stable than all of is immediate neighbors combined.

5. Israel produces more scientific papers per capita than any other nation by a large margin - 109 per 100,000 people —as well as one of the highest per capita rates of patents filed.

6. Israel is one of two countries in the world that entered the 21st cen-

tury with a net gain of (240 million) planted trees, made more remarkable because this was achieved in an area considered mainly desert. That is a sign of a people who are here to stay.

7. What better way to display one's roots, than with the museums of your heritage and culture? One can find more museums per capita in Israel than any other country.

5. ECONOMICALLY

According to Intel's CEO, Intel would have been devastated by the competition, if not for its four research and development centers and two manufacturing plants in Israel, which developed its most advanced microprocessors, Pentium, Sandbridge, Atom and Centrino.

Will Congress rise to the occasion by legislating the US-Israel Water Cooperation Act in the areas of water technologies, water industries, water conservation, water supply and consumption, water quality, irrigation, sewage recycling, desalination, water security, etc.?

Salo added, "The current drought afflicting the United States, which has spread to more than half of the continental United States, is the most widespread drought in more than half a century.... The US government has declared nearly 1,300 counties across 29 states a federal disaster area."

Head of the Desalination Department in Israel's Water Authority claims Israel can help: "Educating people to use less water... The average consumption of water in the US per person is 3 or 4 times of Israel's.... [More] efficient irrigation systems: 90-95% of agriculture in Israel uses drip irrigation as opposed to only 5% in America. Proper maintenance of water pipes - there is a 20% average leakage rate on water pipes in the US, not quite as bad as London's 40% average leakage, nonetheless twice the amount of Israel's leakage.

Regarding sewage water - about 80% is reused in Israel for irrigation, as opposed to America's 1%..." (Arutz 7, Gideon Israel, July 25)."

According to U.S. **Representative Steve Rothman**:

"Under the 2010 U.S. budget, about $75 billion, $65 billion and $3.25 billion will be spent on military operations and aid in Afghanistan, Iraq and

Pakistan during this fiscal year, respectively ($143.5 B). Israel will receive $3 billion, in military aid only. There is no economic aid to Israel, other than loan guarantees that continue to be repaid in full and on time. About 70% of the $3 billion aid must be used by Israel to purchase American military equipment. This provides real support for U.S. high- tech." ...imagine the additional terrible cost in U.S. blood, and the hundreds of billions more of American taxpayer dollars, if Saddam Hussein had developed nuclear weapons, or if Syria possessed them.

"Israel also has permitted the U.S. to stockpile arms, fuel, munitions and other supplies on its soil to be accessed whenever America needs them in the region. This is not only a military advantage but a cost savings to the U.S."

As of 2016 the Obama administration now requires 100% of the aid to be spent in the U.S.

An ally is often additive to a nation's economy as well as security.

Israel supplies Apple with robust miniaturized solid-state memory systems for its iPhones, iPods and iPads, and Microsoft with critical user interface designs for the OS7 product line and the Kinect gaming motion-sensor interface, the fastest rising consumer electronic product in history...U.S. defense and prosperity increasingly depend on the ever-growing economic and technological power of Israel. If we stand together we can deter or defeat any foe... We need Israel as much as it needs us" ("Wall Street Journal", July 5, 2011).

Economic independence is an asset between allies. Allies improve each other's trade and environment. Allies show a positive interaction and most often are win-win relations.

Allies offer aid when possible. Three and a half million tourists visited Israel because they thought it was safe enough during 2010. That is proportionally equal to 138 million tourists visiting the USA, yet only 60 million tourists visited the USA in 2010. From a nearly total reliance on imported energy, Israel can become - by 2014 - a major exporter of natural gas. The annual average of U.S. exports to Israel during 2004-2008 was $11.7BN, more than 4 times the average American aid package!

6. **POLITICALLY (International relations)**

Democracies are characterized by decentralization of power dispersed across different branches and levels of government, intended to give citizens and their elected representatives a bigger say in their lives.

When government officials fear its citizens, we have a democracy, as in the USA and Israel. When the citizens fear the government, we have a tyranny.

Dictatorships are characterized by centralization—power in the hands of one oligarchy, one group, one junta, sometimes one person who leads a subservient bureaucracy.

The team learned that Liberal Democracy (there have been 507 different types of democracy listed in academia) is on one end of the political governing spectrum and Totalitarian control is on the other side. The worst-case scenario for humans is violent anarchy. But that is not a form of governing any more than terrorism is.

How can we define an ally?

In the U.N., only Israel consistently voted with the U.S. better than any other "ally." Nine of top ten countries who are US foreign aid recipients voted against condemnation of Iran's human rights record. It that the sign of an ally or adversary?

Contrast that with the political support of Saudi Arabia who votes against the U.S. 73% of the time in the U.N.

1. Egypt, for example, after voting 79% of the time against the United States, still receives $2+ billion annually in US Foreign Aid.
2. Jordan votes 71% against the United States and receives $192,814,000 annually in US Foreign Aid.
3. Pakistan votes 75% against the United States receives $6,721,000 annually in US Foreign Aid.
4. India, a "democracy", votes 81% against the United States receives $143,699,000 annually. Source: U.S. State Department.

Democracies are natural allies.

America's enemies deeply and intuitively understand that no U.S. goals or resources in the Middle East are remotely important as Israel. To weaken support of Israel is to weaken the influence of the United States in the world. Who will trust a country that is supposed to be an ally but does not act like one?

Israel's population is cramped into a space the size of New Jersey with 80% of its population crammed into a portion much smaller than that. Hemmed in by enemies on three sides, at this time, with over 150,000 Hezbollah and Hamas rockets and missiles at the ready.

ISIS is aiding a very violent upset in Syria and Iraq, attempting to infiltrate Jordan but may soon be dispersed.

Who might Iran be allied with? Iran's nuclear ambitions and genocidal intent are visible on the horizon.

Clearly, Israel needs every acre it now controls. Still, despite its huge technological advances, its survival continues to rely on peremptory policing of the area now called the "West Bank". Israel is forced to depend on an ever-advancing shield of antimissile technology, and on the unswerving commitment of the U.S.

This is no one-way street. At a time of acute recession, debt overhang, "green" versus energy policy and venture capitalists who hope to sustain the U.S. economy and defense with Facebook pages and Twitter feeds, U.S. defense and prosperity increasingly intertwines with the ever-growing economic and technological power of Israel.

Tom's patriotism was aglow. "If we stand together we can deter or defeat any foe. Failure to stand together will doom the U.S. and its allies to a long low intensity war against ascendant jihadist barbarians. International population demographics, fanatic commitment, and nuclear weapons of mass destruction may soon be at our enemies' side. Nuclear capabilities by rogue regimes are a threat to humanity. We have no assurance of victory through delayed or re-active measures. The Western World, specifically the U.S., needs Israel as much as it needs the EU."

7. DEMOCRACY'S NATURAL ENEMIES

Enemies are defined as forms of governance/political systems that are the opposite of democracy called often seen as totalitarianism. It does not matter what the disguise might be: Communism, Leninism, Maoism dictatorships, Nazism, Fascism or Islamism.

Israel is designated by Iran, Hamas, the PLO, Fatah, and the P.A. as well as most Muslim/Arab regimes in the Middle East, as "The Little Satan," due to its values and unconditional alliance with "The Big Satan," the USA.

Unlike Western democracies, Hamas, the PLO and the Arab Middle East enshrine hate-education and fanatic bigotry towards the "infidel" Christian, Jew, Buddhist, Hinduism or a Muslim of different persuasion.

Contrary to the ideal of peaceful co-existence, Hamas, and Islam at-large intend to bring Muslims and all "infidels" to total spiritual and physical submission (the root word for Islam is "al-Silm," which means "submission" or "surrender").

Israel is the only Western democracy in the Middle East, an unconditional ally of the USA, and is confronted daily by the non-democratic Arabs who aligned themselves with America's enemies in the past and present: Bin Laden, Saddam Hussein, North Korea, Hugo Chavez, Khomeini, Khameini, the Communist Bloc and Nazi Germany, as well as with America's rivals: Russia and China.

For simplicity sake, consider this identifier: that which strengthens Israel, will strengthen the U.S. and its true political allies. If it strengthens Israel's democracy, it will weaken violent Zealots of all types.

A signal is sent around the world that the U.S. upholds its commitments. This has been shown to prevent the spread of violence through the fear of a strong retaliation. Additionally, if it strengthens Israel, it weakens Russian and Iranian attempts to dominate the Middle East. This is a growing U.S. concern. If it weakens Israel, it will weaken the U.S. and strengthen the enemies of the U.S.

Simon Says:

It is not now, nor has it ever been a solely Jewish or Israeli issue.

We have enumerated that Israel offers the U.S. low cost intelligence and protection because Israel's troubles are not just a Jewish issue. And the U.S. does the same for Israel in other ways.

Israel's existential threat is dramatic and always imminent.

The same issues face the U.S. but are not dramatic (but could be imminent as we observed on 9/11 or an EMP attack) at this time.

We have seen that both countries provide a safe haven for those who are oppressed and those who crave to live in peace adding to society and not separating from it.

Both countries need clarity about mutual benefits. Clarity is a consolidating and focusing tool. Ambiguity is the opposite of clarity. It is a favorite of TerVol. It becomes diffusing and divisive to the fabric of society and international relations.

We have observed that if we don't have clarity (the ability to discriminate) between who are our allies and who our enemies are, then we will inevitably betray our allies and aid our enemies.

When a country is internally ambiguous, its leaders must rise to the occasion uniting the people and point out the lessons of history, of its heroes, of common values, of a pro-active influential approach, and the clarity of what is an existential threat to bring the people together.

We have seen over and over that clarity is critical to support those who hold the same values. The constructive and destructive dots gave a better picture, but far from complete, so far.

Our job will be to connect more of them to form a picture that anyone can understand.

We must respect the unchanging story of human nature and use the dots of history wisely to create pro-active behavior. With clarity, we can recognize those who are national and sub-national enemies (non-state actors) and internal enemies even as they disguise themselves.

TerVol works by using destructive dots intentionally masquerading as constructive dots. TerVol cannot succeed without them. O.K. team, let's go to work and expose TerVol, humanity's eternal enemy.

#3 Humanity's Eternal Enemy - TerVol Identified (Termites and Volcanoes)

Simon says:

"We had connected thousands of constructive dots to create a picture of the great relationship that the U.S. has had with Israel and the mutual strengths it created. Now we can focus on identifying the destructive dots.

Regardless of the bonds that the U.S. and Israel shared, both internally and externally, we have glimpsed at the deadliest danger to ever hit humanity, TerVol. Religion had vaguely called it the Devil with no direct means of dealing with it. It is critical that we get clarity on what it looks like and the dangers it poses in its various disguises. This means collecting even more dots, some of them invisible without the special lens of education, history, and the illumination by very bright minds."

"You mean we have more research to do?" they belted out simultaneously to Simon. "More?"

They started brainstorming and quickly discovered what was stopping them. The team discovered that TerVol's most powerful secret weapon is a look-you-in-the-eye hypocrisy often attired in the blinding disguise of virtue.

TerVol could undermine a society like termites undermine a building and even create plagues and starvation claiming that overpopulation would ruin the planet. It could attack like a violent volcano, tornado or hurricane. That is how the monster earned its name, TerVol. This is how it achieved its anti-democracy, anti-exceptionalism and antisemitic goals.

Sophocles warned, "What people believe prevails over truth," thus propaganda itself became an issue to study.

Salo's broad, overblown research identified that humanity's most violent tendencies are and have been, a simmering volcano of ancient adventitious hatred.

The best way to define any dangerous monster is by its behavior, regardless of its attire: Identifying the dots and connecting them to create the motion picture.

TerVol fights liberal democracy and personal freedoms.

It attacks minorities, particularly Jewish communities and Jews. Historically this has been seen as a first step to foment hatred towards others, and today, it nibbles away at the exceptionalism of the U.S. and Israel.

The cowardly TerVol is too intimidated by the enormous strength and girth of the U.S. democracy with its exceptionalism in economic and military affairs. In the U.S., TerVol will occasionally use its violent force to launch riots, but it more often uses daily stealth of propaganda and hypocrisy. This is seen as a crowbar called divisiveness.

Salo's broad conceptualization realized that Israel is again a perfect model for us to study.

Israel is sometimes called the "Little Satan," just as the U.S. is called the "Big Satan." Israel and Jews are small and more easily attacked. Does a bully attack the bigger or the smaller? Does the bully attack the soft target or the hard target? This makes Israel a perfect case study.

Salo saw this paradigm was useful to predict challenges that will soon face the U.S. Israel also represents a radar system or predictor for the U.S., alerting us to the threats of totalitarian, despotic, and theocratic states.

We can recognize TerVol at work. The chimera poses as others who apologize for intentional rocket attacks on civilians, defend suicide bombings, aid in smuggling weapons, terrorists or drugs, using innocents as human shields, murdering innocent children, teaching innocent children to hate and kill. The apologists for terror explain why blowing up public buses is necessary. Directly or indirectly they creat a fifth column, co-abuse with the media, urge UN General Assembly charges against Israel and thereby try to weaken a liberal democracy's freedoms. Stooping lower, TerVol uses racially motivated boycotting, sanctions and divestment attacks under the guise of promoting goodness.

Salo spelled it out, "This clever monster's most powerful secret weapon is "hypocrisies," creating corrosive relations. Hypocrisy is a tiny step away from lying. These collaborators often disguise themselves as the 'Moral High Ground' crowd, or those who are so sanctimonious that they claim to only want to save soul of the U.S. or the soul of Israel. They should be called Pecksniffians, named after Dickens character, Seth Pecksniff, a sanctimonious surveyor and architect "who has never designed or built anything", and one of the biggest hypocrites in fiction. Oops, before you yell at me, let me explain. They are those who are hypocritically and unctuously feign benevolence or high moral principles. Pecksniffians are like the termite colonies in a healthy building and they are found in every society. They destroy and demoralize society's cohesiveness."

The team had to decide on how they would describe the toplofty position of those who had hidden agendas. How did TerVol make the common sense of the common man seem immoral?

First off, they found that the dots exposed the definition of a "double standard" because it added ambiguity, not clarity.

They reviewed hundreds of events that were inaccurately reported. They realized that they needed a hundred more dots to create a clear picture. They argued for quite a while and finally decided to measure hypocrisy by documenting a four-tiered standard of hypocrisy. They could no longer use the oversimplified term, "double standard." Again, Israel was their model.

A quad-standard of affairs means that the Jews or Israel are held to be responsible for:

1) A standard considerably above the norm.
2) While some of the big countries can't be held accountable to any norm.
3) Other countries are held to a standard norm of behavior, sometimes called International Law.
4) And for other nations and subnational groups the standard is set below the norm and they are not held responsible for behavior at the lowered level. That standard, below the norm, is relevant to dictatorships, terror groups and totalitarian states.

Because this last norm, so often seen, it is in direct violation of the U.N. Charter. It demonstrates the hypocrisy.

The beginning of "Quadpocrisy"

"I got it," said Kelsey, "Let's call it **quadpocrisy.**" And a new, more accurate term was born.

One of the easiest ways to recognize quadpocrisy is in the area of self-defense. World bodies greatly elevate, distort or redefine international law when it comes to Israel, and Israel alone, when defending itself.

Hypocrisy is the quad-standard bearer. Not admitting this, is intellectually dishonest or gullibly hypocritical. The double standard fails again as an explanation.

Simon's fiancé Yael, pushed back her long, jet black hair and began to spill dots all over their giant table with the following information: Hypocrisy hides and rewrites history and current events with a gruesome smile. Hypocrisy takes on active and passive forms with a wink and a "Who knew?".

At this time, the fighting in Syria has killed hundreds of thousands of their own people and displaced more than four million. "Who knew" that the expanding Arab Spring would have such foul, destructive weather?

Yael learned why historians had called the Jewish People the "miner's canary" of humanity. Miner's carry their equipment and a canary down into the mines. Escaping poisonous gases cause the very sensitive canary in the cage to stop chirping and then fall off its perch, comatose. If the miners see this, they act and survive. If the miners do not see the warning or abide by that warning, they die! The "mine" of democratic countries is quite deep. Looking back at World War II we can see that the bigger the mine, the deeper the shaft, the worse the disaster. The Jewish People would have served as the miner's canary in WW II if the world would have only cared about the warning signs, then perhaps sixty million people would not have had to die.

Hypocrisy is used to hide the warning signals of danger by shrouding the life-protecting cage in a burka (a Muslim female ambulatory full body bag that completely hides identity). Hypocritical spokespeople start with placating excuses and stories so that the multitudes will not be aware of the danger. Hypocrisy also hides the dots by the use of political conformity, political casuistry and moral superciliousness. It puts the thinkers on the defensive. It inverts facts and time sequences.

John Milton warned long ago, "Hypocrisy is the only evil that walks invisible."

Yael threw out a post: by **Avi Benlolo** on 9/21/11, in The Huffington Post, Canada. "The contempt and hatred heaped on Israel, has been documented in such forums as the UNGA, UNESCO, UNRWA, the OIC, ICESCO, the Arab League, etc., is in fact, contempt and hatred of Western Democracy and Civilization."

Some argue that on a personal level we should forgive an individual's mistakes or hypocrisies. Give the criminal, liar, or cheater another chance. If numerous violations become visible as intended for personal benefit, one's integrity is called into question. Integrity is a pervasive character trait and not a one-time deal. There is no reliability without integrity. On an international level, trusting well-known deceivers and their narratives becomes a suicidal leap of faith. Call them a current asset, or even a "frienemy" if necessary, but it has always been wiser to distance oneself from them or incapacitate their ability to do harm.

On a national basis, too many lives are at stake not to expose the hypocrisy! This takes courage to go against the ice block of popular political contagion. Internationally, under the guise of urging another nation to do what is good for itself, only to cause damage, reveals a hidden agenda, creates misunderstandings of every magnitude, and trust is lost. Inconsistency, cunning, lying, duplicity, deception, subterfuge in diplomacy have all been allies of TerVol's hypocrisy.

Observed in its volcano aspect, TerVol can thrust its molten breath through wherever the earth's moral crust is thinnest or weakest. The moral crust is thinnest today at the U.N. Examples abound as the U.N. focuses condemnations on Israel's peccadilloes and the lies about Israel, while downplaying many major, tragic and severest problems around the planet.

Around our world, for example, many nations in the U.N. are known by a religious title yet Israel is not allowed to be called a Jewish State! Even Great Britain has an official state religion.

That is clear hypocrisy.

Watch TerVol's cloak of hypocrisy in action: Since Israel is the world's only Jewish state, (and since Zionism is the Jewish people's national liberation movement), anti-Zionism as opposed to criticism of specific Israeli policies or actions means denial of the Jewish right to national self-determination.

Such a discriminatory denial of this basic right to only one nation (and one of the few that can trace their corporate identity and territorial attachment to antiquity), while allowing this right to all other groups and communities, is pure and unadulterated anti-Jewish racism, or anti-Semitism.

This is a clear example of the quad-standard by the hypocrites again. Isn't it inconsistent if not hypocritical to demand that all other countries delete the use of religion in their name if Israel cannot be called a Jewish State. Remember that the UNGA Resolution # 181 used the term "Jewish" over 40 times yet that is today ignored.

Fortunately, there are those who have objectively studied antisemitism. The Canadian government researched a paper called the "Ottawa Protocol to Combat-Anti-Semitism" that was signed in September of 2014.

As **Prime Minister Stephen Harper** has noted, "Those who would hate and destroy the Jewish people would ultimately hate and destroy the rest of us as well."

The well-respected jurist, **Professor Irwin Cotler** added that antisemitism is not only the longest known form of hatred in the history of humanity — it is the only form of hatred that is truly global! http://www.antisem.org/archive/Ottawa-protocol-on-combating-antisemitism/

TerVol has so locked up the UN that it fiercely denies its quadpocrisy exists. Raging denial is a separate technique.

"From a psychiatric standpoint, quadrapocrisy is a powerful weapon used against Israel. It produces a form of mass hysteria supported by hate," qualified Kelsey.

"Wait until you see how I prove that with logic and facts," challenged Salo.

Kelsey smiled because she had gotten Salo to do her dirty work.

"Is it not hypocritical that Israel is the only state in the world whose right to exist is constantly challenged? Far less successful countries, including numerous states who are known human rights violators, are considered legitimate and their right to exist is not challenged. Observe the quad-standard again."

Here is an example to turn your head, exposing the antisemitism of a supposed NGO, in Israel, B'Tselem:"Israel is committing humanity's worst atrocities," **Liz Sagie** wrote, on her personal blog, (No longer with B'Tselem).

Jessica Montell, B'Tselem's one-time executive director, lied and attacked Israel: "Israel is proving its devotion to Nazi values. . .. Israel exploits the Holocaust to reap international benefits." "Israelis," she noted, "don't erect gas chambers and extermination camps, but if there were any, how many people would actually resist it, and not only in their hearts?" And she admonishes, "In the name of the State of Judaism we have stolen lands, murdered, starved others . . . have created ghettos [for] all kinds of 'others' [and] allowed fascists to raise their heads."

Everyone knows how very small Israel is, and that is why TerVol finds it easier to mount a campaign to delegitimize it and attack it for being a Jewish State.

Other major human tragedies around the globe are barely addressed. This highlights why there is this irrational hatred or perhaps economic benefit to denying Jewish self-determination or self-defense even though it is encoded in law. It is a form of bigotry that ultimately threatens all individual Jews, whether or not they think of themselves as Jews or Zionists.

Hatred threatens the peace in the world because it undermines the essential international principle that states, "Pacta Sunt Servanda", that treaties are to be obeyed. When TerVol denies international law and treaties to one small country, every small country should be concerned.

In Israel's neighbor, Jordan, King Hussein of Jordan killed more Palestinian Arabs in the course of a single month than decades of Arab-Palestinians fighting with Israel, yet the world declared King Hussein as a "man of peace".

Why was Israel's response to Hezbollah attacks from Lebanon in 2006, covered intensely, yet at the same time Ethiopia invaded Somalia, and an estimated 3,000 deaths were going on in Iraq, yet the media paid far less attention to those major tragedies?

"How is it that the press calls Israelis who chose to live in their own land, 'settlers' implying they do not belong or are often described as "Jewish, ultra-orthodox, or right wing, or messianics, or fanatics? Why are they not called pioneers like those brave individuals who settled the United States?" questioned Tom.

If the US adamantly refuses to apologize to Pakistan, half way around the world, for the accidental killing of 24 Pakistani soldiers, Israel certainly need not be pushed by the American President to require Israel to publicly apologize to Turkey for the ship of the Mavi Marmara deaths? They had occurred under battle like conditions and a legal effort to enforce the laws of blockade developed for the security of its citizens. "How come Egypt's blockade of the same area is not equally condemned?" queried Simon.

Now contrast this with the description of Israel's annihilationist Arabs. Some U.N. officials, heads of governments, and journalists call the terrorists "militants", "radicalized refugees", "frustrated freedom fighters", impoverished, displaced, occupied and disenfranchised. The press rarely mentions that it is Koranic driven hatred from which they model their unrelenting war against any sovereign Jewish presence within what they view as their Moslem Arabian Caliphate.

"Why don't we wake up, have some coffee and look TerVol in the eye?" an exasperated Simon moaned.

On November 22, 2012 U.N. agencies and high officials rushed to intervene the moment Israel began to defend its civilian population from hundreds of Hamas rocket attacks coming out of Gaza, but had turned a blind eye and deaf ear while Israel had pleaded many times for action from the U.N.

On at least 20 separate occasions that same year, the Israeli government turned to the U.N. concerning Arab rocket attacks from Gaza. Israel sent identical letters sent to Secretary-General Ban Ki-moon and the Security Council. Israel urged the United Nations to act, and, at a minimum, to speak out and condemn the attacks. The U.N. was mute.

At the same time, **Russian Ambassador Vitaly Churkin**, who for nearly two years blocked any U.N. Security Council action to stop the Syrian regime of Bashar al-Assad from murdering more than 30,000 of his own people, lashed out at "procrastination on Gaza." This Security Council indifference towards Israel quietly gave Hamas the green light to bomb Israeli civilians, finally prompting Israel's belated response. This is the quadpocrsy in action. TerVol was extremely happy.

Israel took out (extrajudicial assassination) the terrorist mastermind **Sheik Ahmed Yassin,** who murdered (proportionally) more Israelis and Jews than did **Osama Bin Laden** did. Israel is defending its own back yard. The world bodies castigated Israel.

Yet, Americans suffered no condemnation following many extrajudicial assassinations. When Bin Laden was eliminated, the U.S. had violated international sovereignty, thousands of miles from the U.S.

What about the universal quiet under the Obama administration, that there have been 112 U.S. drone strikes and 99 air strikes in Yemen since 2009? It is estimated that 1,000 people have been killed: 700-900 militants, 80-plus civilians, and almost 50 unclassified. Where is the world opprobrium?

Israel saved the world from a nuclear war when it produced a surgical strike on the Iraqi nuclear reactor. Israel was internationally castigated.

Blockade Quadpocrisy

Simon says:

"Israel's right to protect itself with a legal blockade of a life-threatening enemy is disputed. What kind of hypocrisy is this when other blockades are considered legal all over the world?"

He knew how Yael would respond. "Why?" goaded Yael.

Simon replied with a hint of faked pique. "This just demonstrates that there is more evidence of the quadpocrisy. To prove my point, I will give you some examples." There really are numerous precedents of blockades where no one screamed "foul."

1. During the Korean War between 1950 and 1953, far from the U.S. continent, there was a blockade.

2. In 1971, when Bangladesh tried to secede from Pakistan, India applied a blockade.

3. During the Iran-Iraq war between 1980 and 1988, there was a blockade of the Shatt el-Arab.

4. Lebanon was blockaded for several months in the 2006 war between Israel and Hezbollah, and Israel allowed safe passage from Lebanon to Cyprus for humanitarian purposes. Egypt Blockades Gaza, Where Are the Flotillas? by Khaled Abu Toameh 8- 9-13

Hamas has finally admitted that it is the Egyptians, and not Israel, who have turned the Gaza Strip into a "big prison." While the Egyptian authorities are tightening the blockade on the Gaza Strip, a thousand trucks loaded with goods and construction material continue to enter the area through the Erez Terminal from Israel. That has totaled 34,000 truckloads in 8 months.

Ghazi Hamad, a senior official with the Hamas-controlled foreign ministry, was quoted, claiming that the Gaza Strip has been turned into a "big prison as a result of the continued closure of the Rafah border crossing by the Egyptian authorities since June 30." But this is a story that has not found its way to the pages of mainstream newspapers in the West, nor has Egypt been castigated because this blockade does not in any way "implicate" Israel. http://www.gatestoneinstitute.org/3923/egypt-blockades-gaza.

"Quadpocrisy again. Score one for me," smiled Tom and he proceeded to give another example.

'Proportionality" and "Disproportionate Force" type Quadpocrisy

The idea of unnecessary force may have originated in the American sport of football. It was called "unnecessary roughness" spotted by trained, neutral referees. But in professional football the term was applied equally to both teams. Influenced by this term, sophomoric journalist created "excessive force", "disproportional force" and "unnecessary force" which they seem to use routinely ONLY against Israel.

According to international humanitarian law and the Rome Statute, the death of civilians during an armed conflict, no matter how grave and regrettable, does not in itself constitute a war crime.

International humanitarian law and the Rome Statute permit belligerents to carry out proportionate attacks against military objectives, even when it is known that some civilian deaths or injuries will occur. Disproportionate force, a crime, occurs if there is an intentional attack directed against civilians, as we have documented in Iraq, Syria, Russia, Communist China, Pakistan, Afghanistan and with Shiites, Sunnis, Hamas, Hezbollah and Fatah.

Specifically, for Israel, there are bound to be civilian deaths because Hamas uses civilians as human shields and places its arsenal of weapons in civilian areas (like schools, hospitals and mosques), placement of which are considered war crimes.

Technically, the rule of proportionality has to do with the relationship between the damage inflicted and the legitimate military goal. What must be assessed is:

(a) the anticipated civilian damage or injury;

(b) the anticipated military advantage;

(c) and whether (a) was "clearly excessive" in relation to the anticipated military advantage. Another way of phrasing it: **former President of the International Court, Rosalyn Higgins,** explained that proportionality "cannot be in relation to any specific prior injury - it has to be in relation to the overall legitimate objective of ending the aggression."

Israel is frequently accused of "a disproportionate response." Logically, this is the opposite of a "proportionate response" to the immediate and clear threat of or being attacked.

A "proportionate" (the ragged tit for tat) response unambiguously indicates there will be no fear of massive retaliation if the aggressor is caught and that the risk/reward ratio is in the aggressor's favor. It is but the cost of doing business for them. Terrorists send missiles from homes or from public areas, like mosques, schools or hospitals. When Hamas operatives hide in areas that will cause civilian casualties, if there is an Israeli military response to attacks on its civilians, is a cynical propaganda tactic. Hamas, violating international law, is using human shields yet the media only focus on numbers of deaths.

Truly proportionate responses can be messy, but they are effective. In hindsight (the dots), "caring proportionate" responses are dainty, costly and consistently ineffective. This not only lowers the price of aggression but encourages it.

Had Japan known about our atomic power it is doubtful that they would have surprise attacked Pearl Harbor. We had a lesson affirming the value of a very strong response and appear to have not learned it.

Tom was on a fast track of learning and was irritated: "So Israel is incessantly accused of "excessive force or "disproportionate force" by the Arabs, the Muslim world, the U.N. and the press. What is infuriating is that it is a bold, provable, documentable lie. This represents another quadpocrisy as a way to delegitimizing Israel and call for its destruction."

In contrast, even a UN study shows that the ratio of civilian to combatant deaths in Gaza in 2009 was by far the lowest in any asymmetric conflict in the history of warfare! The UN estimates that there has been an average three-to-one ratio of civilian to combatant deaths in such conflicts worldwide. Three civilians for every combatant killed. That is the estimated ratio in Afghanistan: three-to-one. In Iraq, and in Kosovo, it was worse: the ratio is believed to be four-to-one. Anecdotal evidence suggests the ratios were much higher in Chechnya and Serbia. In Gaza, it was less than one-to-one.

Col. Richard Kemp commanded British forces in Afghanistan. The IDF record then, is most extraordinary. (Jewish Chronicle-UK). David Hornick had written similarly in the Spectator. http://spectator.org/archives/2012/03/13/report-from-an-asymmetrical-war.

"Tom and I could share dozens of examples of quadpocrisy with you. But we are going to limit this list," explained Yael.

1   During 2011 brutal U.S. bombing of Libya, terms like "disproportionate force," (routinely applied to Israel) seemed to vanish without a trace.

2.   1929- The British used no force at all and the result was during 4 days of Arab rioting across their Mandate, there were counted 133 dead and over 300 wounded. Hebron, which had been settled by refugees from Spain 400 years earlier, was decimated. Surviving Jews were forcefully expelled from their homes of 4 centuries, by the British and that was not called either excessive force or disproportionate.

3.   1960's - Rioting in Los Angeles, 34 dead; Newark, 26 dead; Detroit, 43 dead.

4.   1987 -2 days in Venezuela rioting left 119 dead.

5.   1992 – 3 days of rioting in Los Angeles left 51 dead

6. 1993- 1 day in Somalia left 100s dead.

7. 1993 -Waco Texas, over 80 people died.

8   1999 -The U.S. with NATO bombed Serbia to its knees for killing ethnic Albanians in Kosovo and NATO even accidentally bombed the Chinese Embassy in Belgrade. NATO and the U.S. used 38,000 combat missions and used Tomahawk missiles although this is thousands of miles from the U.S. mainland. Estimates indicated that there were 10-12,000 deaths in the total population (and of those 1200 had been killed in NATO airstrikes). Europe and the United States were in effect seeking to force a sovereign state to relinquish part of its territory, but there were no press reports of "excessive force" or 'disproportionate force".

9. 1986-1989, it has been estimated that 1-2 million Kurds (of which 50-100,000 were civilians) were killed by Iraq. This Anfal Campaign was a genocidal. Poison gas was used in the city of Halabja in which thousands of civilians were murdered.

Given the reality of quadpocrisy, "disproportionate force" seemed to be missing from journalist's reports in these examples.

Yael wanted to move on. "It is documentable that comparable situations are ignored, demonstrating the quad-standard. And I will give you more examples where there was disproportionate force and that term was not slung around."

10. In 1993 the UN envoy in Somalia, Admiral Howe accused General Aidid of using women and children as shields for gunmen, saying that the general's faction had organized the demonstrations and that he would be held responsible for the deaths. (New York Times, June 18, 1993) **UN Military Spokesman Major David Stockwell** defended firing on the civilians: Everyone on the ground in the vicinity was a combatant, because they meant to do us harm. (Manchester Guardian Weekly, September 19, 1993.)

The US spokesmen denied that excessive/disproportionate force was used, high civilian casualties notwithstanding. The US claimed that it had not used excessive force and the Somalis themselves bore the ultimate responsibility, since they used civilian shields and had started the firefight:

It is they who initiated the firefight and who bear ultimate responsibility for this tragic loss of life. (Statement by US Central Command as reported in New York Times, October 14, 1993.)

Why was the U.S. there if it was not an existential threat like the Arab armies and terrorists hovering in and around Israel? Why was the U.S. not censured in the U.N.?

11. 1976-When **Lebanese Christian militias**, backed by the Syrian Army, massacred 3,500 Arab-Palestinians (mostly civilians) in the Beirut refugee camp of **Tel Zaatar**, the UN slumbered. This was not labeled "excessive force" or "disproportionate force" by the press. The retaliation driven militias and Lebanese soldiers slaughtered hundreds of Palestinians in 1982 in the refugee camps of **Sabra** and **Shatila**, this time under Israel's not so watchful eye. This incurred maximum condemnation to Israel. Israel had allowed the Lebanese Christian Phalange to enter the camps as part of a plan to transfer authority to the Lebanese, and accepted responsibility for that decision. It was the Lebanese Christian Phalangist militia who were responsible for the revenge massacres that occurred at the two Beirut-area refugee camps on September 16–17, 1982. Israeli military commanders, unwilling to commit their soldier's lives in risky city fighting, allowed the Christian Lebanese Phalangists to enter Sabra and Shatila to root out terrorist cells they believed to be located there. It was estimated that there may have been up to 200 armed men in the camps working out of the countless bunkers built by the PLO over the years and stocked with generous reserves of ammunition. Fighting was ferocious.

After two days, Israeli soldiers ordered the Phalangists out, and found hundreds dead (estimates range from 460 according to the Lebanese police, to 700–800 calculated by Israeli intelligence). The dead, according to the Lebanese account, included 35 women and children. The rest were men: Palestinians, Lebanese, Pakistanis, Iranians, Syrians and Algerians. It is reasonable to assume that the killings were perpetrated to avenge the murders of Lebanese President Bashir Gemayel and 25 of his followers, killed in a bomb attack earlier that week. There was a world cry that the Israelis should have protected them.

"Quadripocrisy again," squealed Tom as he scored again while patting Kelsey on the back.

12. **Panama** is thousand miles distant from the United States and never posed a threat to US cities or any substantial number of US civilians. In contrast, Israel's civilian population and even Jerusalem, its capital, have been directly threatened by Arab-Palestinian attacks.

The immediate provocation for the US invasion in 1990 was the killing, by Panamanian soldiers, of an off-duty US Marine and the wounding of another, after the Marines' car got lost and was stopped at a Panamanian checkpoint.

A **60 Minutes** report suggested that the number of dead in Panama may have approached 4,000, and cited a US Army document dated nine days after the invasion began that estimated the number of civilian dead at 1000.

"I got another quadpocrisy point" as Tom made the victory sign with his arms in the air.

13. The Saudis expelled all the Arab-Palestinians because they initially supported Saddam Hussein in the Gulf War. Did the UN condemn them?

14. Tom interrupted again, "It's super quadpocrisy, if there is such a thing! On one day alone The U.N. General Assembly adopted nine resolutions on "Palestinian rights and the Golan," sharply criticizing Israel yet making no mention of Sunday's massacre of Palestinian Arabs by Syrian warplanes firing missiles into a mosque in a refugee camp near Damascus."

On the UN Watch's website **Hillel Neuer**, executive director of UN Watch, underscored the absurdity of the resolution tally. "The U.N.'s disproportionate assault against the Jewish state undermines the credibility of what is supposed to be, an impartial and respected international body. It exposes the sores of politicization and selectivity that eat away at its founding mission, eroding the U.N. Charter promise of equal treatment to all nations large and small," he said. At this time, "With more than 40,000 killed in Syria, and millions of Syrian refugees suffering now in the cold of winter, it ought to shock the conscience of mankind that the U.N. will devote more than 80 percent of this session's resolutions to Israel, and just one, on Thursday, to Syria."

Benighted Hypocrisy or perhaps Extortion

In 1973 the Vatican recognized Yasser Arafat's PLO, a well-known terrorist umbrella group, (read John Laffin's PLO Connections) only 9 years after it was given a name. It is very hard to understand that 45 years (1993) after the founding of Israel, the Church finally recognized the democratic State of Israel, with reservation. The Vatican has continued its policy of supporting the Arabs and undermining Israel's right to exist. It is doubtful that the Church could be that overtly anti-Semitic. This sounded like an extortion game: the PLO won't kill Christians as long as the Vatican doesn't recognize Israel.

This was the same PLO/Fatah who was behind the gasp-worthy slaughter of the Jewish Fogel family in Israel on 11 March 2011. Arabs invaded the Fogel home in the middle of the night and literally and ritually slaughtered the father, the mother, two young sons, and a three-month old baby, who they beheaded! They did not slaughter this family using quick death by gunshot, but ritually slaughtered them with knives. What possible motivating ideology penetrated their diseased brains that could possibly have rationalized their behavior. After being caught the two murderers later proudly confessed to the killings, expressed no remorse, and reenacted the attack before security officials. The attack was condemned by virtually all world bodies…and then it was business as usual.

One has to wonder where the protestors and the TV coverage stations were during the long-running genocide in Darfur, with its estimated 300,000 dead and at least 2.5 million refugees; or where were the street protests over the war in the Congo, with over 4 million dead or driven from their homes?

None of these barbaric tragedies saw protesters flock onto the streets of New York, Berkley, London, Paris or Vienna. Hypocrisy in action: But if Israel builds apartment buildings, there is an outcry and protesters with enormous TV coverage. "I call that quadpocrisy," concluded Tom.

University Quadpocrisy.

You don't have to be college material to recognize this. It is one of TerVol's prized accomplishments in the U.S. and European Universities, a trophy of emotion over facts in institutions that are supposed to be guided by facts over emotions.

It is easier to see the quad-standard or hypocrisy on university campuses where young, gullible students are so energized and so disinformed. There are demonstrations all over Europe and U.S. in universities and on the streets creating incredible fabrications about Israel. But there are never any demonstrations of outrage against the acts of terrorism committed against Israel.

Is it not hypocrisy when we don't see student or left-wing demonstrations against Islamic dictatorships from London, Paris, Barcelona or demonstrations against the Burma/Myanmar dictatorship?

Are they so blind as to confuse support of the Arab goals while defending Arab terrorism by renaming them demonstrations?

Why is there a totally illicit, totally fabricated Apartheid Week on so many campuses against a democracy, Israel, which is the only country in the Middle East that can prove no apartheid?

Why aren't there demonstrations against the enslavement of millions of women who are forced to have genital mutilation and live without any legal protection?

Or why aren't there demonstrations against the use of children as human bombs where there is conflict with Islam?

Or why do we not see university leadership in support of the victims of Islamic terrorism in Iraq, Afghanistan, Sudan, Nigeria or Kenya?

This is the hypocritical termite approach: ignore the evil and undermine the successful democracies.

The E.U. Quad-standard

This is another prized accomplishment for TerVol in Europe.

"This is a good example," said Salo. "Cyprus had declared its independence in 1960. Cypriot independence was recognized in International law.

However, in 1974 the Turkish army began an aggressive invasion the State of Cyprus. Tens of thousands of Greek Cypriots were expelled by the Turks in what was viewed as a deliberate policy of ethnic cleansing. The Turks then illegally occupied the northern 37% of Cyprus and transported tens of thousands of Turks on this conquered land."

In the aftermath of this invasion, the U.N. Security Council adopted Resolution 353 which demanded "an immediate end to foreign military intervention" and called for "the withdrawal without delay from the Republic of Cyprus of foreign military personnel."

Ignoring UNSC 351, the Turkish Cypriots declared their independence in 1983 by forming the "Turkish Republic of Northern Cyprus". The U.N. condemned this as "null and void" and did nothing to enforce their resolution. Over the years, an estimated 160,000 people became resettled from Turkey into Northern Cyprus.

It appeared that the international community should have judged the dispute over Northern Cyprus far more severely than the way it viewed the dispute over Israel's "West Bank," where Israel had multiple rights that it could exercise if it decided to do so.

The European Union blindly reiterates, with barely any legal substance, that (Israeli) settlements are illegal under international law and constitute an "obstacle to peace." Ironically, while the EU releases harsh statements of this sort against Israel for any construction activity within West Bank towns, it has nothing to say about tens of thousands of Turkish settlers that have moved into Northern Cyprus.

The EU knowingly and purposefully provides substantial direct financial assistance to settlements in Turkish-occupied Northern Cyprus. That makes it clear that the EU funds the occupation of an EU member state. The EU maintains an entire separate program to direct funds to Northern Cyprus. The grants are pursuant to a 2006 regulation adopted by the EU to "end the isolation of the Turkish Cypriot community," and allocated 259 million Euros over five years, and now operates on an annual 28 million Euro allocation (a sum that amounts to roughly 0.8 percent of Northern Cyprus' GDP.)

The Northern Cyprus program is only the most glaring example of the broad EU funding for settlement activity of occupied land. Agreements just inked this summer with Morocco would continue to fund its occupation of Western Sahara, for example. And of course, many European businesses and universities openly operate in the occupied territories, from French oil companies in Western Sahara to British universities in Northern Cyprus. Yet these companies are not disbarred from EU funding, while similarly situated Israeli ones would be. Hypocrisy or hatred? http://www.jpost.com/Opinion/Op-Ed-Contributors/How-the-EU-directly-funds-settlements-in-occupied-territory-327329 and The Difference Between Northern Cyprus and Judea, Samaria;

The Quadpocrisy Giant, the U.N.

This was another trophy in TerVol's ever expanding trophy room.

During the first sixty-seven years of the existence of the United Nations, no circumstances

not the murders of seventy million people by the Red Chinese;

not the mammoth horrible prison of the Soviet Gulag archipelago;

not the brutalization of North Koreans;

not the oppression of Burmese;

not the loot-motivated wars in Africa

not the genocide in East Timor;

not the genocide in Rwanda;

not the genocide in Cambodia,

not all of them together — has been of greater concern to the U.N. international community than "the Jewish problem."

"Check it out" charged Salo: The 59th Session (2004-05) of the UNGA, for example, enacted nineteen anti-Israel resolutions, but not a single one on Sudan's ongoing genocide in Darfur where hundreds of thousands of blameless civilians perished.

There were 22 UN General Assembly Resolutions targeted against Israel in 2012; 4 for the entire rest of world. "Maybe we should call this emboldened hatred rather than quadpocrisy," suggested Yael.

In a UN-sponsored "International Day of Solidarity with the Palestinian People," an official picture of Secretary-General Kofi Annan, flanked by UN senior officials, sat on the podium beside an Arabic-language "Map of Palestine" that showed a "Palestine" completely replacing Israel. This is flagrantly against the founding principles of the U.N.; quite heinous, map murdering hypocrisy.

There were so many other examples of hypocrisy that Yael was moved to tears. Most were not well known. The United Nations, itself, has been condemning Israel for its attempt to protect its citizens from sniper attacks and terrorism by building a security fence and also a small segment of wall in response to shootings of its civilians and terrorist bombing attacks. Condemning Israel for its security fence is vulgar and hypocritical because Israel has a right to defend its citizens.

During the 1930's the graffiti on Europe buildings was "Jews, Go to Palestine!" In 2012, the walls were filled with graffiti that read "Jews, Get out of Palestine!" The Europeans have demonstrated once again not only how short their memories are but how enduringly endemic antisemitism is in their culture.

"Wall" Quadpocrisy

Many countries besides Israel build walls to protect their interests. None are condemned like Israel is.

- Italy built a wall in 2006 to keep gang members away from the public;
- Spain built a fence in 1998 to protect against illegals;
- Iran –Pakistan wall was planned for 435 mi, 2007;
- India - Pakistan concertina wire fence finished in 2004 of 330 mi.;
- Saudi Arabia on Iraqi border put up a berm with electrified concertina wire;
- Afghanistan-Pakistan fence 2005;
- Kuwait-Iraq fence;
- Baghdad, Iraq: a concrete wall was built within 2007
- The U.S. and Mexico have a huge barrier fence.

- Other current barriers (found in Wikipedia):
Afghanistan,1.2 Botswana,1.3 Brunei,1.4 China,1.5 Cyprus,1.6 Egypt, 1.7 Greece,1.8 India,1.9 Iran,1.10 Iraq,1.11 Israel,1.12 Korea,1.13 Mo rocco,1.14 Northern Ireland,1.15 Pakistan,1.16 Russia,1.17 Saudi Arabia, 1.18 South Africa, 1.19 Spain, 1.20 Thailand, 1.21 United Arab Emirates, 1.23 United States, 1.24 Uzbekistan

"Occupied lands"
Quadpocrisy Run Amuck

This atomic quadpocrisy was laid out by Simon.

- Let's understand what "Occupied Territories" really means. For there to be an occupation at international law, there has to be an occupying and occupied power both of which are members of the community of nations. As an example, the only conceivable occupying power for the West Bank was Jordan (despite its illegality in international law). Jordan, long ago (1988), renounced all claims over the West Bank and took back citizenship for the Arabs living in that area. Therefore, it can't be occupied.
- By definition of the 1949 Fourth Geneva Convention (FGC), article 6, an occupying power can only be considered this to the extent that it exercises the function of government in such territory.
- The term 'occupied territories' is a misleading, politically loaded pejorative – a red herring designed to rob Israel of any legal or moral rights and empower Arab- Palestinians with the right to "use all measures" to expel Israel. ©2009, Eli E. Hertz Page 4.
- Israel did not want the land and asked to give it away to the Arab world if there could be peace. Judea and Samaria were not lands of any High Contracting Power at the time of the war because Jordan's annexation of same was not recognized by the world save for Britain

and Pakistan. It follows that they are not "occupied territories" pursuant to the FGC. In Aug 1967, in Khartoum, the official Arab response to a step dealing with this disputed area and to peace was "No Recognition, No Peace and No Negotiations"

- "Occupied territories" are defined by international law as those lands which are taken over by an act of aggression from another signatory country or High Contracting Party. The "West Bank" was regained from the Arabs during a defensive war. It therefore can't be occupied according to international law!

- Since the end of World War II, no border dispute in the world has been defined as "occupied territories," except in Israel's case! In virtually every other disagreement concerning borders and territories the most common terms applied are "territorial disputes" or "contested borders." This includes Bosnia-Herzegovina, East Timor, even the Western Sahara and Kashmir.

- As pointed out by Aaron Lerner of IMRA, "The US condemns the recent occupation of residential buildings in the neighborhood of Silwan, Jerusalem". White House spokesman Josh Earnest - October 1 2014 http://www.timesofisrael.com/us-hammers-israel-over-east-jerusalem-housing-plans/ Why use the term "occupation"? Israelis had legally purchased the properties, albeit via third parties - just as Walt Disney purchased swampland in Orlando through a series of third parties. Did Walt "occupy" Orlando? No. He bought the land fairly. "Occupation" is a very incendiary term. Turkey's presence in Northern Cyprus is not branded "occupied territory".

- There is an obvious hypocrisy and bias for journalists or the U.N. The West Bank was never called occupied territory when Jordan had ILLEGAL control before the 1967 war. But it must be said in Jordan's defense, the land did not belong to a sovereign and was only under a mandate, despite gaining the land in an act of aggression.

- The use of the term 'occupied territories' thus endows the Arab-Palestinians with an aura of bogus statehood and a false history designed to rob Israel of any legal or moral rights and empower Palestinians with the right to "use all measures" to expel Israel.

- 'The definition of the term "occupied territory" that appears in the U.S. Defense's Dictionary of Military Terms demonstrates an awareness of the widespread misuse of the term 'occupied territory' and notes the inappropriateness of the term in situations applicable to territory being administered pursuant to peace terms, treaty, or other agreement, express or implied, with the civil authority of the territory."

- **Great Britain** still occupies 17 provinces of Ireland, Gibraltar and is holding on to the many residual symbols of her former colonial glory around the world.

- **France** is still holding on to many overseas territories like New Caledonia and French Guinea.

- **Spain** has no intention to give independence to the Basque people, the oldest indigenous living group known in Europe.

- **China** - The international community has done nothing to stop occupation of Tibet by China.

- **Indonesia** - It was "painful" for Indonesia to allow freedom to East Timor. International pressure was applied only because of the huge oil reserves off the coast of East Timor were found. But there is no pressure in relation to the continuous occupation of Bali, West Papua and numerous islands that would love to obtain independence from the Muslim tyranny of Jakarta.

- **Russia** has no plans to return the Eastern part of Poland it has occupied since before WW2 and end occupation of eastern Prussia, the Kuril Islands and Southern Sakhalin. Russia still retains its status as an imperial power by holding on to the Crimea of the Ukraine, Chechnya, Dagistan, North Ossetia, Tatarstan and many other national enclaves which were occupied by Tsar.

- **USA** - There is no intention of even talking about compensation or returning, the occupied land which used to be, not long ago, a part of Mexico. .

- It should be remembered that most countries around the world (including USA, UK, France, Germany, China and Russia) were forged and established their current borders during the last 300 years. Their creation was accompanied by dramatic conquests and destruction of unique and independent cultures. <u>Duplicity of "Occupied" Lands</u>. September 19, 2011 by **Steven Shamrak**.

- An extensive legal report, *The Levy Report in 2011-12* has come out in Israel. It strongly suggested that the "West Bank" can be called a disputed territory to which both the Jewish state and the "Palestinians" (individual residents) may assert a claim. Those claims can best be resolved by negotiations that could end the conflict.

Quadpocrisy: European countries offered no two-state solution for themselves.

Why do European countries demand from Israel what they do not even expect from themselves?

There is hardly a major country in Europe that isn't facing increasingly defiant secessionist movements which could eventually redraw the map of the entire region.

Their hypocrisy is astonishing: they want to force Serbia and Israel to do what they themselves are unwilling to countenance.

- The international community demands a two-state solution which is detrimental to Israel.
- No comparable demand is made for a two-state solution as detrimental to Spain and France, concerning the Basque country.
- Or detrimental to the Philippines, concerning Mindanao.
- Or detrimental to Cyprus, concerning the Greek and Turkish parts of the island.
- Or detrimental to Georgia, concerning each of Abkhazia and South Ossetia.

There was no demand by the international community that there should have been a two-state solution detrimental to Sri Lanka, concerning the Sinhalese and the Tamils.

Simon could not be silenced. That is nothing: "Get how the French are over the top imperialistic hypocrites." France is going to war in Mali because it says "we cannot have a terrorist state at the door of Europe," but when Israel launches a defensive operation to protect its citizens from missile attacks from terrorists in Gaza, the French newspapers and television commentators scream about Israeli aggression.

The distance between Bamako in Mali and Paris: 6266km. The distance between Gaza and Israel: 0 km. This situation starkly exposes the hypocrisy of the Europeans in their attitudes towards Israel's right to defend itself. Mali is France's Gaza JANUARY 14, 2013 Le Monde; Ron Agam

Nauseating Quadpocrisy:
No two-state solution from many other countries.

1. **Morocco** snatched the massive and resource-rich Western Sahara in 1975 without firing a shot. The Moroccan invasion was met with a UN Security Council condemnation, which Rabat shrugged off. Although no nation has recognized Moroccan sovereignty over the occupied area, Morocco remains a close ally of the U.S. and the EU.

 U.S. policy now supports Moroccan proposals to retain the occupied territory under Moroccan sovereignty with local autonomy. Moreover, European companies happily help Morocco exploit Western Sahara's resources, and recent treaties with Europe even acknowledge and engage with Moroccan control.

2. In 1975 **North Vietnam** wiped South Vietnam off the map and Indonesia seized East Timor. All nations now recognize Hanoi's sovereignty over all Vietnam. And despite a hostile Security Council resolution, the West quietly supported Indonesia's Timor position for decades.

3. **Armenia** successfully conquered parts of Azerbaijan in the 1990s, a move condemned by the EU but that seems unlikely to be reversed.

4. **Russia** snagged parts of **Georgia** and the **Ukraine.**

5. In **Great Britain,** Scottish nationalists are gearing up for another attempt to break free of English rule.

6. **China** will not negotiate its sovereignty over Taiwan, Tibet, the Spratly Islands, and the Paracel Islands. There is no two-state solution for Taiwan. China does not refer to Taiwan as the Republic of China, in the manner of the reference by the government of Israel to Judea, Samaria and Aza as Palestine. China refers to Taiwan as Chinese Taiwan.

7. **Russia** maintains its claim to Chechnya. No two-state solution there. No negotiations. No releases of Chechnian prisoners.

8. **India** and **Pakistan** retain their respective sovereignties in Jammu and Kashmir. No negotiations, and no independent Jammu and Kashmir.

Putting forth her degree in psychiatry, Kelsey pronounced that once you have identified an entity as hypocritical, it can no longer be trusted to support your interests and can be suspect of attacking or undermining your interests.

Salo's mind stored massive amounts of trivia, but important trivia. "Talk about quadpocrsiy," Salo exploded. He remembered that Josh Rapps explained, in Nov. of 2001, that the Taliban in Afghanistan used attacks during Ramadan as an excuse to scuttle the U.S. led "Coalition" under the pretense that if the U.S. responded with violence, it would offend Moslem religious sensibilities and prove that in the end this was a Christian Crusade against Islam.

Egypt and Syria, and its other Arab allies had no such reservations about attacking Israel on its most solemn day, Yom Kippur, in 1973. They also had no qualms about fighting during the month of Ramadan.

Quadpocrisy in the Press

This is a self-degrading, and truly immoral form of propaganda. Their excessive, disproportionate, repetitive glancing attacks on Israel occupy columns of prominent space, while not giving the same space to real tragedies around the world.

One has to assume the **NYT** would not have questioned whether the outlooks of Hitler and Stalin to "vanquish the Jews entirely" were genuinely held. But they have been hypocritically silent with President Morsi of Egypt who was essentially representing the anti-Zionist, anti-democratic, antisemitic, **Muslim Brotherhood!**

In the news media, positing itself above the fray, we read terms like "moral equivalence", "cycle of violence", "excessive force", "tough love", "use restraint", "Arab victims", "collective punishment", "overreacting", and " illegal settlements" to **only** refer to the "Israeli condition"…especially by attention seeking journalists. Often, they hold themselves to be gods, selectively applying these labels almost solely to Israel and with scant, second hand narratives to support use of those words.

Kelsey commented that moral relativism was the subconscious negation of right and wrong. It protects the ego of the individual from their conscience. It is used to spread a pre-existing bias. Moral relativism is defense for those who need to be excused by their bad behaviors. With moral relativism, one could use any terms to describe something as simply being relative; as in no right or no wrong. Sometimes this was purely profiteering, face saving, political correctness, or ignorance.

The equivalence being drawn in the coverage of the Israeli exchange of one soldier kidnapped in an illegal act of aggression by Hamas, and the return of a thousand of those who had been tried and convicted under the due process of law, reflects the morally bankrupt "tit-for-tat" analysis of the Arab war against Israel.

Before Israel's re-establishment in 1948, Israel has only launched military operations against the Arabs in response to actual or imminent Arab attacks. Yet many refuse to acknowledge the difference between murderous aggression and the defense against it.

There is a quadpocrisy of moral relativism used in one direction observed as (non-reciprocal) multiculturalism. For those in love with multiculturalism, the sins of the non-West are mostly ignored or attributed to Western influence, while those of the West are peculiar to Western civilization. This becomes evident when the multiculturalist person professes that all cultures are equal and in the next breath condemns Western culture because, in his view, it is unfairly exclusive, intolerant and bigoted.

Imagine tens of thousands of Japanese Americans responding to Pearl Harbor by engaging in wholesale violence against their fellow Americans. While that never happened, it did not prevent the American government from interning thousands of American citizens of Japanese origin for much of the war as suspected members of a 'fifth column'. But when Israel faced insurrection-like Arab riots (not an act of social protest) in the October 2000, Israel had to defend its citizens. Many died. Israel dealt with it directly and did not indiscriminately incarcerate thousands of Arabs but was condemned for "excessive force" while merely protecting its citizens.

Aiding a fifth column in Israel by ignoring it or supporting it, the press does not report that some Israeli Arabs belong to a terrorist organization called **The Galilee Liberators** and the **Northern Branch of the Islamic Movement (Murabitun and Murabatat)** affiliated with **Hamas,** another fifth column. It has continuously and openly engaged in subversive activity with the goal of destroying Israel and establishing an Islamic State. It has infiltrated Bedouin schools in the Negev while regularly organizing demonstrations and riots by spreading anti-Israel propaganda to the Bedouins who have been loyal to Israel in the past. Once a year it (with aid of groups like the Muslim Brotherhood) holds a mass (tens of thousands) anti-Israel propaganda festival in Umm al-Fahm declaring that the al-Aqsa mosque is in danger. They urge the believers to prepare to give their lives to prevent the mosque from being damaged. All this has been documented in the Or Commission following the riots in October 2000.

The Galilee Liberators organization was formed by Arabs living in northern Israel in 2002, when the Palestinian suicide bombings on Israeli towns of the Second Intifada were at their peak. In the subsequent 12 years, **the Galilee Liberators** developed ties with Palestinian terrorist organizations such as the extremist Popular Front, the PFLP-General Command, Hamas and Al Aqsa Brigades. Parts are allied with the Lebanese Hezbollah and others with al Qaeda. There have been few arrests and several murders.

Israel has never called for annihilation of its Muslim citizens.

The press hardly touches this:

Muslims are only 5% of the population in England yet one in 5 inmates in high security prisons are Muslim and 1 in 5 teenage crimes are committed by Muslims. Muslim children are persecuting children in British schools, in fact, a 9-year-old British boy committed suicide rather than face continued persecution by them. In 2007 a 15-year-old British schoolboy named Henry Webster was beaten with a hammer by a gang of Muslim pupils and was left brain-damaged. Since then the school was the scene of numerous violent incidents involving Muslim youth.

Muslim men threaten British schoolgirls daily. Muslim gangs have raped young British girls and forced them into prostitution. Women are being told to cover up in Islamic garb or else. Yet the government inaction is not called disproportionate inaction. Muslim Patrols have been accosting residents in London, demanding they abide by the laws of what they claim to be Muslim areas. Posters have been appearing in England which read: "You are entering a Sharia-controlled zone, Islamic rules enforced."

Where is accurate, timely press coverage for these situations?

Quadpocrisy of Expulsions and marking territory

As early as the mid-1950s, Iraq, Saudi Arabia, and Libya expelled masses of striking "Palestinian" workers. No international condemnation.

In 1970, Jordan expelled some 20,000 "Palestinians" and demolished their camps. No international condemnation.

In 1994-95, Libya expelled tens of thousands of long-term "Palestinian" residents in response to the Oslo process. No international condemnation.

After the 2003 Iraq war, some 21,000 "Palestinians" fled the country in response to a systematic terror and persecution campaign. No international condemnation.

As recently as 2007, Beirut effectively displaced 31,400 "Palestinian" refugees when the Lebanese army destroyed the Nahr el Bared refugee camp during fighting between the militant Fatal al-Islam group and the Lebanese army. No international condemnation!

In 1991, Kuwait expelled most of its "Palestinian" residents in retaliation for the Palestine Liberation Organization's (PLO) endorsement of Iraq's brutal occupation of the emirate (August 1990-February 1991): From March to September 1991, about 200,000 "Palestinians" were expelled from the emirate in a systematic campaign of terror, violence, and economic pressure while another 200,000 who fled during the Iraqi occupation were denied return. This expulsion was largely ignored by the international community with no condemnation, nor effort from the U.N. Security Council to do anything to assist the newly displaced refugees and punish their ethnic cleanser. "Kuwait Expels Thousands of Palestinians" by **Steven J. Rosen** Middle East Quarterly Fall 2012, pp. 75-83

The **CIA** and **European governments** condone torture in countries thousands of miles away during the hunt of "approved" terrorists like Bin Laden. Yet the U.S. State Departments publicly scolds Israel for employing similar methods to discover and preempt terrorist acts against its citizens hundreds of feet away. What revealing quadpocrisy prevented the International Community or U.N. Security Council from acting when **Hafez Assad**, decimated the town of Hama in1982 and used 10,000-20,000 bodies of its citizens as land fill?

Yet Israel is excoriated by the International Community when it is forced to enter selected Palestinian settlements to arrest known terrorists, a responsibility that the PA is obligated to by a signed agreement, but refuses to do.

When Gilad Shalit, an Israeli soldier, was kidnapped by Hamas on Israeli soil, he was held in isolation for five years until his release. He was denied any and all visitation rights from lawyers, family, and even the International Red Cross in violation of his human rights and international law. But there was no international outcry for Shalit.

Dr Michael Nazir-Ali , the Bishop of Rochester, England said that if a lost Englishman enters a Muslim "no-go" area he is beaten up for trespassing.

Mark Tapson wrote that in the Tower Hamlets in East London or as the Muslims there refer to it, "the Islamic Republic of Tower Hamlets", imams known as the "Tower Hamlets Taliban", issue death threats to unveiled women, and gays are attacked by gangs of young Muslim men.

"Muslims Against the Crusades" has launched an ambitious campaign to turn twelve British cities into independent Islamic states, including Birmingham, Leeds, Liverpool, Manchester, and what the group calls "Londonistan."

It is well known that a large percentage of Muslim immigrants who enter the European Union arrive illegally via Greece or Italy. Greece built a fence to keep them out that is patrolled by European Union police or armed forces.

Israel created a fence and a wall, to provide safety for its citizens as a direct result of terrorism and shootings. The Europeans patrol the Greek fence to keep out immigrants seeking a safer life, yet deny Israel the right to build a fence to keep its citizens from being murdered.

Immigration and Integration, the Social and Psychological Problems

Now the five were getting into a discussion that was turning heated. Being an experienced forensic psychiatrist, Kelsey had a more professional way of looking at things.

"Look what I discovered," Kelsey said in a kindly teacher tones, "These examples fit in with the type of psychological workings of the world's hypocrisy when Israel was forced to build a security fence to reduce the terrorism and carnage.

One would think that a British citizen who had to flee his home because it became a no-go area claimed as their own turf, by Muslim immigrants, would be skeptical of Muslim claims of sharing Jerusalem. One would expect that British victims of Muslim riots would sympathize with Israeli victims of the Palestinian Intifada. One would think that having been victims of Muslim terrorism the British would sympathize with Israeli victims of Muslim terror."

This morning Dr. Landmark was dressed in a new black two-piece pant suit covering a high collared red blouse. Sleek and meaning business, she took over.

She began to talk about the research of **Nicolai Sennels,** a psychologist, in 2009 and the Danish State's Bureau of Statistics.

"Sit down everyone. I have to share this with you. Why are different standards of behavior allowed, based on religion, values and ethnicity? We need clarity to define these problems. Are you aware that hypocrisy can be built on ambiguity and bias? If we had one standard, that has some clarity, instead of a quad-standard, we would make better decisions."

"But don't worry, I am only giving you a synopsis of his book, <u>Among</u>

<u>Criminal Muslims: A Psychologist's Experiences form the Copenhagen Municipality</u>, and his article published on April 27, 2012, "Report from the Therapy Room: Why are Muslims more violent and criminal?"

What Sennels found after working with 150 Muslim and 100 Christian Danish youths in the youth prison for over 10 years, was that cultural differences that were based in religiously held beliefs, influenced Muslims in a way that makes them more likely to become criminal and display what we call anti-social behavior towards whoever they considered other. Naturally "criminal behavior" is a Danish legal system definition and 'anti-social" is a Judeo-Christian value system.

The facts are that 7 of 10 inmates in Danish youth prisons are immigrants, almost all Muslim. http://avisen.dk/unge-efterkommere-er-de-mest-kriminelle_6193.aspx The second generations represented a higher percentage of incarcerated criminals. http://politiken.dk/indland/article560520.ece

Sennels dissolved some ambiguity and found some clarity noting the differences of cultural impact had on the criminals. I will quickly share them with you for a better understanding of what we face.

1. Anger versus weakness: Muslim clients saw these normal Western social tools for negotiation during social conflicts as signs of weakness.

2. Honor versus insecurity: In the Judeo-Christian culture meeting criticism with hostility and threats, are seen as signs of insecurity and a lack of self-confidence. In the Muslim culture, demands for integration into the new civilization are constantly fueling many resident Muslims' feeling of being criticized and feeling enmity towards their non-Islamic surroundings. In their culture reacting with hostility and threats is seen as a sign of strength and self-confidence.

3. Victim mentality vs. personal responsibility: In Western societies we are told that we ourselves, in the main, are the ones responsible for our lives. Muslim clients mainly saw the sources for their suffering as outer factors. Sometimes they claimed it was those who they attacked who were the problem because he or she had "provoked", "insulted" or tempted them beyond their means and they felt "forced" to attack

those they injured. They insisted that they were the victims. Those whom they attacked were almost always non-Muslims.

4. Muslims vs. non-Muslims: Sennels' experiences made it clear that Muslims do not only experience themselves as only belonging to a different group of people, they also see themselves as superior and entitled to special respect. This is probably inspired by the Islamic scriptures, in which the term "infidel" (non-Muslim) appears 347 times. According to a survey made in 2008, only 14 percent of the Muslims living in France feel more French than Muslim.

5. Sexuality: Men vs. women: Muslim men have a superior position in the world, according to Islam and Muslim customs. Societies suppressing the feminine thus become less empathic, creative, intuitive, peaceful, democratic and social. Such a society aims at hierarchical, aggressive patriarchal structures. When it comes to crimes, defined by Western laws, this shows itself in especially the rape statistics. Among many examples is what had happened in Oslo, Norway, where 100 percent of all so-called assault rapes (rapes where the rapist and his victim did not know each other beforehand) committed from 2006 to 2008 were committed by non-Western immigrants and there was a 30 percent rise in rapes in Oslo in 2011.

6. Anti-social behavior, education and poverty: Here is a chicken or the egg argument. Sennels conclusion was that anti-social behavior (including crime) leads to poverty - not the other way around. Explaining other people's destructive behavior based on their bank account is a product of a very materialistic (almost communistic), not humanistic, one-dimensional view of human beings. People are more than what they own. People who consciously do things that lead to criminal records simply have a harder time getting accepted on the job market.

7. The Islamic culture focuses too little on knowledge and education. In Denmark, 64 percent of all schoolchildren with Arabic backgrounds are so poor in reading and writing after 10 years in the Danish school system that they are not able to go on with their education. In our

high-tech knowledge societies, it is simply necessary to have an education and be willing to continually and flexibly develop one's skills throughout life. To support this, Nature magazine reported in 2003, the world average for production of articles per million inhabitants was 137, The 57 country OIC (Organization of the Islamic Conference or Cooperation) countries, the average was just 13.

"Sennels posited a model for understanding. A democratic society has natural demands for integration and adaption to Western standards of behavior for immigrants. This leads to Muslims' feeling of victimization under this pressure to accept their new society's mores. Thus anti-social Muslims and socially unacceptable behavior are related to perceived demands for integration and socially acceptable behavior, until they either adapt, are repatriated, are in prison, or take over.

Integration vs. Muslim culture: Sennels observed that immigrants need three things to be able to integrate. They need to want it. They need to be allowed, and they need to have the capacity. There is an exceedingly strong social control in the tight Muslim society. Everybody is keeping an eye on everybody, and if someone does not follow the cultural or religious code they are met with criticism and risk severe consequences, such as being banned from their community or even from their own family. In the worst cases, and there are many of those, Muslim women in particular, live under a death threat. Most of Sennels' Muslim clients saw their religious and cultural background as the height of civilization and morality, superior to the Danish society. Leaving it would be seen as a kind of cultural and religious apostasy and degradation by their kinsmen.

As an example, in Sweden and other European countries, it has taken only one charismatic Muslim leader to declare a Muslim neighborhood to be a small Islamic area by rejecting the rule of that country. They then declare it their own turf forever."

Kelsey was now on a roll.

"In part, this explains why the Arabs, most of whom who had never set foot in Israel, demanded a 'right of return' into Israel proper. Of course, there is a legitimate idea of fair compensation for any human beings who were accidentally or maliciously displaced from any country! Israel's defensive War of Independence in 1948 had two choices: survival or annihilation. That was it.

In 1947, 1948 and 1949 the Arab High Command demanded the Arabs leave. Some were told that they must leave to make way for the invading Arab armies. Then they were told they could come back and take over the land of the Jews who would be driven into the sea. Others fled due to the fears of war.

Compensation is due those who can/must prove ownership of property lost and have chosen not to return with a willingness to live in peace with their neighbors.

Around the same period over 850,000 Jews left behind an estimated $300 billion in assets when they were forced to flee or be slaughtered from many Arab, Muslim and Persian countries when Israel became a state. Compensation demands are not being made of the Syrians, the Iranians, the Libyans, the Iraqis, the Yemenis, and the Egyptians who displaced (or more specifically murdered and expelled) their Jews.

An explanation of this persecution is legitimized when one reads "Terror and Liberalism," by scholar **Paul Berman** who quotes **Sayid Qutb,** the leading theoretician of the Muslim Brotherhood: 'most evil theories which try to destroy all values and all that is sacred to mankind are advocated by Jews.'

Elsewhere in the book, Berman painstakingly documents Qutb's frankly Hitlerian view of the Jewish role in world history, including his repeated assertions that Jews had conspired against Muslims from the dawn of Islam. This frightening and prevailing attitude is why Jewish refugees do not want to return to those lands in which their forefathers had lived for centuries.

What Sennels and Berman found are the ideological foundations of the Muslim Brotherhood and they remain firmly in place now. They are represented in Europe and the USA. Any compromise with the Jews, such as a peace treaty with Israel, would therefore be another twist in the same conspiracy. According to Qutb and his followers, the only honorable path is to vanquish the Jews entirely for no reason other than they're being Jews.

This exposes enormous ignorance about the origins of antisemitism in the Muslim world, connections to Nazism and its centrality to the Muslim Brotherhood's world view in the United States.

There is a misguided view that antisemitism is essentially a European phenomenon, and thus an alien import into the Muslim world. That false premise posits that antisemitism will disappear once the Arab/Muslim-Israeli conflict is resolved. That premise has been wrong for 1400 years.

Simon says:

We have exposed a few of the disguises of TerVol such as quadpocrisy. Had you not been fooled like so many others? There are many more disguises that we must uncover. We need more information to balance our decision making. We need greater quantities of valid information and statistics to confidently tie down what we have learned. We will apply those findings to our values as part of the problem dissolving process. Poor research produces disastrous decisions and fatal results. We can't afford that any longer because the stakes are getting higher. History can provide hindsight. The past is the father of the present, just as the present is the father of the future. Accurate measurements can aid in creating worthwhile decisions based on our values and recognizing other cultures' values.

Let's go back in time and learn how to build a stable platform for thinking out the problems.

#4 Hypocrisy Engorged

Simon says:

We have to go deeper and explore what happened with the positions that governments have taken and what their results were. To repeat, knowing history is important, but learning the right lessons can only be done in context. We can contrast government positions with what really happened. It is one of the values of hindsight because we can connect more dots. To fervently deny damaging positions to Israel or actions recognizable as antisemitism makes for hypocrisy and another trophy for TerVol.

Rave Reviews and then U.S. Hypocrisy and Contradictions Hurt

U.S. President Woodrow Wilson credited ancient Israeli society with being "a divine precedent for a pure democracy," and said that it was "distinguished from monarchy, aristocracy or any other form of government" in depending on "the principle, 'that rebellion to tyrants is obedience to God.'"

Wilson responded to the Balfour Declaration, which proclaimed Britain's support of a Jewish homeland in British Palestine, by saying, reverently, "To think that I . . . should be able to help restore the Holy Land to its people."

U.S. President Warren Harding said, "It is impossible for one who has studied at all the services of the Hebrew people to avoid the faith that they will one day be restored to their historic national home and there enter on a new and yet greater phase of their contribution to the advance of humanity."

U.S. President Calvin Coolidge said that "the Jewish faith is predominantly the faith of liberty," and that he had "sympathy with the deep and intense longing which finds such fine expression in the Jewish National Homeland in Palestine."

Think of the U.S. hypocrisy by demanding that Israel give up its 3,000-year-old homeland to sworn enemies, when the U.S. government denied Mexican repatriation of parts of the U.S.

The Mexican Repatriation refers to a mass migration that took place between 1929 and 1939, when as many as 500,000 people of Mexican descent were forced or pressured to leave the U.S. The event, carried out by American authorities, took place without due process. Some 35,000 were deported, amongst many hundreds of thousands of other immigrants who were deported during this period. The Immigration and Naturalization Service targeted Mexicans because of "the proximity of the Mexican border, the physical distinctiveness of mestizos, and easily identifiable barrios." Authors have estimated that the total number of repatriates was about one million, and 60 percent of those were citizens of the United States. http://en.wikipedia.org/wiki/Mexican_Repatriation

In 1938, after the Kristallnacht Nov 9-10 pogroms in Germany, the governor of the U.S. Virgin Islands, **Lawrence Cramer**, backed by the territory's legislative assembly, publicly offered to accept Jewish refugees fleeing the Third Reich. "The U.S. immigration quotas did not apply to our territory," **Rep. Donna Christensen**, a Democrat who currently (2014) represents the Virgin Islands, "So refugees could have been admitted on a temporary basis, on tourist visas, for as long as they were in danger."

The U.S. State Department pressured President Roosevelt to resist sanctuary for refugees fleeing Hitler during WW II, essentially helping the Nazis with their "Final Solution" and war effort. Outspoken Jewish leadership did not fight this with the excuse that it would cause antisemitism in the U.S. This was a sign of things to come.

The **U.S. State Department** has a well-documented history of creating excuses which turn against Israel and the Jews' safety and security. The State Department has displayed a type of antisemitism it thinks can be hidden in the pages of history, while claiming balance to the U.S. only reliable democracy in the Middle East.

Harold Ickes, Secretary of the Interior, supported the proposal to let refugees in, but the State Department strongly opposed it.

President Roosevelt sided with State, vetoing the plan on the grounds that Nazi spies might disguise themselves as Jewish refugees and sneak into the mainland U.S. via the islands. In fact, no cases of Nazis posing as Jewish refugees to get into America were ever discovered.

Professor Stephen Norwood, in <u>The Third Reich in the Ivory Tower</u>, noted at least 50 instances in which American colleges offered scholarships to European Jewish Refugees, but the Roosevelt administration blocked their entry. U.S. officials claimed the students could not prove they had a safe address in Europe to which they could later return – and thus constituted a "risk" to become financially dependent on the federal government.

This this hidden double standard continued as demonstrated by the U.S. State Department's efforts. Working behind the scenes, tensions grew in 1956 between the U.S. and Israel following the British, French Israel incursion into Egypt. They would continue over the next four months as Israel demanded specific assurances once it pulled back. As letters continued to go back and forth at the highest levels, Ben-Gurion wrote on February 8, 1957 to President Eisenhower:

"I have to record with regret that in this matter the United Nations has applied different standards to Egypt and to Israel. For eight years Egypt acted in disregard of the [1948] Armistice Agreement…and pursued a policy of belligerency towards Israel. … Those who have the power and authority to intervene took no effective steps whatever to end these flagrant violations of international obligations. … It is unthinkable that now that we have recovered our independence in our ancient homeland we should submit to discrimination. … The question is not a legalistic one. It affects the very foundations of international morality: will the United Nations apply one measure to Egypt and another to Israel?" (Ibid., pp. 166-8)

Royal Hypocrisy Hurts

Winston Churchill emphasized the issue of "rights." He wrote in 1922: "When it is asked what is meant by the development of the Jewish National Home in Palestine, it may be answered that it is not the imposition of a Jewish nationality upon the inhabitants of Palestine as a whole, but the further development of the existing Jewish community, with the assistance of Jews in other parts of the world, in order that it may become a centre in which the Jewish people as a whole may take, on grounds of religion and race, an interest and a pride. But in order that this community should have the best prospect of free development and provide a full opportunity for the Jewish People to display its capacities, it is essential that it should know that it is in Palestine as of right and not on sufferance."

Sir Nicholas Winton's (known in England as "the British Schindler) letter to the President of the United States, written in May 1939, remains a tragic reminder of the desperation not just of Jews trying to flee Hitler, but of those working so hard to save them. And the Roosevelt Administration's response remains a symbol of a government that looked for every reason to say "no" to Jewish refugees, even when the law itself offered numerous options to save lives by opening the doors just a little.

Demonstrating a more contemporary, on-going hypocrisy, **Melanie Phillips** clobbers the British Prime Minister with some logic and facts in a letter on May 5, 2011:

Dear Prime Minister (Rt Hon. David Cameron MP) "…I wonder whether you might explain: …to both Britain and the Jewish people why you do not insist that Mr. Abbas engage seriously in a meaningful peace process by unambiguously renouncing in both English and Arabic his repeated assertions that his people will never accept Israel as a Jewish state…why you implicitly endorse the racist ethnic cleansing inherent in the putative "State of Palestine" which the PA says it will declare a state in which Mr. Abbas has repeatedly declared that not one Jew will be allowed to live, but which you have now threatened to support…Why the British set out to undermine and reverse their own government's policy to re-establish the Jewish National Home in the land of Israel when the British reneged on their internationally binding treaty obligation to settle the Jews throughout Palestine including the areas currently known as the West Bank and Gaza with the result that they kept out desperate Jews trying to flee Nazi Europe, causing thousands to be murdered in the Holocaust. At the same time, the British encouraged Arab illegal immigration from neighbouring countries and turned a blind eye to the pogroms carried out by these Arab newcomers against the Jews whose land it was supposed to be thus laying the groundwork for the false claim that the Arabs were the rightful inheritors of the land. And all the time, the British cloaked this vicious treachery in the honeyed fiction that they were the true friends of the Jewish people and had their interests at heart.

…For Arab aggression against the Jews has been rewarded and encouraged from the start, by robbing the Jews of their rightful inheritance and giving great chunks of it to their aggressors. But if aggressors are rewarded, the inevitable result is more aggression until they achieve their final terrible aim."

Even the brilliant **Tony Blair,** a former prime Minister of Great Britain, would himself apply different standards by saying that there could be no lasting peace in Northern Ireland until the Irish Republican Army destroys its hidden weapons, renounces violence and commits to a political process and then push ahead with the "Road Map" without making similar demands on the Palestinians?

TerVol's active hypocrisy is also the barometer of the world's health.

So often, when the World has had totalitarian fever, the Jew was the first to have suffered: Spanish Middle Ages, in Christian persecutions, in Russian pogroms, in European Fascism, in Islamic fundamentalism.

There seems to be an attitude that shedding a minority's blood is more acceptable than the measures required to prevent it. That has become an element that appears to be increasingly internalized into the discourse on the Israel-Palestinian conflict.

Hypocrisy forges facts: TerVol's's sham amnesia of history.

Yael's research produced a short history undermining the quadpocrisy of an amnesiac history. **Jews are the oldest of any people on earth who have kept their national identity and cultural heritage intact.**

Making his intention clear, in 1906, **David Ben Gurion** (later the Prime Minister of Israel) stated: "The Jewish settlement is not designed to undermine the position of the Arab community; on the contrary, it will salvage it from its economic misery, lift it from its social decline, and rescue it from physical and moral degeneration. Our renaissance in Palestine will come through the country's regeneration, that is: the renaissance of it Arab inhabitants." This was the position of the Jews returning to their historic homeland.

In part, Israel's Declaration of Independence reads:

"WE APPEAL in the very midst of the onslaught launched against us for months now – to the Arab inhabitants of the State of Israel to preserve peace and participate in the upbuilding of the State on the basis of full and equal citizenship and due representation in all its provisional and permanent institutions.

WE EXTEND our hand to all neighbouring states and their peoples in an offer of peace and good neighbourliness, and appeal to them to establish bonds of cooperation and mutual help with the sovereign Jewish people settle in its own land…"

"I wish I had known this before. What is with this bogus amnesia? These were public statements! They are part of the public record! So many of us have been misled by propaganda and outright lies", an exasperated Tom said somewhat under his breath.

Going back many years, the first known modern positions were established as the Balfour Declaration in 1917 and the Emir Faisal-Weitzman agreement of 1919 at the Paris Peace Conference. They were recognized by the world community. Clearly, they supported the creation of a Jewish State in the British Mandate of Palestine and encouraged Jewish immigration immediately, and in large numbers, to settle the Mandated area because it made moral, legal, and physical sense. The Mandate of Palestine was reserved exclusively for the Jewish People to reconstitute the ancient Jewish State of Judea destroyed by Rome, as stated by **Lord Arthur James Balfour** himself.

Even I didn't know that following WWI, the Arabs had gotten 99% of the land distributed by the allies from the defeated Ottoman Empire", apologized Salo.

The San Remo Resolution is the single most important international law concerning contemporary land redistribution following a war.

A resolution was adopted at the San Remo Peace Conference on April 25, 1920 by the Prime Ministers of Great Britain (**David Lloyd George**), France (**Alexandre Millerand**) and Italy (**Francesco Nitti**), as well as Japan (**Ambassador, K. Matsui**).

The express purpose of the conference was about carving up the defeated Ottoman Empire and distributing mandates (an authority granted by a law to act according to that law as a trust) for the new states that were then being created. It adequately met Arab national aspirations by creating the new states of Syria, Mesopotamia later re-named Iraq. Others were established in the Arabian Peninsula, Egypt and North Africa, numbering 21 in all.

At the San Remo Convention, there was a newly carved territory taken from the Turks to be labelled "Palestine." It was assigned to Great Britain to carry out this Mandate [for Palestine] under the League of Nations as its fiduciary. This was a legal trust for Britain. By international law, Britain was required to facilitate the immigration of the Jews, but no other peoples were mentioned.

Article 5 provided that The Mandatory shall be responsible for seeing that no "Palestine territory" shall be ceded or leased to, or in any way placed under the control of, the Government of any foreign Power.

Article 6 of the Mandate, charged Britain with the duty to facilitate Jewish immigration and close settlement by Jews in the territory which then included Transjordan, as called for in the Balfour declaration, that had already been adopted by the other Allied Powers.

As a trustee, Britain had a fiduciary and moral duty to act in good faith in carrying out the duties imposed by the Mandate. Furthermore, as the San Remo resolution has never been abrogated, it was and continues to be legally binding between the several parties who signed it. But the story goes on.

Dividing the Mandate in defiance of intent

The Mandate's terms were finalized and unanimously approved on July 24, 1922, by the Council of the League of Nations, which was the "Mandate for Palestine" document although it did not set final borders. It left this for the Mandatory to stipulate in a binding appendix to the final document in the form of a life changing memorandum.

Here is how it happened:

Using the muscle of intense political and economic pressure, Britain forced an addition, called Article, # 25, of the "Mandate for Palestine." This entitled the British Mandatory to change the terms of the Mandate in the territory east of the Jordan River. They could then ingratiate themselves with the oil rich Arab countries. The Jewish leadership was powerless to argue against Britain. The Jews were coerced and threatened to accept or lose it all and finally accepted with vehement protest over the broken promise and international law of San Remo. It became legally binding.

The picture changed greatly. All the clauses concerning a Jewish National Home would no longer apply to this new territory, despite its essential contradiction of the meaning [Trans-Jordan] of the original Mandate, as is clearly stated:

"The following provisions of the Mandate for Palestine are not applicable to the territory known as Trans-Jordan, which comprises all territory lying to the east of a line drawn from … up the centre of the Wady Araba, Dead Sea and River Jordan. … His Majesty's Government accept[s] full responsibility as Mandatory for Trans-Jordan."

The creation of an Arab state in eastern Palestine (today Jordan) on seventy eight percent of the landmass of the original Mandate intended for a Jewish National Home should in no way change the status of Jews west of the Jordan River.

There was never any intention by the members of the San Remo group to create an Arab state in the British Mandate of the territory of Palestine.

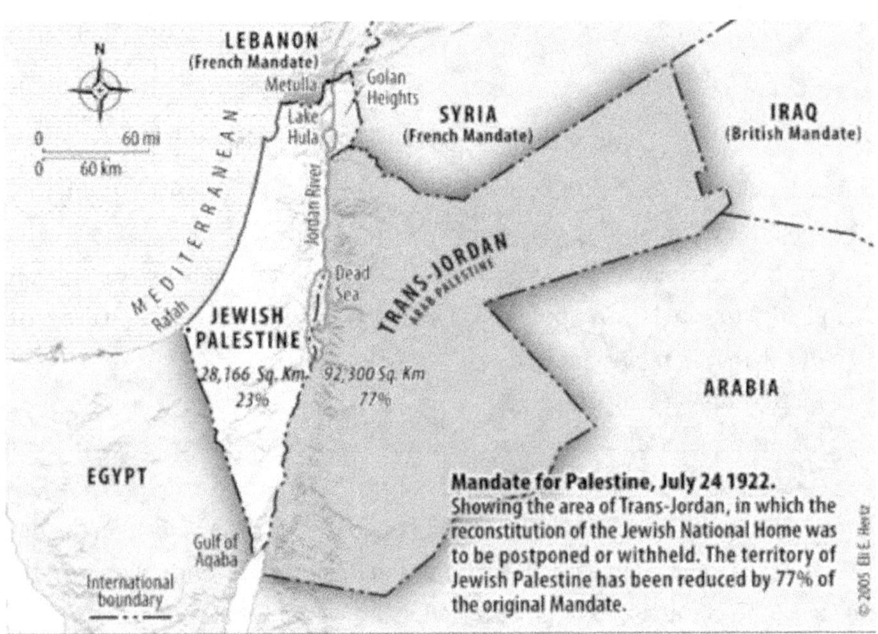

Mandate for Palestine, July 24 1922. Showing the area of Trans-Jordan, in which the reconstitution of the Jewish National Home was to be postponed or withheld. The territory of Jewish Palestine has been reduced by 77% of the original Mandate.

© 2005 Eli E. Hertz

While Jewish legal rights are firmly implanted in international law, there is, on the other hand, no binding document of international law that provides for the creation of an additional, new Arab state in former Mandated Palestine.

UN resolutions cannot constitute a change in international law, nor does the "Performance Based Road Map".

Howard Grief, Esq, an international legal expert, developed a seven-hundred-page legal treatise entitled "The Legal Foundation and Borders of Israel Under International Law" in 2008. It is the basis of the original "Palestine Mandate for the Homeland of the Jewish People."

As is clear, Judea and Samaria were never lands of a High Contracting Power at the time of the war because Jordan's annexation was not recognized by the world save for Britain and Pakistan. It follows that they cannot be "occupied territories" pursuant to the Fourth Geneva Convention.

Malicious Quadpocrisy from the EU

How can E.U. not be considered hypocrites by recently celebrating 25 years of the reunification of Berlin and at the same time calling for the dissection of another country's capital, Jerusalem? http://www.huffingtonpost.com/2012/02/23/la-apologizes-for-deportation_n_1295052.html

Giulio Meotti wrote How Much Does the War On Israel Cost Europe? (January 28, 2013). He pointed out that they spend billions of Euros to keep the fires lit at the same time that their economies are sputtering. He wondered how far the hatred will take people. "The EU has become the largest single donor to the Arab-Palestinians, contributing about Euros 500 million ($720 million) yearly, yet their own economies are in horrible, inexcusable shape.

"Britain, in 1989 refused to sell gas masks to Israel because they could be used for "offensive purposes". The reasoning is preposterous.

"In 1991 a subsidiary of Thames Water Plc., the British company that supplies water and sewage services to most of London, refused to do business with Israel because it has "many and valued Arab clients."

"...How much is Europe investing in Israel's destruction? By financing the Palestinian war and sponsoring the Arab rejectionist anti-Semitism, Europe is reawakening the centuries-old beast of Judeophobic bigotry. European taxes are used to fund antisemitism of an intensity unseen since Nazi Germany.

"…The European Union just allocated 60 million Euros to 'support the Palestinian National Development Plan by helping the PA to finance its budget deficit and implement its reform agenda". This fund perpetuates the chronic Arab dependence and corruption.

"…From 1994 to 2011, the EU donated 4.26 billion Euros to the Palestinian Authority through various channels and this figure does not take into account individual EU states donations to the PA.

"Europe also channels an ocean of money to the anti-Israel NGOs.

"There is a fourth way Europe funds Palestinian terrorism and anti-Semitism: school textbooks and television channels. This is a kind of software of the holy war against the Jews.

"The textbooks funded by the European Union call for Jihad: "Palestine" is shown to encompass all the Jewish State, Judaism's most holy sites (such as the Temple Mount) have been erased, the Jews are demonized and Arab martyrdom is praised. In these texts, Jews are described as cunning, locusts and wild animals.

"To the poor in Europe, giving away hundreds of millions of Euros yearly to support a war effort against Israel, implies a bizarre antisemitism not seen since Hitler."

Haters are seen by the ways they express themselves. Most Arabs support a policy of kidnapping Israeli soldiers and holding them hostage. The PLO, Fatah and Hamas openly exist to ultimately destroy the Jewish state of Israel.

"I would consider that hateful," thought Simon.

Would you consider someone a "peace partner" who steadfastly declared that they would kidnap your child?

A Pew Global Attitudes Project survey found that almost no one in the Muslim Middle East has anything nice to say about Jews. Researchers found that the percentage expressing "favorable views" about Jews was uniformly low: Egypt, 2 percent; Jordan, 2 percent; Pakistan, 2 percent; Lebanon, 3 percent; Palestine, 4 percent; Turkey, 4 percent.

Why is it that 48 percent of Israeli Muslims had favorable opinions of Jews?

Expressions of antisemitism and anti-Israel can also be found in well-known individuals. Some of them are Jewish.

It seems hypocritical to call oneself Jewish and expend their energy to condemn just the Jewish State when there are so many other tragedies going on around the world.

Simon and Yael read "Jewish Enablers of the war Against Israel" by **Professor Steven Plaut, (**www.frontpagemag.com, copyright 2011) for a short list of Jews who mercilessly single out and attack Israel on issues that are dubious to start with and do not apply the same standard of the same issues to any other country. Here is that quadpocrisy again.

Here are some names to remember of those who have disparaged the existence of the Jewish State of Israel, called for damaging moves, either directly or in terribly misguided fashion. There is an attempt to conceal their hypocrisy as most claim their Jewish authenticity as a shield against being called antisemitic:

Peter Beinart; Judge Richard Goldstone; Prof. Norman Finkelstein, Richard Falk,(Prof. emeritus of international law at Princeton headed the UN Human Rights commission to report human rights violations by Israel against the Palestinians in 2008 and compared Israel to Nazi Germany); George Galloway; Ken Livingstone; Yossi Beilin; MJ Rosenberg; Lula de Silva(Brazil); Cristina Fernandez (Argentina); Harold Pinter (N.P.lit, 2005); Catherine Ashton (EU's foreign policy chief); with Amoz Oz; and A.B. Yehoshua; Oren Yiftachel, a professor of "political geography" at Ben-Gurion University. Yiftachel is one of Israel's most outspoken anti-Zionists and calls his country "an ethnocratic regime" and a "Judaization project [that] has caused the pervasive dispossession of Palestinian-Arabs."

Additionally, check out the track records of: Professors Stephen Walt and John Mearshimer, of academia, wrote "The Israel Lobby and US Foreign Policy" (2007); Professors Steven Levitsky (Harvard) and Glen Weyl (U. Chicago); President Jimmy Carter; President;Ahmadenijad of Iran; the Ayotollah Khameini of Iran; Adolf Hitler; Bishop Desmond Tutu; Charles Enderlin; Prof. Francis Boyle; Rep. Paul Findley; Career Foreign Service Officer, Andrew Killgore; Former U.S. Foreign Service officer Eugene

Bird; John Conyers; Nick Rahall; Former Amb. to S.A. James Akins; Juan Cole; George Soros; Haj Amin al Husseini; Yasser Arafat; Mahmoud Abbas; countless actors; Prof.Noam Chomsky; Ellis Goldberg; Juan Cole; Joel Beinin; Illan Pape; Zachary Lockman; Lauren Booth; Prof. Neve Gordon; Prof. Shlomo Sand, the radical author of "The Invention of the Land of Israel." (Sand and Oren Yifachtel sit behind the protective wall of the academic ivory tower in Israel); Journalist Amira Haas; Screenwriter Tony Kushner ("I have a problem with the idea of a Jewish state. It would have been better if it had never happened… I think it was a mistake." He figures prominently on the website of the rabidly anti-Israel polemicist, Norman Finkelstein.).

New York University professor Tony Judt (himself a Jew), remarked that as far as he was concerned, there was "no place in the world today for a "Jewish state," and the idea of Jewish statehood was "not just an anachronism but a dysfunctional one."

"Today, non-Israeli Jews feel themselves once again exposed to criticism and vulnerable to attack for things they didn't do," Judt wrote in 2003.

There has been a measurable increase in the incidence of attacks on Jews in Europe and elsewhere that is primarily attributable to their misdirected efforts, naive students and young Muslims, who use Israel as a subterfuge.

The UN and associated "NGO" Hypocrisy tops them all

This is where might makes right: The permanent members of the Security Council are all the mighty victors following World War II: China, France, Russia, Britain and the USA. This might give them the right to have a permanent veto.

Let's review the Founding Principles of the United Nations:

- Maintaining international peace and security;
- preventing and removing threats to peace;
- suppressing acts of aggression;
- respecting the principle of equal rights and self-determination of peoples;

- strengthening universal peace; and
- promoting and encouraging respect for human rights and fundamental freedoms for all.

What has become of the ideals upon which the U.N. was founded? We find thousands of examples of anti-Israel, anti-Democracy, and anti-exceptionalism criticism from religious organizations, the United Nations General Assembly (currently193 member countries and two observer states), UNESCO, UNHRC, ISESCO, OPEC, OIC, Arab League, Islam, OCHA, UN's Office for the Coordination of Humanitarian Affairs in Occupied Palestinian Territories.

Other Israel attack groups are Amnesty International, UNRWA, ICRC, EU, JStreet, CAIR/MPAC, Doctors without Borders, Hezbollah, ALBA, Oxfam, Students for Justice in Palestine and the New Israel Fund, to name a few. Their focus on condemning Israel while ignoring human rights defilement, such as religious intolerance in many countries belies their supposed humanitarian goals.

The evidence reveals that there is hypocrisy by those who declare that the U.N. today acts for its founding principles in clear contradiction to the facts.

The 51 founding members of the UN in 1945 were roughly balanced between democracies and dictatorships. According to the **Economist's 2014 Democracy Index** measuring the state of democracy in 167 countries, there were 24 full democracies, 52 flawed democracies, 39 hybrid regimes and 52 authoritarian regimes. That means that sixty years later, the number of full democracies has not increased.

The average UN representative is statistically less likely to be speaking for a democratically elected government and far more likely to be there as the personal representative of a tyrant or an oligarchy...Every tyranny is equally represented at the UN. Every king, dictator, sheikh, colonel, prince, beloved leader and president-for-life has a seat at the table.

And since there are many or more tyrannical states as there are full democracies, simple majority rule always favors tyranny and the hybrid. The U.N. has become the voting hall of tyrannies.

This is not part of the Founding Principles! The U.N.'s identity has been buried along with its integrity. Only the exceptional effort and funding of the

United States and some of its allies has the Charter and its ideals been kept alive even though The U.N. has become occupied territory. http://www.un.org/depts/dhl/unms/founders.shtml

"I am so disappointed in the UN", sighed Kelsey. "It started off with such noble aspirations and now cannot even live up to its founding principles. I quickly found eighteen countries that can't live up to the U.N.'s founding principles. But I will only share a few with you."

1. **Cuba**, which jails people for circulating the Human Rights Declaration, became vice chair of the U.N. Human Rights Council.

2. **Iran**, which sentences adulteresses to death, was elected to the U.N. Commission on the Status of Women.

3. **North Korea** (nuclear-armed) was appointed head of the U.N. Council on Disarmament.

4. No U.N. resolutions were taken against the ongoing Arab slave trade in **Sudan** or for the rights of women and minorities in places where these were denied.

5. The 1988 **UN General Assembly** recommendation - supported by 132 countries - to recognize a Palestinian state, without applying any of the credentials normally presented or described in international law.

6. A number of the **50 original signatories** were already on the verge of being made satellites of the Soviet Empire. The 51st, Poland, was delayed from joining the 50 by a Soviet-backed Communist takeover. Even as the ink was drying on a charter of world peace, the second signatory to that charter was forging the chains that would bind a tenth of the other signatories into a totalitarian empire. http://www.un.org/depts/dhl/unms/founders.shtml http://graphics.eiu.com/PDF/Democracy_Index_2010_web.pdf

7. **UNESCO**: Bashar al-Assad of Syria was chosen to be the Arab representative on the UNESCO committee that deals with issues relating to the implementation of human rights. "UNESCO's decision comes after Assad's regime managed to kill 3,500 demonstrators and arrest

tens of thousands, without any due process whatsoever." From Maariv: "On Wednesday Nov16, 2011. http://www.24-7pressrelease.com/press-release/new-book-exposes-us-and-un-for-funding-terrorism-236520.php

8. On September 21, 2011 /EIN Presswire/ — A new book exposes US and UN for Funding Terrorism. It is well documented that the United Nations refugee policy funds the teaching of terrorist ideals and practices within refugee camp schools. This claim is one of many veteran news reporter and commentator **David Bedein**, Director of the Israel Resource News Agency & The Center for Near East Policy Research, examines in his eye-opening new book, WHERE HAS ALL THE FLOUR GONE: WHIMS AND WASTE OF UN PALESTINIAN. "Give me four years to teach the children and the seed I have sown will never be uprooted." Vladimir Lenin

9. **Russia** is a permanent member of the Security Council. Russia invaded **Hungary** against the premises of the U.N. in 1956. The last telex out of Hungary during the invasion of 1956 was: "We are quiet, not afraid. Send the news to the world and say it should condemn the Russians. The fighting is very close now and we haven't enough guns. What is the United Nations doing? Give us a little help. We will hold out to our last drop of blood." No help came from the U.N.

Over the next decade, millions more would die in new conflicts. And the list of genocides would continue to steadily grow adding up to some 50 million dead on the UN's watch.

But the United Nations operates under the umbrella of political interests which prioritize alliances over atrocities and power over human priorities. Only when a consensus among the "democracy of tyrants" is reached can any meaningful action be taken.

There are other areas where TerVol has triumphed: the trick of "Plausible Deniability"

When is an NGO not an NGO, but a GONGO or a Congo line? NGOs are supposed to be free of government support or direction. By definition, Non-Governmental Organizations (NGOs) are autonomous, non-profit and politically unaffiliated groups that claim to promote an agenda based on universal moral values, such as human rights, democracy, the environment, etc.

There are even more examples of political hypocrisy. And there are Government Orchestrated NGOs who should be known as GONGOs.

"What happened to the original morality invested in NGOs? How do we explain the oxymoron of GONGO? Why do they focus almost exclusively on one country when there is so much inhumanity all around the globe?" Simon rhetorically asked.

Salo could not help responding, "Termites are smart enough to dress in butterfly's clothing. They are then adored despite the damage they are about to do." He did have a sense of irony.

TerVol's use of Lawfare

"Wake up everyone," Simon commanded. "We have been deceived! I have to tell you about the many NGOs that are not non-governmental organizations if governments support them to attain political goals.

Sometimes significant practical impact on government policy can be achieved by interim injunctions, the publicity (usually negative for Israel) generated by the lodging of the petition itself, out-of-court settlements reached to avoid drawn-out legal proceedings, irrespective of the substantive merits of the petitions, and so on.

The ample financial resources of political NGOs, with agendas often inimical to the democratic vision of preserving Israel as the nation-state of the Jewish people, allow them to lodge frequent petitions with a like-minded High Court of Justice. This is known as "Lawfare," just like warfare.

When the GONGO's use Boycott, Divest and Sanction (BDS) of Israel only, that should be sufficient, but for the international hypocrisy, to destroy their credibility.

BDS is actually not new. Arab nations forced boycotts against pre-state Israel in 1945 to try to eliminate the nascent State.

The ultimate goal of the BDS movement is the elimination of Israel and the violation of Jewish rights. The movement has a central demand for a "right of return" of millions of Arab-Palestinians and all their progeny.

Even **Norman Finkelstein**, an infamous critic of Israel has stated that BDS is "not really talking about rights. They're talking about [how] they want to destroy Israel".

"I don't ever remember reading that anyone in American NGO movements ever proposed to blacklist South African professors during real apartheid. Today the BDS groups propose blacklisting Israeli professors despite the provable facts that there is no apartheid. I am disgusted at the heinous hypocrisy", declared Simon.

A group's goal to cause a people or country to disappear deserves no better comparison than to the Nazis. As a political position, it is a legal and moral disaster. It is not politics; it is a tantrum—and perhaps a lethal one http://tabletmag.com/jewish-news-and-politics/186468/bds-politics-radical-gestures?utm_source=tabletmagazinelist&utm_campaign=d920ce0dd2-Monday_October_27_201410_27_2014&utm_medium=email&utm_term=0_c308bf8edb-d920ce0dd2-206994993

The **NGO Monitor** (https://www.ngo-monitor.org) is the most reliable, factual, accurate body, that continues to document and expose the immoral exploitation of universal human rights for political objectives.

So many NGOs and UN agencies use the façade of human rights and humanitarian aid while callously ignoring indiscriminate rocket attacks against Israeli civilians – every one of which is a war crime. 6-14-12 NGO Monitor report, www.ngo.monitor.org

GONGOs often try to hide government support to appear to be a neutral NGO because they are supposed to be NOT politically affiliated. Transparency is nil! The hard work of the NGO Monitor documented that the European Union gave their support to proxies whose efforts were to undermine the elected government of Israel. A number of powerful groups receive more than 70% of their annual donations from or through foreign governments. The GONGOs, quite simply, are a fraud. (https://www.ngo-monitor.org/)

For example, there are groups that frequently single out and attack Israel. Some are: **Rabbi's for Human Rights** (6% of their funding is from foreign governments), **Physicians for Human Rights-Israel** (53% of funding is from foreign governments), the Israeli, **Yesh Din** whose budget is NIS 5 million" foreign donations in NIS 4.7 million.Of this 25% of this money is from foreign governments. According to NGO Monitor, in the past decade the New ISrael Fund has transferred $22 Million Dollard to Adalah, B'Tselem and Yesh Din. (www.israelnationalnews.com **Gabe Kahn** Nov 14, 2011).

These anti-Israeli NGOs are very active externally in the delegitmization and political warfare against Israel. With a pretense of morality, they pursue only one democratic country, Israel. That is TerVol's hypocrisy in action.

This campaign was crystallized at the **2001 UN World Conference Against Racism in Durban, South Africa**. At the Conference 1,500 so called NGOs adopted a document and plan of action calling for the total isolation of Israel. To achieve this goal, NGOs frequently scream false accusations that Israel is an apartheid state, make unsubstantiated allegations of war crimes, promote anti-Israel BDS (boycotts, divestment, and sanctions), and bring lawfare cases against Israeli officials, amongst other tactics. December 7, 2011 NGO Monitor.

"From the look on your faces I can't tell if you are not clear yet, or if you are in shock. I guess I need some ice water to spill on your heads. I will share more information with you. Don't let yourselves feel overwhelmed just yet", Simon smiled.

One illuminating example that NGOs exist is that the Dutch Foreign Ministry under Rosenthal has begun to institute sweeping reforms to stop Dutch charities from funding anti-Israel boycott, divestment and sanctions (BDS) activities and NGOs that deny Israel's right to exist. He'll work to stop funding estimated, at 10 million euros, organizations calling for divestment, boycott, thereby denying Israel's right to exist. http://campaign.r20.constant-contact.com/render?llr=rfhybieab&v=0015U2tEoPRVkiuO1R4PmvXxrfJhx9 Bu41yO2TRdS4Ff3JZW_-GWRcOn8Gdef5qi-1v3W8gYkUyzm0n U6VVPlr0K1kb8jX7USHkp6nVz9HT-rz5ZtUCFHwOPQ%3D%3D

The CIDI **(Center for Information and Documentation on Israel)** report named many Arab and Dutch NGOs that were dependent on subsidies from the Dutch Foreign Ministry. The northern European countries, said CIDI, are also funding the same NGOs as the Dutch Foreign Ministry. Norway, Denmark, and Sweden are key financial providers of anti-Israel groups. Switzerland was also cited by CIDI.

The governments of several countries such as the United Kingdom, Ireland, the Netherlands, Switzerland, Spain, Finland, Belgium, and France were also funding anti-Israel NGOs. That makes them GONGOs, not NGOs. That should destroy their moral credibility to reasonable people. For those who want peace, pursuing lies and delegitimization of Israel alone proves hypocrisy. "EU-Funded Yesh Din Provides Building Blocks for Lawfare." http://campaign.r20.constantcontact.com/render?llr=rfhybieab&v=001EgdY2 fhRL-XRXmGRhtBJ2hMYkss6YHVbYEEvlWyS3b85pyudf OZJsX6JOOC-PUztcRPOT3DUpCLZ8AZvS4aedMRyt0gTmzjAKwq8r2Ga_54wTL_8MZ bkg%3D%3D

Why do foreign governments provide so much money to anti-Israeli political advocacy NGOs?

The bottom line is that they attempt to further the delegitimization of the Jewish State of Israel, making it vulnerable to political jackals and aggressive militant bodies while those governments appear blameless. TerVol's trick is called "credible deniability", a tactic implying forethought by setting up conditions to plausibly avoid responsibility for future actions.

Transparency is almost non-existent on the part of European funders, Israeli NGOs, and major indirect funding via "aid' organizations. **NGO Monitor** has discovered that over 27 million NIS annually was provided to Israeli political advocacy NGOs by foreign governments which make them GONGOs. The reports for 2012 show that a total amount of 34,355,579 NIS annually is being provided to 30 NGOs from a number of foreign governments. (Additional foreign government funding goes to Palestinian and international NGOs active in delegitimization campaigns.)

These GONGOs often make unsubstantiated allegations and misrepresent the law. For instance, many GONGOs screamed that there was a massacre in Jenin in 2002. It was proven to be a total propaganda fabrication to be used a bludgeon.

Can the role of GONGOs funded by foreign governments be unique to Israel? Both the amount of money given to NGOs and the quantity of these types of NGOs are not found elsewhere! Only Israel has hundreds of NGOs operating under a facade of human rights whose credibility and impact are artificially amplified by massive foreign funds.

As shown in NGO Monitor's study, in 2007-2010 (the last available data), NGOs in Israel and the Palestinian Authority received over 11 million Euros through the European Instrument for Democracy and Human Rights (EIDHR); 57% of EIDHR funding directed at the Middle East, while projects in Syria, Iraq, Iran, Oman, Saudi Arabia, and the UAE are largely ignored by EU frameworks such as EIDHR. The decision making and evaluation processes by which EIDHR provides this large-scale funding for political advocacy NGOs is entirely hidden from public view, in violation of basic transparency requirements for democratic governance. http://www.ngomonitor.org/article/evaluating_funding_for_political_advocacy_ngos_in_the_arab_israeli_co nflict_the_european_instrument_for_democracy_and_human_rights_eidhr_

Trócaire, an Irish church-based NGO, is a government funded BDS (they are really a GONGO) that they describe themselves as "humanitarian" aid, like an NGO. It received over one-third of its income from governments (€ 18 million from Ireland in 2012). Trocaire launched a campaign lobbying the EU "to end trade with illegal Israeli settlements." Documented by the NGO Monitor 10-18-12

How U.S. Government Funding for Mideast Political NGOs Undermines U.S. Policy

This is more than hypocrisy. It is short sided and self-destructive of U.S. interests. It is hate in the disguise of morality which is one of TerVol's best deceits.

A 13-page report , <u>The Negative Impact of U.S. Government Funding for Mideast Political NGOs</u>, with a 38-page appendix by NGO Monitor was presented to Members of Congress. It shows that U.S. Government is funding several political NGOs in the Palestinian Authority and Israel that contradicts U.S. policy, has a negative impact on the peace process, and lacks the independent oversight necessary to prevent abuses."Some of the NGO grantees are like the "MIFTAH Windows". They fund political advocacy NGOs that demonize Israel, promote the infamous blood libel and promote campaigns targeting Israel. This activity is entirely inconsistent with U.S. policy and laws. HTTP//U.S.%20Governmen t%20Funding%20forMideast%20Political%20NGOs%20Undermines%20U.S. %20Policy%20.htm An incredulous example of the hatred of Israel was seen in response of 50 NGOs and UN agencies that demanded that Israel end its totally legal blockade of Gaza. This is in spite of the UN Secretary General's Palmer Committee and other legal experts who also have declared that Israel's blockade of Gaza is completely legal under international law.

Since the beginning of the evil violence in Syria in April 2011, Oxfam International and its branches have released only 3 statements and petitions condemning the ongoing violence in Syria. At that time the violence has reportedly led to the deaths of at least 10,000 civilians. As of July, 2014 the death total was above 160,000. By mid-June of 2015 it was over 200 thousand dead. In comparison, Oxfam has condemned Syria's immediate neighbor, Israel, in at least 9 statements over that last year-and-a-half and made 10 condemnatory statements during the three-week 2008-2009 Gaza War. That makes Oxfam a deceitful enemy of Israel. Initial information supplied by the NGO Monitor in September 12, 2012. This made TerVol laugh heartily. It was doing such a good job. GONGOs are aided by foreign governments to affect Israel's policies by circumventing accepted diplomatic practices in manners which are far from transparent – either to their own domestic publics or to the Israeli electorate. NGOs are not supposed to be government funded in order to get special status and credibility.

Second, it permits electorally inconsequential segments of the population to short-circuit public debate and to influence events far beyond their domestic weight, using the resources of official alien sovereignties whose interests are very different – indeed often diametrically opposed – to those of Israel. The protection of minority rights is an important element of liberal democracy, but the right to subvert, indeed supersede, the will of the majority is quite another.

There should not exist a notion of the rule of the minority. The symbiotic interaction between an indisputably politically biased judiciary and organizations funded largely by governments with interests divergent from those of Israel, bestow inordinately disproportionate influence on an electorally insignificant minority.

Voting blocks in the U.N. –Intergovernmental Organizations. There are five powerful voting blocs within the U.N.

Three of the political voting blocks, created by TerVol's tactics, have a very strong influence on U.N. voting, particularly since so many countries that are not democracies and are ruled by an oligarchy, theocracy or dictator. OPEC, in this grouping, uses it personal oil wealth for power. Here are five examples.

1. **The Non-Aligned Movement (NAM),** institutionalized in 1961, is a group of states which are not aligned formally with or against any major power bloc. As of 2012, the movement has 120 members and 17 observer countries. The proclaimed basis of the Non-Aligned Movement five principles were:

   - Mutual respect for each other's territorial integrity and sovereignty
   - Mutual non-aggression
   - Mutual non-interference in domestic affairs
   - Equality and mutual benefit
   - Peaceful co-existence

But how does one understand this? The 120-nation Nonaligned Movement handed its host, Iran, a diplomatic victory, unanimously decreeing support for the disputed Iranian nuclear energy program and criticizing the American-led attempt to isolate and punish Iran with unilateral economic sanctions. Israel was not invited. The unanimous backing of the final document undercut the American argument that Iran was an isolated outlier nation. "Nonaligned Nations Back Iran's Nuclear Bid, but Not Syria" by Thomas **Erdbank,** August 31, 2012

2. **"Is the OIC a GONGO?"** by Elizabeth@horowitzfreedomcenter.org

The Organization of the Islamic Conference, is **now called the Organization of Islamic Cooperation** (OIC). The OIC is a religious and political organization made up of 57 States.

The OIC is a unique organization, one that has no equivalent in the world. It unites the religious, economic, military, and political strength of 56 states. By contrast, the European Union represents half as many states and is a secular body only.

The OIC is strictly tied to the principles of the Koran, the Sunna, and the Sharia. Close to the Muslim World League of the Muslim Brotherhood, it shares the Brotherhood's strategic and cultural vision: that of a universal religious community, the Ummah, based upon the Koran, the Sunna, and the canonical orthodoxy of Shari'a. The OIC currently represents **56** countries and the Palestinian Authority (considered a state by them), the whole constituting the universal Ummah with a community of more than one billion three hundred (up to six hundred) million Muslims.

The facts are that the UN General Assembly is driven largely by the largest bloc of countries. The OIC is also one of the largest intergovernmental organizations in the world. The OIC has a unique structure among nations and human societies. In a word, it appears that the OIC seeks to become the reincarnation of the Caliphate ruling the entire world.

If Islam rules over the world as the OIC would want, we will see the removal of music, operas, almost all literature of the West, Western concepts of Civilization, movies and art. The world will be bereft of what makes Western Civilization what it is.

The Vatican and the various churches are to be de facto devoid of political power.

The distinguished author and researcher, Bat Ye'or, has written thoroughly about the OIC Organization of Islamic Cooperation: Asian religions do not represent systems that bring together religion, strategy, politics, and law within a single organizational structure whereas Islam does.

The OIC enjoys unlimited power through the union and cohesion of all its bodies, but also to this it adds the infallibility conferred by religion. Bringing together 57 countries, including some of the richest in the world, it controls the lion's share of global energy resources.

Among its targets, the OIC Charter specifies the propagation, promotion, and preservation of Islamic teachings and values, the spread of Islamic culture, and the preservation of the Islamic heritage (article I-11). Article I-12 promotes the protection and defense of the true image of Islam, the fight against its defamation, and the encouragement of dialogue between civilizations and religions.

The OIC supports all the jihadist movements considered to be resisting "foreign occupation," including those in "occupied" Indian Kashmir, and condemns the "humiliation and oppression" of Muslims in India.

It implies that the covenants which do not conform with Islamic values will not be followed.

To give an idea of the difference in our belief systems, the Sudanese President Omar al Bashir, accused (according to Western criteria of justice) of genocide committed in southern Sudan and Darfur, has not been troubled by the **Islamic Court of Justice.**

The OICs combined political and religious institution is at the very outer rim of Western thinking, which is anchored the separation between politics and religion. Rooted in individualism, Europeans, Americans and Israelis cultivate the search for happiness and cherish freedom of thought and of rational, scientific exploration, which are perceived as a human being's greatest privilege and finest adventure.

Aspiring to a worldwide Caliphate indicates the longing for their supreme authority over all others, owing its infallibility to Allah and Allah's human intermediary, Mohammed.

According to **Ibn Khaldoun**, this institution placing politics at the service of worldwide, religious expansionism was created as instrument for the mandatory Islamization of mankind. From ATLAS Shrugs, November, 2011.

3. **ISESCO,** is separate bloc but part of the **OIC:** the Islamic Educational, Scientific, and Cultural Organization (52 member states and 3 observer states). It seeks to impose on the West the Islamic perception of history and civilization through the **Observatory of Islamophobia**, and the newly created **Islamic International Court of Justice.**

4. **The Arab League** is a regional organization of Arab countries in and around North Africa, the Horn of Africa, and Southwest Asia. It was

formed in Cairo on 22 March 1945. Currently, the League has 22 regular members and covers 5,000,000 square miles and untold oil wealth. They vote as a block in the U.N.

5.   **OPEC** is the acronym for the Organization of the Petroleum Exporting Countries. It was created in 1960 as a cartel to influence world oil prices. Currently they have 12 members of which 6 are in the Middle East, 4 in Africa and 2 in South America. They produced an oil embargo in 1973 which raised the price of a barrel of oil by 4 times, produced a global economic recession and raised unemployment. This is real political power.

Simon says:

We can see that the game has been stacked by wealthy poseurs, hypocritical profiteers and opaque dissimulators. This is hypocrisy taken to an international level.

Most of these TerVol guided voting blocks and NGOs have one thing in common, they barely hide their hatred as they espouse their anti-Democracy, anti-exceptionalism, anti-Israel and anti-Zionism as being for the betterment of the world.

But as bloody history has shown, these groups can be linked by plain Jew hatred or antisemitism. The same trend has been linked with the downfall of societies. No wonder the Jews are so concerned. The mystery of what the connected dots will reveal can be lit by the brightest brains even to the dimmest of people.

There are scholars who have illuminated that there is a small group, who have particular concerns, the Jewish People. We need to see how this happened to the Jewish Nation because we know it is the precursor to attacks on others, human rights and democracy itself.

Some may ask why we should be concerned just because the Jews are threatened. We are about to find out why it is important to everyone!

Let's find out.

#5 Democracy's Dilemmas:
Dealing with Bullies and Canaries

Simon says:

"Look out the window. Do the dark clouds pushed by strong winds across the sky make you uncomfortable again? We need to seek out more clues from the past using our model of the ancient Jewish People. Is this our savior canary? We have shown how TerVol tries to cripple and destroy smaller countries and peoples first. The Jewish People are about the smallest religious nation that for millennia that TerVol has not been able to destroy. Most already know that what starts with antisemitism never ends with antisemitism. We can put many examples together to show those with an open mind that our thesis is correct.

Antisemitism can be seen as a generalization about bullies who do not respect any others' rights, first picking on those who they think are Jewish. These examples help us gain clarity by illuminating the destructive dots of antisemitism, plus its cohorts, anti-Israel, anti-Zionism, anti-Exceptionalism and anti-Democracy.

Besides the thousands of books and academic studies, the EU and the U.S. State Department have composed working definitions of antisemitism. It covers all forms of classic antisemitism as well as their contemporary applications.

The definition states, in part: "Anti-Semitism is a certain perception of Jews, expressed as hatred toward Jews. Manifestations are violent rhetorical, economic and physical directed toward Jewish appearing or even non-practicing Jewish individuals, their personal property and toward Jewish community and religious institutions..."

The haters always presume guilt for whatever pretext they can imagine. Some contemporary examples include blaming all Jews for the wrongs committed by Jewish individuals, denying the Holocaust, and accusing Jews of controlling the media, economy, government or other societal institutions to everyone else's detriment.

Today anti-Zionism or anti-Israel often serve as cover for antisemitism. It should be easy to see through TerVol's hypocrisy. Apply this guide: Only the Jewish people are denied their right to self-determination, right to security and Israel's the right to exist. This has to be antisemitism. This is a preview of what could happen to the U.S. when anti-American and anti-exceptionalism flourish in the U.N. The basic principle demonstrating antisemitism or anti-Israel or anti-Zionism is not to treat Jews or Israelis or Zionists the same as you would treat others.

Let's see how some scholars can clear this up for us."

What might some Western scholars, historians and experts say about how antisemitism can affect all of us in the USA and Israel?

Arieh L. Avneri thoroughly documented the legitimacy of Jewish land settlement in the Mandate of Palestine and before. As one stands back to view the years from 1878 to 1948, the conclusion is that an overwhelming antisemitism infects, sometimes cloaked as anti-Zionism, to prevent the Jews from having a state like all other peoples. The issue of stable Arab possession or roots in the land is debunked in his esteemed book, <u>The Claim of Dispossession</u>, with overwhelming facts and statistics. Anyone denying the Jewish Peoples historic claim to the land could not stand up to the information he shares.

Tracts upon tracts of land were purchased by Jewish philanthropists and Jewish funds long preceding the actual formation of the Jewish State. Tens of thousands of children, parents and grandparents would put spare change, pennies, into a box known as the Jewish National Fund to purchase land and plant trees. He demonstrates that Zionism embodies the Jews right to self-determination in their ancient homeland.

Martin Sherman shined a klieg light on this bias. "The Jews are being told that they can only legitimize the existence of their nation-state if they agree to expose it to mortal danger. They are being told that for their own right to political independence to be embraced by the democratic nations of the world, they must consent to the establishment of (yet another) Muslim tyranny, unswervingly dedicated to its destruction, and surrender to it areas vital to its national security and survival."

"No sensible nation would submit to that. We, in the USA, certainly wouldn't as long as we remain powerful enough," a piqued Tom pointed out.

Simon popped in, "Once I began studying this, it was not difficult to grasp the validity that there has always been a molten core of hatred lying deep in human psyches that can erupt violently like a destructive volcano as anti-exceptionalism, or anti-stranger, anti-independent thinking, antisemitism, or anti-democracy.

I learned that there were other terms for antisemitism like misoJudaism, Judeoschadenfreude, Judeohatred, Judeopsychosis, Judeopathology, Judeohostility, Judeophobia, and Systemic Jew Hatred."

"If you think about it," commented Salo, "The overlap of antisemitism and hypocrisy is fairly easy to see. Denying a person or nation's right to legitimacy (to life) but willing to take advantage of the myriad of advances (the Jewish People can proudly call it exceptionalism) in every arena that the Jew, Israel or the U.S. has given the world certainly fits the definition of hypocrisy. More wickedly, some have even called it 'tough love' to conceal its deadliness. The anti-Israel crowd finds it so easy to create rights of a non-existent people to complete the hypocrisy that they are morally right destroying Israel. It is a form of pack mentality, brutish jealousy."

Yael's years of research supported this. Antisemitism to Jews is often like the volcano of TerVol. Other times in Western society it exists as the voracious termite colony of TerVol.

First TerVol confuses people.

The word "Semitic" entered the vocabulary for the study of languages only, not a race in 1871. "Antisemitism" was first coined 1879 by **Wilhelm Marr** to replace the German word "Judenhass" (Jew hatred) for "polite company." Wilhelm Marr observed and hysterically feared Jewish exceptionalism. On a deeper level, the Jews represented equal civil rights and the ability to benefit where "merit" was in essential conflict in a rigid class society.

To fool many, TerVol got on an academic high horse. He knew that "Antisemitism" had nothing to do with the academic endeavor of Semitic linguistics. Wilhelm Marr went on to form the League of Anti-Semites in 1879. He publicly concealed his political movement from the religiously based anti-Jewish ferocities that had preceded it. To portray himself as a hero defending the West, Marr preached, "The Jews are unstoppable!" Marr resounded that the Jews had fought against the Western world for almost two millennia and were now poised to conquer the continent: France was already Judaized (a fearful claim of the Arabs today about Israel). Germany was about to be skinned alive. As Marr wrote, "We have among us a flexible, tenacious, intelligent, foreign tribe that knows how to bring abstract reality into play in many ways. Not individual Jews, but the Jewish spirit and Jewish consciousness have overpowered the world." Guided by TerVol, he wanted to appear noble, the same cloak and mask of today. However, he was jealous of the consistent basis displaying exceptionalism of the Jewish people to survive and be productive.

Anthony Julius, the legal genius, sums it up in <u>Trials of the Diaspora: A History of Anti-Semitism in England:</u> "…The kernel of truth that allowed for Marr's paranoid analysis was that Jews were highly competitive in all areas— except national politics… Wherever they were offered enough freedom to compete on more or less equal terms, Jews did well enough to lend credibility to inflated images of their "power." But since collective Jewry lacked and never sought precisely the kind of political reach with which they were credited, the disparity between image and reality made them an ideal target for those who really did want to flex their power."

Prof. Ruth R. Wisse is quite good at succinct clarity: "Antisemitism is not directed against the behavior of Jews but against the existence of Jews." Antisemitism often shows up as scapegoating. That means a generalized blame from local or personal problems, blaming from the few to the many. It persisted over the millennia, as an excuse robbing, plundering, raping, humiliating, stealing legal rights, distraction from local problems, and mass murdering Jews.

The lowest common denominator spanning countries large and small, which constitute the international community, appears to be Jew-hatred. It is an excuse to plunder from a minority. To blame Jews for antisemitism is as rational as saying skin color is responsible for anti-black racism.

A few Jews, who themselves hate the expression of Jewish self-determination in the form of the State of Israel, present their credentials under the auspices of their being Jewish. History is full of examples that you can be Jewish and still hate other Jews and Zionism.

"These examples are not actually Jewish self-hatred" explained Kelsey, "but they do hate their connection to Judaism. They do love themselves."

Zionism is the Jewish People's national liberation movement. Antisemitism is manifest as anti-Zionism and Anti-Israel. This is a singular denial to the Jewish right to national self-determination and self-defense which is granted to every legitimate People.

Some have asked what makes antisemitism different from all the other racisms? It seems to be around forever. Antisemitism can be seen as a millennial genocide. And it tends to destroy indiscriminately.

Frits Bolkestein, a former European Commissioner, went so far as to recommend that practicing Jews in Holland immigrate to Israel because he doubted the government's ability to protect them from the increasing onslaughts from Islamic immigrants. He does not understand that he is next.

As **David Harris** has said, "By all standards of civilization and modernity, Israel should be admired and emulated by the rest of the world. Instead, the Jewish state is hated and is a pariah among nations, just as Jews themselves are pariahs in most of the world outside America today."

Simon reminded the others that this is truly quadpocrisy and would be overtly used against America if the USA was not so powerful.

Yael seconded Simon explaining that "the haters and antisemites are a taffy twisted group. They often justify their irrational hatred, hypocritically behind the excuse of saving the rest of us. Some excuse the Holocaust because people said Jews are sinister, rootless, cosmopolitan people, who are not citizens [with] allegiance to a conventional nation state. This idea contradicts normative Jewish Law. When the few remaining Jews who were left following the violent pogroms and the Holocaust, had to fight to retain what had been legally promised to them: a conventional nation state, the antisemites hated them for that, too."

The intellectual class in Europe that is able to swivel so swiftly, from hating Jews for one reason in the 1930s to hating them in the second half of the

20th century, for seeking equal rights amongst the nations, says far more about Europeans than it does about Jews. It displays an irrational, prejudged distaste.

Mark Steyn, a deep thinker and journalist, wrote, ".... One of the most fascinating things about the new (facet) of antisemitism in Europe is the number of people who blame the Jews for the Islamization of Europe, the number of people who say, 'We wouldn't have all these mosques in Antwerp, Rotterdam, Hamburg, and Malmo if we hadn't been so riddled with post-war Holocaust guilt. Those Jews did it to us!' "As I said," recalled Simon, "taffytwisted."

The **World Zionist Organization** surveyed the level of anti-Semitism among French citizens. One survey revealed that more than 40% of the French population holds anti-Semitic beliefs. The survey also found that 47% of the population believes that "French Jews are more loyal to Israel than the country where they live." TerVol applauded the media bias.

A P*ew Research Center's Global Attitudes Project* found that 46% of Spanish residents held an unfavorable view of Jews, thanks to the media.

Meanwhile, 47% of Germans are of the opinion that Israel is exterminating the Palestinians, according to a poll undertaken by the Friedrich Ebert Foundation, affiliated with the German Social Democratic Party. TerVol is puffing out his chest at putting that one over on the Germans thanks to the help from the media.

Forty-four percent of Italians are prejudiced or hostile toward Jews, according to a study recently issued by the Italian Chamber of Deputies' Committee, thanks to the media.

The same trend is appearing all over Europe. Half of the population holds deep anti-Jewish feelings. More thanks to the media.

Britain has just included Israel on a list of 28 countries whose human rights record is of "concern" to the government. The media is so slanted on this issue that it has the power to impact government leaders. There has to be something else motivating these unsupportable anti-Semitic beliefs.

Virtually all the human rights moralizers seem to be disregarding the frightening plight of the Arab-Palestinians and Christians in the ghastly Syrian civil war and in all the other Arab countries like Lebanon and Jordan. They busy themselves away from the ghastly massacres going on in Africa. There are no demonstrations about the brutal Muslim on Muslim or Muslim persecution of Christians killings in Iraq. Perhaps the media finds there is no anti-Israel angle to the story. It appears that the mainstream Western media are sometimes delicately anti-Israel and other times heavy-handed. There is no other way to explain the fact that all these high-and-mighty moralizers are ignoring the frightening plight of multiple brutalities that are infinitely more disgusting than Israelis building homes in the cities and neighborhoods.

"Here is how it boiled down," claimed the psychiatrist, Kelsey. "The antisemitic hypocrite starts by proclaiming with utmost confidence in his source that the Jews are the evil in the world. Then, the antisemite postures himself on the moral high ground assuming the role of protector of humanity from the evil, called Judaism. It is not the Jewish presence in the Middle East. It is Jewish presence in the world. To solve the problem, they argue the Jews must be transmutated, converted or eliminated. This paranoid attitude is called projecting one's feelings as coming from the other."

A well-respected German academic ***Matthias Kuntzel*** observed, "…As with the Nazis, the jihadists' aim is to eliminate this source of evil that {they argue} threatens all of humanity." (Jihad and Jew-Hatred: Islamism, Nazism, and the Roots of 9/11, trans. Colin Meade (New York: Telos Press, 2007), p. 149.)

Here is a sample of what some influential Islamic leaders and TV programs say about hating Jews.

Muhammad Hussein Yaqub the noted Egyptian cleric, delivered a televised diatribe revealing the jihadists' ideological position. He represents a majority position: "If the Jews left Palestine to us, would we start loving them? Of course not! They are enemies not because they occupied Palestine. They would have been enemies even if they did not occupy a thing. Our fighting with the Jews is eternal, and it will not end until the final battle until not a single Jew remains on the face of the earth." (Muhammad Hussein Yaqoub, "We Will Fight, Defeat, and Annihilate Them," al-Rahma TV, Jan. 17, 2009, Middle East Media Research Institute, Washington, D.C., Special Dispatch No. 2278, Mar. 12, 2009.)

"Most people don't know the reality that I found. I am still reeling from the unabashed, unfounded hatred," shared Tom. "Listen to this."

HonestReporting.com: The Big Lie is spread with massive repetition. In 2003 a private Syrian film company created a 29-part television series Ash-Shatat ("The Diaspora"). This series originally aired in Lebanon in late 2003 and was broadcast by Al-Manar, a satellite television network owned by Hezbollah. This TV series, based on the antisemitic forgery, "The Protocols of the Learned Elders of Zion," to show the Jewish people as engaging in a conspiracy to rule the world. They represent the Jews as people who murder Christian children, drain their blood and use this blood to bake matzah. When the world stood by quietly as these hate inspiring lies were spread, the silence lent credibility to lies.

"Hold your breath" shot in Yael. On **al-Jazeera** (2000) radio, an episode of The Opposite Direction was dedicated to the question, "Is Zionism Worse than Nazism?" Of the 12,000 viewers who called in to Al Jazeera, 85 percent answered in the affirmative, 11 percent saw both as equally bad, and 2.7 percent ventured that Nazism was worse. " Zionism and Nazism: A Discussion on the TV Channel Al-Jazeera," Middle East Media Research Institute (MEMRI), June 7, 2001, quoted in Rubin, The Tragedy of the Middle East, p. 213.

The miner's canary has been ignored because of hate-laden paranoia.

"Antisemitism is a psychiatric problem. I have studied it," reported Kelsey with an air of confidence. "Those who despise Israel have been successful with one propaganda approach that would make Hitler proud. It is a mass paranoia caused by clever brainwashing with the use of the media. For instance, most citizens understanding of issues comes from the media. They quickly inverted the reality to make Israel (pop. About 6 million Jews) the 'Goliath', and the Arab/Muslim (pop. About 1.5 billion people) world the 'David.'"

"Like old fashioned Jew-hatred, anti-Zionism inverts the reality of Jewish vulnerability and victimization in order to justify irrational hatred of Jews and deny basic rights of self-defense to Jewish victims It is the giant entire Arab/Muslim (about 1.5 billion people) effort to destroy Israel (about 6 million Jews) that reveals the true David and Goliath."

"For us in the U.S., whether we are Jewish or not, and thousands of miles away from Israel, why is it so important to examine Jewish concerns or those of Israel? You are losing us. How does this compute?" begged Salo.

Kelsey focused her eyes on Salo and Yael hoping to snare their interest. "Remember the ties of exceptionalism between the U.S. and Israel make those who are envious, angry with us? Do you remember the miner's canary? The bigger the mine is, the bigger the risk. And the more valuable is the bird. The tiny bird will be felled by noxious gases before the strong, miners are aware of their impending doom. If the miners notice, they have a chance to protect themselves. We in the U.S. should have paid attention to the miner's canary instead of watching the racist Nazis and doing nothing.

In the very recent past, Israel can recall the hate and actual attacks that followed the passage of UNGA 3379 on Nov. 10, 1975, and the Durban Conferences that bellowed that Zionism is racism. The Conference had established a plan for delegitimizing Israel by undermining Jewish national claims and rewriting history. Zionism is, in fact, the opposite of racism."

"And we also have modern day Cassandras, blessed with the ability to forecast and cursed that she would never be believed. There will be a horrible price to pay if we do not heed Cassandra's warning about the dangers of a nuclearized, genocidal Iranian theocracy! There are specific reasons for particularly Jewish and Israeli concerns, but actually, they directly or indirectly apply to all of humanity!" exhorted Kelsey.

The sharpened survival sensitivities of the Jewish People became a sort of natural selection during the long course of their history. Listen, world, listen.

Israel, because of its small size and lack of geographic buffers acts like a magnifying glass on the human drama that highlights the ultimate risk the U.S. and the West must face. Of all the states in the world, Israel is one of the smallest states, surrounded by enemies, so its existence is threatened by the same forces that attempt to bring down the U.S. Israel is a predictor of the attacks on human rights. Today democracies don't smell the gasses emanating from Iran, alone.

If we lose another miner's canary, our civilization may have lost our last chance and end up in a nuclear war.

An accounting of history suggests answers

The memory of millennial massacres, persecutions and violent expulsions, serves to sensitize people. Kelsey recommended looking into her stuffed notebook. Part is found in the appendix of this book. This history often demonstrates that these violent events were frequently a result of other's failures which were then blamed on the Jews, just like the lies hurled at Israel today.

Paul Johnson, author of **A History of the Jews** concluded that the Jews, not for the first time, are blamed for the persecution they suffer. Like the Israelis, the world is tired of the endless antagonism directed by the Arabs and wishes that the Jews and their state would just fade away. During those war years ordinary Germans were aware that the Jews were being "sent east," a clear euphemism employed for Auschwitz and were furious at the rattling of the vast trains of cattle cars packed with doomed Jews, which disturbed their rest thought the night, and cursed "those damned Jews for never letting us get a decent night's sleep."

For instance: In **1290 King Edward I,** separated British Christians from Jews by issuing an edict expelling all Jews from England. Jews were only allowed back in England 350 years later because the civil wars in Britain had hurt the economy and Oliver Cromwell hoped that importing Jews would help the economy recover. Contrary to popular belief, England and not Germany was the first European country where Jews had to wear apartheid badge that distinguished them from non-Jews. Massacres against Jews, such as the massacre of York in 1190, took place in England hundreds of years before the Nazis even existed!

The brilliant **Rabbi Jonathan Sacks** urges us to see the positive, "that the Jewish people are a "symbol of hope for every small country, for every persecuted people...Jews, having been through as close as you get to 'hell on earth,' have come through, have not looked back, have looked forward, have not nurtured feelings of resentment and revenge, have gone out and built the future. And if that is not a testament to the power of faith, I don't know what is…"

Today, Israel is surrounded by enemies internally and externally. They are fighting wars on every front, infiltrated by terrorists and confronting the wet dreams of genocidal regimes such as Iran whose prime ministers have sworn to cause Israel's annihilation. Israel has been under international attack of delegitimization carried out through the United Nations, the World Council of Churches, the OIC, spurious NGOs, "peace" organizations, Arab and Islamic groups, labor unions, university campuses, and a hostile European Union.

This seems like an extension of a legitimate Jewish concern.

Looking back a few centuries, the lessons of the super violent Czhmelnicki (Bohdan Khmelnytsky of the Ukraine) massacres that resulted in 100,000 Jews murdered. This was ignored by the world. It didn't matter that the Jews had lived in this very same area for eight centuries. Nor did it matter that they were the indigenous population. They weren't immigrants or new comers. Muslim Turkey saw how Czhmelnicki got away with the slaughters and figured the world would not interfere with what they did to Armenians.

Jews suffered in Arab countries in the recent past. The word in Arabic word for massacre or pogrom is "farhud" and means "violent dispossession."

In the modern era, over a dozen major farhuds occurred in Baghdad, Iraq, on June 1–2, 1941, Djerada, in Morocco in 1948, in Aleppo and Damascus, Syria in 1947 and 1948, in Benghazi and Tripoli in 1948, in Bahrain in 1949, in Egypt in 1952, and in Libya and Tunisia in 1967. There were arrests and expulsions in Egypt in 1956, economic strangulation by spoliation in Iraq in 1951, in Syria in 1949, in Libya in 1970, or by exclusion in Syria and Lebanon in 1947, in Libya in 1958, in Iran in 2000, or by allowing Egyptian business only in Egypt in 1961. Looking back a half century, Jews fled Iran during the Khomeini Muslim Revolution. This Iranian regime's constitution calls for the "continuation of that revolution both inside and outside the country."

To this end Iran has supported terror groups such as Hezbollah, Hamas, the Muslim Brotherhood, al-Qaeda, Osama Bin Laden, and Ayman Zawahiri, Bashar Assad of Syria, N. Korea, Chavez's Venezuela, http://www.israelbehindthenews.com/bin/content.cgi?ID=872&q=1

When the canary stopped singing there was a rejection
of peace and a resurrection of Jihad and Farhud

Dr. Mordechai Kedar brings some recollections from an article: "Islam owes its growth to butchery and barbarism". http://www.israpundit.org/ archives/63601513

Memory and hindsight count.

An abridged list of Muslim massacres of Jews riddle the history of Islam. Even a sample of dates abound: 712 AD, in Samarkand (now Uzbekistan) and Sind (now Pakistan); 940 AD, 1049, in Armenia; 1011,1013,1019, 1026, in India; 1066, in Granada (Spain); 1381, in Asfahan (Iran); in many Persian cities up to the year 1400.

And this is but a partial list.

As we get closer to the modern period, we have the Muslim massacre of the Sikhs in 1826; a massacre of Christians in Damascus, 1860; the massacre of the Jews of Fez, Morocco in 1912; the Christian Armenian genocide in Muslim Turkey 1915; the massacre of the Jews of Hevron, 1929; the Iran-Iraq War of 1980-1988 with a million victims; the civil war I Algeria 1992-1998; the massacre of 2 million Christians and Animists in southern Sudan during the second half of the 20th century.

Dr. Yael Marano recalled, **"Dr. Kedar** is an incredible researcher. How can we not understand the abundance of facts? Let me share current examples of the manifest hatred through rejection, not peace. Even the European Union stands guilty."

"This picture of human history emphasizes that genuine peace and stability between peoples requires far more than signed agreements. It requires bona fide mutual trust, respect, and a psyche of peace to prevail throughout all levels of society. However, this must emanate from the elected, academic and clerical leadership through the main stream media. The proper lesson that Israel should have learned is that it can expect rejection."

"I have collected a series of rejections and violation of agreements dealing with Israel's sustainability that should offer a big clue for the clueless, and I will share just a few if you will listen," pleaded Yael.

1. **UNGA resolution 181** the partition resolution chopping apart the

remaining 20% of the original mandate for a Jewish Homeland again was not enough and was **rejected** by all the Arab states.

2. By law and treaty, remember that the **Palestinian Authority** (PA), a temporary ruling body, which only exists through the provisions of the Oslo Accords in 1993, made the choice in 2000 when the P.A. joined forces with Hamas to wage terror (against civilians) wars against Israel: Intifada I and Intifida II. The P.A. **rejected** Israel's offer of peace and Palestinian statehood. This was their choice.

3. The PA made the choice in 2005 again when it responded to Israel's unilateral withdrawal from Gaza with a tenfold increase in the number of rockets and missiles it fired on Israeli civilian targets in the Negev and close by cities. The Arabs in Gaza **rejected** Israel's offer for prosperity.

4. **The P.A. made the choice in 2008 when their Prime Minister Abbas rejected then-prime minister Ehud Olmert's offer of statehood, land and peace.**

5. On the official P.A. map, of the Middle East, there is no Israel. This is a clear rejection of Israel's right to exist.

6. "Zionism is going to come to an end, as it "has no future in the Middle East," Balad chairman and Israeli Knesset Member, **Jamal Zahalka** said in an interview with The Jerusalem Post on Sunday (4-7-13). "I am not a Zionist, I am an anti-Zionist," he said. 'No peace without an end to the Zionist regime, rejecting Israel's right to exist. Zahalka sees the conflict as unsolvable as long as Israel exists as a Jewish state. At a recent conference in Canada he exclaimed: "In the long term there is no chance for democracy, peace and freedom without ending the Zionist regime." "Give me my land and take your democracy with you," he said addressing Israel, telling the Post this was the theme of one of his speeches he gave in Canada, titled, "Debunking the myth of Israeli democracy."

7. In the 1949 Israel-Jordanian Armistice, Article VIII, Jordan promised free access to holy places. It **never happened**. The Jordanians demolished 58 synagogues and their contents, uprooted the tombstones of Jewish cemeteries, and used them for paving or building latrines,

and built a latrine against the Western Wall of the Temple Mount, the single most holy site for Jews. Is this not **rejection** of peace? http://www.palestinefacts.org/pf_1948to1967_holysites.php http://www.jcpa.org/JCPA/Templates/ShowPage.asp?DBID=1&LN GID=1&TMID=111&FID=443&PID=0&IID=3052

8. During the attack on Israel in 1947-1949, the Jordanians killed a large number of Jews and then mass expelled all the Jewish inhabitants of eastern areas of Jerusalem, rejecting the obligations of the treaty and it became, as Adolph Hitler liked to say, Judenrein, or cleansed of Jews. http://en.wikipedia.org/wiki/WesternWall.

Abdulla el-Tal, Jordan's military governor of the Old City and an uninhibited antisemite, proudly proclaimed that "for the first time in 1,000 years, not a single Jew remains in the Jewish quarter... and as not a single building remains intact, this makes the return of the Jews here impossible." Christians were also maltreated, with over 60 percent of them emigrating from Jerusalem during that period.

9. **General "Bogie" Ya'alon** explained, "During talks with world powers, the Iranians have managed to enrich 750 kilograms of uranium to 3.5 percent, and 36 kilograms of uranium to 20 percent." Hatred prevailed over dialogue violating and **rejecting** the agreement.

10. **Fatah means "Conquest"** in Arabic. It is clear what they represent, conquest! It is also a reverse acronym of the Arabic for "Palestine Liberation Movement", the core movement of the larger body, the Palestinian Liberation Organization and also its Palestinian wing in the administered territories was a major part of the Unified National Leadership of the Intifada, which managed that uprising in 1987-93. If this is what Fatah means they are demonstrating their choice against peace. Isn't it clear that the name, itself, is a **rejection** of peace?

11. There are **17 official Palestinian Authority security elements**, 10 of them under the Palestinian Police or General Security Service and two of them independent. Why are they not creating 17 schools or

17 hospitals? There are additional reports of other small units of various sorts, and these do not include the armed Tanzim of the Fatah movement. The original name for Fatah's armed wing was al-Assifa (The Storm), and this was also the name Fatah first used in its communiques, trying for some time to conceal its identity.

Other militant groups associated with Fatah include: Force 17, Black September (the Munich Olympics attack),

Fatah Hawks- The Fatah Hawks was an armed militia active mainly until the mid-90s., Al-Aqsa Martyrs' Brigades- created in the Second Intifada to bolster the organization's militant standing vis-à-vis the rival Hamas movement, The Brigades, but not Fatah proper, are listed as a terrorist organization by the United States.

The P.A. "Constitution" calls for the destruction of Israel (Article 12) and the use of terrorism as an indispensable element in the campaign to achieve that goal (Article 19). Clearly a **rejection** of peace is within their covenant.

Hamas, calls (in its Charter) for the destruction of Israel (article 15) and the murder of Jews (article 7). This is another core **rejection** of peace. PM (sic) Abbas is making it clear that he is promoting a Palestinian state for the purpose of continuing the war against Israel.

The Long Overdue Palestinian State, New York Times, May 16, 2011.

12. In the PLO's (think Arafat and Abbas) original founding Charter (or Covenant), Article 24 states: "this Organization does not exercise any regional sovereignty over the west Bank in the Hashemite Kingdom of Jordan, in the Gaza Strip or the Himmah area." They **rejected** Israel's minimal geography at that time. Their clear aim was to destroy Israel. The Jews simply have no place in Palestine, which must be made Judenrein.

Furthermore, the implication of article 22 is that there is no place for the Jew anywhere: "Israel is the instrument of the Zionist movement and geographical base for world imperialism Israel is a constant source of threat vis-a-vis peace in the Middle East and the whole world." Just as the Nazis would deliver humanity from the Jewish evil, so the PLO would save humankind. They did as the Nazis by giving the appearance of negotiations in the run up to World War II.

13. Then there is the Phased Plan, formally adopted by the PLO on June 9, 1974 in its 12th session by the Palestinian Nation Council. As of this writing, it is still in effect. "First, to establish a combatant national authority over every part of Palestinian territory that is liberated." (Art. 2). Second to use that territory to continue the fight against Israel (Art.4). Third, to start "a pan Arab War to complete the liberation of all Palestinian territory: that is, to annihilate Israel" (Art. 8)"

In Islamic parlance, all war dictated by the shari'a is necessarily holy.

Israel's existence is thoroughly **rejected**. "Failure to Amend the PLO Covenant" **Likoed Nederland**

Holocaust survivor **Elie Wiesel's** timeless admonition, "Always believe the threats of your enemies and not the promises of your friends".

14. **Wafa al-Biss** is a young Arab-Palestinian woman from Gaza, received emergency – probably life-saving care- at Beersheba's Soroka University Medical Center in 2005. Her parents and her Gaza doctors all praised the dedication of the staff and the quality of the treatment she received from the Israelis. She was allowed return for periodic check-ups to monitor her progress. On one of these visits, she was caught at a border crossing, trying to smuggle more 10 kg. of explosives in her clothing. Her goal was to blow herself up in an attack intended to kill the very doctors who had saved her life, along with as many patients and bystanders as possible. Now, while Wafa al-Biss's conduct may not be a template that all Arab Palestinians to embrace, judging from the enthusiastic reception she received on her return, it certainly seems to be extremely popular, even in official PA circles. Is this not a clear rejection of peace?

And polls asking Arab-Palestinians if the implementation of an agreement that meets Palestinian demands is actually a final arrangement or simply a step towards the ultimate creation of a sovereign Palestinian state from the Jordan River to the sea also finds that the Palestinian street sees the "Palestinian state side by side with Israel" as no more than a stage in the march towards the final goal.

Palestinian Authority officials said that the PA President Mahmoud Abbas had considered asking for a UN vote on November 15 or 29, 2012 to create a sovereign. The Palestinian Authority could then consider itself free of all its commitments under the agreements signed with Israel, including economic and security obligations.

It should be clear that for the Arabs/Muslims, military struggle is not a tactic but part of a strategy, and the military revolution of an Arab-Palestinian nation is a decisive component in the struggle for the destruction and the removal of the Zionist entity; the struggle will not be complete until the Zionist state is destroyed and Palestine, in its entirety will be liberated. "Fatah: Oslo Accords will cease to exist after UN bid" by **Khaled Abu Toameh,** The Jerusalem Post 11/08/2012

That canary has stopped singing. Does this sign make international law and business conveyances about the Golan heights a dead issue?

Salo had researched who owned what and when. This was very important if legal titles to land or international law were to be followed.

In 2013 Israel's antennae perked up due to tens of thousands of fighting foreign jihadists coming into Syria and lesser numbers, into Jordan and Lebanon. Israel's major geographic defense line from Syrian attacks is the Golan Heights. In order to weaken Israel's defenses, many deny Israel's legal and historical right to the Golan. There are multiple security reasons from the Golan area.

"Syria: The Growing Power of Jihadist Groups" 2-27-13 by **Stuart Ramsay** was Chief Correspondent Sky News when he learned how much the Golan was worth to Israel from a security standpoint, from the standpoint of water and prosperity (the Golan is one of Israel's most important sources of domestic beef, fruit, and wine. Additionally, there may even be oil on the Golan. On

Saturday, February 23, 2013, Saudi Gazette reported that Israel has awarded its first license to drill for oil on the Golan Heights to a US energy company.

Naturally Salo came up with T.M.I. again: "Golan" is the name of a city mentioned in the Bible as a "City of Refuge". Throughout the Golan Heights, 29 ancient synagogues were found dating back to the Roman and Byzantine (4th to 15th century) periods.

The team found that in 1891, **Baron Rothschild** purchased land. It was approximately 18,000-20,000 acres of land in the Hauran area of the Syrian Province owned by the Ottoman Empire (Daily Globes Jan 1996.

Immigrants of the First Aliyah (1881–1903) established five small communities on this purchased land, but were physically forced to leave by the Ottomans in 1899. The Pasha of Damascus expelled the Jews from Rothschild's settlement on the Golan.

"Rothschilds' Land On Syrian Golan Heights" (http://www.camera.org/index.asp?x_ar...04&x_context=7) TruthInMedia .org12-28-01. Finally, the Rothchilds transferred the deeds to the Jewish National Fund (JNF) in 1957. - Daily Globes Jan 1996).

Following WW I, the Golan Heights became part of the French Mandate for Syria, while the Sea of Galilee was placed entirely within the British Mandate of Palestine.

In 1942, the Syrian government illegally confiscated the land. As a result, in 1944, the Golan Heights and Golan plane was claimed as part of the newly independent state of Syria.

During the period 1948-67, when Syria controlled the Golan Heights (about 459 sq. miles). It used the area as a military stronghold from which its troops randomly shelled and mortared Israeli civilians in the Huleh Valley (Israel's richest agricultural area) below, forcing children to sleep in bomb shelters and reducing the agricultural harvests.

In May 1967 **Hafez Assad, then Syria's Defense Minister** declared: "Our forces are now entirely ready not only to repulse the aggression, but to initiate the act of liberation itself, and to explode the Zionist presence in the Arab homeland. The Syrian Army, with its finger on the trigger, is united... I, as a military man, believe that the time has come to enter into a battle of annihilation." Almost immediately following Syria's war of aggression in June of 1967, and its loss of the Golan Heights, Israelis began settling the Golan.

The topography and printed existential threats to Israel

This topographical map of a hypothetical 'demilitarized' 'Palestinian state' clearly shows the risks. One does not need a college education to see what could happen in this very vulnerable area.

One-third of Israel's valuable freshwater supply originates in the Golan Heights, from which it travels to the Sea of Galilee and the Jordan River.

In this arid region, water takes on giant importance.

Ceding control of the Heights to Syria or a Palestinian state would give them access to the Sea of Galilee's eastern shore and one of Israel's two key sources of water in this parched area of the world.

(**Ariel Zirulnick** June 07, 2011http://www.miftah.org)

The **Palestinian National Covenant** is also the founding charter of the PLO, delineating the organization's stated aims and goals. **Article 19** states, "the establishment of Israel is fundamentally null and void, whatever time has elapsed."

Article 22 asserts that, "the liberation of Palestine will destroy the Zionist and imperialist presence and will contribute to the establishment of peace in the Middle East."

The Covenant also denies the existence of the Jewish people as a nation and any ties that it might have to the Land of Israel (Article 20). It declares that "armed struggle is the only way to liberate Palestine and is therefore a strategy and not tactics" (Article 9).

Since the Covenant is a legally binding document, declaring a willingness to alter it does not amount to amending it. No changes were adopted and implemented by the PNC, nor was there any specific mention of articles to be amended.

Article 33 of the Covenant states that the only body empowered to change the document is the Palestinian National Council (PNC) and that such changes must be approved by a two-thirds majority of the PNC in a special session. Thus, Chairman Arafat's letters are insufficient. Under the procedure outlined by the Covenant itself, Arafat's letters have no legal bearing on the text of the document. The PLO's obligation to convene the PNC in order to amend the Covenant remains unfulfilled.

Nabil Shaath, a high-level minister in the P.A. made their goal clear: "The story of 'two states for two peoples' means that there will be a Jewish people over there and a Palestinian people here. We will never accept this." Abbas added: "Don't order us to recognize a Jewish state. We won't accept it."

So far, the canary is still chirping.

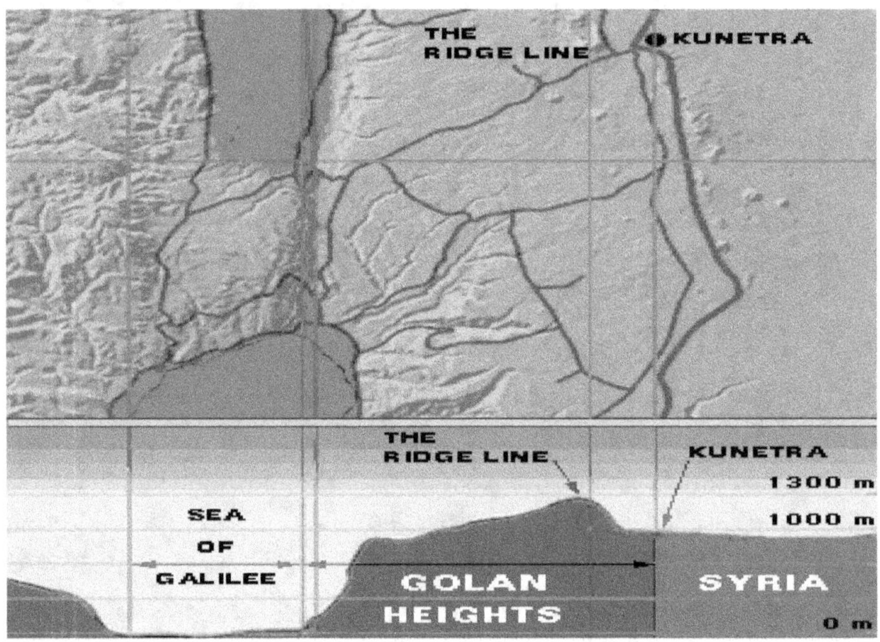

Bully power and perfidy made it tough for a Jewish State: important points.

1. In 1887, the **Turkish Sultan** prohibited Jewish immigration into his country in the area now called Israel.
2. With wages for Arab workers double or more the wages in Syria, Jordan, and Iraq, in 1936, a **British Royal Commission** could report: "The whole range of public services has steadily developed to the

benefit of the [Arab] fellaheen...the revenue for those services having been largely provided by the Jews."

3. In July of 1937 the **British Peel commission** proposed partitioning the land again giving the Jews 4% of the land that they were promised in both the Balfour Declaration and international law at San Remo.

4. **Neville Chamberlain** violated the Mandate trust by announcing he would stop all Jewish immigration into "Palestine" in spite of the known Nazi atrocities. His White Paper in May of 1939 allowed up to 15,000 a year or a total of 75,000 fleeing refugees entry into safety from Hitler before completely cutting several million Jews entry to safety.

Former British Prime Minister Lloyd George, in a 1939 address, called the White Paper "An act of national perfidy that will dishonor the name of Britain."

The British White Paper violated international law as established by the Balfour Declaration, the San Remo Accords, and the Faisal-Weitzmann agreement of 1919. These agreements, recognized by the world community, supported the creation of an Arab-Jewish State and encouraged Jewish immigration, immediately and in large numbers.

http://www.mfa.gov.il/MFA/Foreign+Relations/Israel+and+the+UN/Speeches+-+statements/Amb_Waxman_Statement_UN_Security_Council_25-Jul-2012.htm

5. At the same time, the new opportunities in Palestine attracted hundreds of thousands of Arab immigrants, who were allowed to enter these communities without British restriction, from Iraq, Syria, Jordan, and the desert. By 1948, the Arab population in the Mandate area had grown to some 1.35 million, an increase of 60% since the 1930s.

6. **UNESCO** (the United Nations Educational, Scientific and Cultural Organization) renamed the "Western Wall" or "Wailing Wall" regarding the loss of the Jewish Temple, the al Buraq wall, giving it to Islam. UNESCO is also attempting to claim that Hevron is not a Jewish site. Hevron was the first Jewish city in the land of Israel, home of Jewish patriarchs and matriarchs, Abraham, Isaac and Jacob and Sarah, Rebecca and Leah. King David ruled from Hevron for more

than seven years before moving the capital to Jerusalem. Jews have lived in Hevron almost continuously for thousands of years. Article by Eli Hertz August 6, 2009.

7. **UNGA Resolution 194,** adopted by the UN General Assembly on December 11, 1948, addressed a host of issues, but only one paragraph out of 15 dealt with all the refugees created by the conflict. Resolution 194 attempted to create the tools required to reach a truce in the region. The resolution **only established a conciliation commission** with representatives from the United States, France and Turkey to replace the UN mediator.

The Resolution's "refugee clause" is not a standalone item as some would have us think, nor does it pertain specifically to Arab refugees. But one paragraph, paragraph 11, has drawn the most attention specifically from the Arab countries.

Paragraph 11 of UNGA 194 alone, addressed the issue of refugees. It did not guarantee a Right of Return and certainly did not guarantee an unconditional Right of Return (that is the claimed right of Arab-Palestinian refugees to return to Israel. Nor did it specifically mention Arab refugees, thereby indicating that the resolution was aimed at all refugees, both Jewish and Arab. Instead, Resolution 194 recommended that refugees be allowed to return to their homeland if they met two important conditions:

a. That they be willing to live in peace with their neighbors;

b. That the return takes place "at the earliest practicable date"

Arab publicists have sought to detach entirely the flight of Jews from Arab lands from the Arab-Israeli conflict, claiming they are two separate phenomena, and that Israelis should take up the issue with each respective Arab state that was involved, not with the Arab-Palestinians.

The resolution also recommended that for those who did not wish to return, "Compensation should be paid for the property ... and for loss of or damage to property" by the "governments or authorities responsible." Although Arab leaders point to General Assembly Resolution 194 as proof that Arab refugees have a right to return or be compensated, it is important to note that the same Arab States: Egypt, Iraq, Lebanon, Saudi Arabia, Syria, and Yemen, voted against Resolution194.

General Assembly resolutions are not binding, and only serve as advisory statements, therefore there can be no obligation or enforcement of Resolution 194.

Israel is not even mentioned specifically in the resolution.

The fact that plural wording also is used – "governments or authorities" – suggests that, contrary to Arab claims, the burden of compensation does not fall solely upon one side of the conflict.

Because five neighboring Arab armies and armed Arabs within the country chose to fight and go to war, Israel could not possibly be responsible for creating the refugee problem.

8. **The UNSC resolution #1701** (Aug. 2006) intended goal was to cease hostilities created by **Hezbollah** in Lebanon on Israel. It demanded that Israel leave southern Lebanon and that the area be completely demilitarized except for Lebanese forces. The United Nations Interim Force in Lebanon (UNIFEL) had been placed there to assure the peace, originally failing in 1978.

It failed to prevent Hezbollah from attacking Israel in 2006. Billions of dollars were required to fund it and the U.S. picked up 25% of the tab. Yet it did not prevent the next war on Israel.

9. When hundreds of thousands of Arab Jews, under threat of death, attacked and under other forms of persecution, were forced to flee Arab communities, the State of Israel absorbed the majority of them into the then-fledgling nation.

"I just don't understand it. The language is clear so clear. Why have the Jewish refugees from Arab countries not been included in this discussion?" asked Tom, whose background in the area was less than average.

"It is hard to understand," explained Yael, "Jews had been living in some Arab countries for over one thousand years, perhaps 2,000. And overnight they are expelled, without compensation, from their homes, their synagogues, their cemeteries and businesses, and many had to pay large sums of money just to leave.

"Israel, as well as the world community has failed to raise the issue of the mammoth injustice done to almost a million Jews from Arab countries. The scale and the premeditated state-sponsored nature of persecution that prompted the 1948 flight of close to 900,000 Jews from their homes has only recently begun to emerge."

Yael then cited a report that caused everyone to gasp as they had no knowledge of the enormity:

The World Organization of Jews from Arab Countries **(WOJAC)** estimated in 2006, that Jewish property abandoned in Arab countries would be valued at more than $100 billion, later revising their estimate in 2007 to $300 billion. They also estimated Jewish owned real estate left behind in Arab lands at 100,000 square kilometers. That is four times the size of the state of Israel! "Jews forced out of Arab countries seek reparations". www.jpost.com."Expelled Jews hold deeds on abandoned property in Arab lands". www.jpost.com.

One only needs to reexamine the almost prophetic article in The New York Times two days after Israel declared independence ("Jews in Grave Danger in all Moslem Lands") to confirm the lie.

The New York Times reported on May 16, 1948: "For nearly four months, the United Nations has had before it, an appeal for 'immediate and urgent' consideration of the case of the Jewish populations in Arab and Moslem countries stretching from Morocco to India." The country-by-country table estimated the Jewish population-at-risk as 899,000 souls.

Yael needed to drive home the point, "The article cited the dismissal of Jews in the civil service in Syria; per capita ransom payment of $20,000 by Iraqi Jews seeking to leave Iraq. There was a forced levy on the Lebanese Jewish community to support the Arab war effort parallel to incitement and physical attacks on Jews, and Jews fleeing to India from Afghanistan. It quoted the UN Economic and Social Council report as saying: "The very survival of the Jewish communities in certain Arab and Moslem countries is in serious danger, unless preventive action is taken without delay." Hostility and oppression only grew, ultimately leading to the exodus of almost all Jews from all Arab and Moslem countries from Casablanca to Karachi. Using oil power

(OPEC), Arabs claimed that Israel allowing Jewish refugees a Right of Return, is groundless.

More of The U.N.'s Record

UNSC Resolution #69, adopted on March 4, 1949, having received and considered Israel's application for membership in the United Nations, the Council decided that in its judgment Israel was a peace-loving state and recommended to the General Assembly that they grant membership to Israel. The resolution was adopted by nine votes to one (Egypt against).

UNGA Resolution #237 admitted Israel to the United Nations on May 11, 1949, "taking note of the declarations and explanations made by the representative of the Government of Israel" in respect of implementation of resolutions 194 and 181, to which Israel did not commit itself to any specific action or timeframe. Israel has since rejected any resolution calling on it to allow the extranational Arabs to come to Israel.

Below is a map of the suggested partition by the General Assembly.

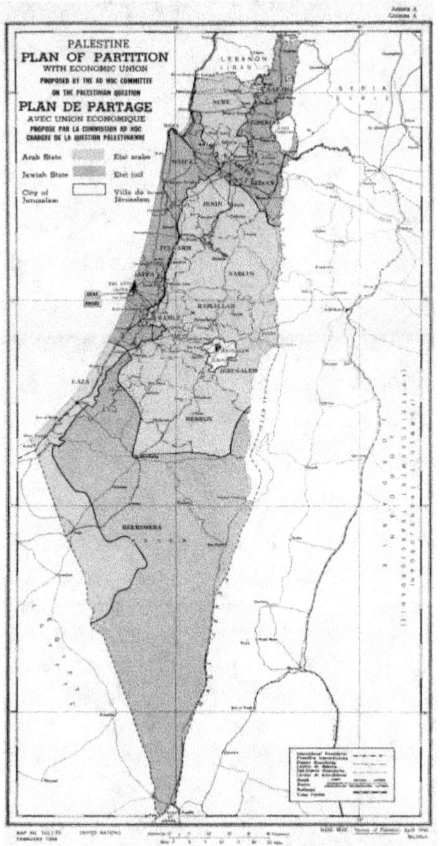

UNSC resolution 242 adopted on June 14, 1967 followed the Six-Day War, which called upon the government of Israel to ensure the safety and welfare of the inhabitants of the areas where military operations had taken place and to facilitate the return of those inhabitants who had fled. The resolution also recommended the governments concerned to respect humanitarian principles governing the treatment of prisoners of war and the protection of civilian persons in times of war contained in the Geneva Conventions. The Council also requested the Secretary-General to follow the effective implementation of this resolution and report back. Muslim countries flexed their oil money power and spoke openly and with unabashed sincerity of world domination as a required goal. All these Muslim countries want to bring about a world-wide Caliphate under Islam. They say it publicly over and over.

UNSC Resolution #446, adopted on 22 March 1979, concerned the issue of Israeli settlements in the "Arab territories occupied by Israel since 1967, including Jerusalem." This refers to the claim of Palestinian territories of the "West Bank"," East" Jerusalem and the Gaza Strip as well as the Syrian Golan Heights.

Assuming ownership of land by a non-existent sovereignty cannot exist in international law.

But, in the Resolution, the Security Council determined: "that the policy and practices of Israel in establishing settlements in the Palestinian and other Arab territories occupied since 1967 have no legal validity and constitute a serious obstruction to achieving a comprehensive, just and lasting peace in the Middle East" The Resolution was adopted by 12 votes to none, with 3 abstentions from Norway, the United Kingdom and the United States of America.

The 1949 Lausanne Conference (27 April-12 September) convened by the UN Conciliation Commission for Palestine (UNCCP) is when Israel officially proposed a return of 100,000 displaced Arab persons into Israel if all the Arab States would sign a peace treaty with Israel and repatriate the remaining estimated 550,000 refugees to their countries of common language, religion and culture.

All the Arab States **rejected** this proposal. A little bit of **oil wealth history** helps understand what motivated the Western powers. American companies developed the huge petroleum reserves in Saudi Arabia in the 1938. Reserves of oil in the Persian Gulf were being systematically uncovered: Iran(1908), Iraq(1923), Bahrain (1931) Kuwait (1938), the AE is a federation of seven emirates (equivalent to principalities)1950s. These countries speak openly and with unabashed sincerity of world domination as a required goal. All these Muslim leaders want to bring about a world-wide Caliphate under Islam. They say it publicly over and over.

Kelsey concluded, "The Jews and Israelis have a right to be gravely concerned about their survival or getting justice in the world. Facing and confronting an ugly reality is not paranoia. To confront facts is not an act of prejudice, but to intentionally ignore them is suicidal. This inversion of reality is a masterpiece of TerVol in action."

ANNEX - of massacres.

Yael asked if anyone could hold their breath long enough to have a list read out loud. A good memory can be hard to live with. This list stops before the creation of the State of Israel even though were several massacres that followed. Here is a list that could make Jews concerned.

By **Rabbi Levi Brackman** and **Rivkah Lubitch**

Appended-This is just a brief listing which should keep matters in prospective.

Jewish Persecution | Timeline of Judaism | History of AntiSemitism and some of the Lesser Known Highlights of Jewish International Relations In The Common Era (an Abbreviated sampling)

DATE	PLACE	EVENT
250 C.E.	Canhage	Expulsion
224 C.E.	Italy Forced	Conversion
325 C.E.	Jerusalem	Expulsion
351 C.E	Persia Book	Burning
357 C.E.	Italy Property	Confiscation
379 C.E.	Milan Synagogue	Burning
415 C.E.	Alexandria	Expulsion
418 C.E.	Minorca Forced	Conversion
469 C.E.	Ipahan	Holocaust
489 C.E.	Antioch Synagogue	Burning
506 C.E.	Daphne Synagogue	Burning
519 C.E.	Ravenna Synagogue	Burning
554 C.E.	Diocese of Clement (France)	Expulsion
561 C.E.	Diocese of Uzes (France)	Expulsion
582 C.E	Merovingia	Forced Conversion
612 C.E.	Visigoth Spain	Expulsion

628 C.E.	Byzantium	Forced Conversion
629 C.E.	Merovingia	Forced Conversion
632 CE	King Dagobert	expelled all Jews
633 C.E.	Toledo	Forced Conversion
638 C.E.	Toledo	Stake Burnings
642 C.E.	Visigothic Empire	Expulsion
653 C.E.	Toledo	Expulsion
681 C.E.	Spain	Forced Conversion
693 C.E.	Toledo	Jews Enslaved
722 C.E.	Byzantium	Judaism Outlawed
855 C.E.	Italy	Expulsion
876 C.E.	Sens	Expulsion
897 C.E.	Narbonne Land	Confiscation
945 C.E.	Venice	Ban on Sea Travel
1009 C.E.	Orleans	Massacre
1012 C.E.	Rouen, Limoges & Rome	Massacre
1012 CE	Mainz	Henry II of Germany expelled all Jews
1012 C.E.	Mayence	Expulsion
1021 C.E.	Rome	Jews Burned Alive
1063 C.E.	Spain	Massacre

The 1066 Granada massacre took place on December 30, 1066 (9 Tevet 4827) when a Muslim mob stormed the royal palace in Granada, which was at that time in Muslim-ruled al-Andalus, assassinated the Jewish vizier Joseph ibn Naghrela and massacred many of the Jewish population of the city. Muslim mobs stormed the royal palace where Joseph had sought refuge, then crucified him.

In the ensuing massacre of the Jewish population, many of the Jews of Granada were murdered. The 1906 Jewish Encyclopedia claims that "More than 1,500 Jewish families, numbering 4,000 persons, fell in one day. Jewish persecution source: P.E. Grosser & E.G. Halperin, Anti-Semitism: Causes and Effects, New York

1095 C.E.	Lorraine	Massacre

Date	Place	Event
1096 C.E.	Northern France & Germany	1/3 of Jewish Population Massacred
1096 C.E.	Hungary	Massacre
1096 C.E.	Ralisbon	Massacre
1099 C.E.	Jerusalem Jews	Burned Alive
1100 C.E.	Kiev	Pogrom
1121	Belgium	Jews were driven out until they repented of killing Christ;
1140 C.E.	Germany	Massacres
1146 C.E.	Rhine Valley	Massacre
1147 C.E.	Wurzburg	Massacre
1147 C.E.	Belitz (Germany)	Jews Burned Alive
1147 C.E.	Carenton, Ramenu & Sully (France)	Massacres
1171 C.E.	Blois Stake	Burnings
1181 C.E.	France	Expulsion
1181 C.E.	England Property	Confiscation
1182	France	King Philip expelled the Jews & turned synagogues into churches;
1188 C.E.	London & York	Mob Attacks
1190 C.E.	Norfolk	Jews Burned Alive
1191 C.E.	Bray (France)	Jews Burned Alive
1195 C.E.	France	Property Confiscation
1209 C.E.	Beziers	Massacre
1212 C.E.	Spain	Rioting and blood bath against the Jews of Toledo.
1215 C.E.	Rome	Lateran Council of Rome decrees that Jews must wear the "badge of shame" in all Christian countries.

		Jews are denied all public sector employment, and are burdened with extra taxes.
1215 C.E.	Toulouse (France)	Mass Arrests
1218 C.E.	England Jews	Forced to Wear Badges
1231 C.E.	Rome	Inquisition Established
1236 C.E.	France	Forced Conversion/Massacre
1239 C.E.	London	Massacre & Property Confiscation
1240 C.E.	Austria	Property confiscation. Jews either imprisoned, converted, expelled, or burned.
1240 C.E.	France	Talmud Confiscated
1240 C.E.	England	Book Burning
1240 C.E.	Spain	Forced Conversion
1242 C.E.	Paris	Talmud Burned
1244 C.E.	Oxford	Mob Attacks
1255 C.E.	England	Blood libel in Lincoln results in the burning / torture of many Jews & public hangings.
1261 C.E.	Canterbury	Mob Attacks
1262 C.E.	London	Mob Attacks
1264 C.E.	London	Mob Attacks
1264 C.E.	Germany	Council of Vienna declares that all Jews must wear a "pointed dunce cap." Thousands murdered.
1267 C.E.	Vienna	Jews Forced to Wear Horned Hats
1270 C.E.	Weissenberg, Magdeburg, Arnstadt, Coblenz, Singzig,	Jews Burned Alive

	and Erfurt	
1270 C.E.	England	The libel of the "counterfeit coins" – all Jewish men, women and children in England imprisoned. Hundreds are hung.
1276 C.E.	Bavaria	Expulsion
1278 C.E.	Genoa (Spain)	Mob Attacks
1279 C.E.	Hungary & Poland	The Council of Offon denies Jews the right to all civic positions. The Jews of Hungary & Poland are forced to wear the "red badge of shame."
1283 C.E.	Mayence & Bacharach	Mob Attacks
1285 C.E.	Munich	Jews Burned Alive
1290 C.E.	England	King Edward I issues an edict banishing all Jews (16,000) from England. Many drowned.
1291 C.E.	France	The Jewish refugees from England are promptly expelled from France.
1292 C.E.	Italy	Forced conversions & expulsion of the Italian Jewish community.
1298 C.E.	Germany	The libel of the "Desecrated Host" is perpetrated against the Jews of Germany. Approximately 150 Jewish communities undergo

		forced conversion.
1298 C.E.	Franconia, Bavaria & Austria	Reindfel's Decree is propagated against the Jews of Franconia and Bavarai. Riots against these Jewish communities, as well as those in Austria, result in the massacre of 100,000 Jews over a six-month period.
1306 C.E.	France	Expulsion Philip the Tall expelled 100,000 Jews from France
1308 C.E.	Strasbourg	Jews Burned Alive
1320 C.E.	Toulouse & Perpigon	120 Communities Massacred & Talmud Burned
1321 C.E.	Teruel	Public Executions
1328 C.E.	Estella	5,000 Jews Slaughtered
1348 C.E.	France & Spain	Jews Burned Alive
1348 C.E.	Switzerland	Expulsion
1349 C.E.	Worms, Strasbourg, Oppenheim, Mayence, Erfurt, Bavaria & Swabia	Jews Burned Alive
1349 C.E.	Heilbronn (Germany)	Expulsion
1349 C.E.	Hungary	Expulsion
1354 C.E.	Castile (Spain)	12,000 Jews Slaughtered
1368 C.E.	Toledo	8,000 Jews Slaughtered
1370 C.E.	Majorca., Penignon & Barcelona	Mob Attack
1377 C.E.	Huesca (Spain)	Jews Burned Alive
1380 C.E.	Paris	Mob Attack
1384 C.E.	Nordlingen	Mass Murder

1388 C.E.	Strasbourg	Expulsion
1389 C.E.	Prague	Mass Slaughter & Book Burning
1391 C.E.	Castille, Toledo, Madrid, Seville, Cordova, Cuenca & Barcelona Forced	Conversions & Mass Murder
1394 C.E.	Germany	Expulsion
1394 C.E.	France	Expulsion
1399 C.E.	Posen (Poland)	Jews Burned Alive
1400 C.E.	Prague	Stake Burnings
1407 C.E.	Cracow	Mob Attack
1415 C.E.	Rome	Talmud Confiscated
1422 C.E.	Austria	Jews Burned Alive
1422 C.E.	Austria	Expulsion
1424 C.E.	Fribourg & Zurich	Expulsion
1426 C.E.	Cologne	Expulsion
1431 C.E.	Southern Germany	Jews Burned Alive
1432 C.E.	Savory	Expulsion
1438 C.E.	Mainz	Expulsion
1439 C.E.	Augsburg	Expulsion
1449 C.E.	Toledo	Public Torture &. Burnings
1456 C.E.	Bavaria	Expulsion
1453 C.E.	Franconia	Expulsion
1453 C.E.	Breslau	Expulsion
1454 C.E.	Wurzburg	Expulsion
1463 C.E.	Cracow	Mob Attack
1473 C.E.	Andalusia	Mob Attack
1480 C.E.	Venice	Jews Burned Alive
1481 C.E.	Seville	Stake Burnings
1484 C.E.	Cuidad Real, Guadalupe, Saragossa & Teruel	Jews Burned Alive
1485 C.E.	Vincenza (Italy)	Expulsion

1486 C.E.	Toledo	Jews Burned Alive
1488 C.E.	Toledo	Stake Burnings
1490 C.E.	Toledo	Public Executions
1491 C.E.	Astorga	Public Torture & Execution
1492 C.E.	Spain	Expulsion
1495 C.E.	Lithuania	Expulsion
1497 C.E.	Portugal	Expulsion
1499 C.E.	Germany	Expulsion
1506 C.E.	Lisbon	Mob Attack
1510 C.E.	Berlin	Public Torture & Execution
1514 C.E.	Strasbourg	Expulsion
1519 C.E.	Regensburg	Expulsion
1539 C.E.	Cracow & Portugal	Stake Burnings
1540 C.E.	Naples	Expulsion
1542 C.E.	Bohemia	Expulsion
1550 C.E.	Genoa	Expulsion
1551 C.E.	Bavaria	Expulsion
1555 C.E.	Pesaro	Expulsion
1556 C.E.	Sokhachev (Poland)	Public Torture & Execution
1559 C.E.	Austria	Expulsion
1561 C.E.	Prague	Expulsion
1567 C.E.	Wurzburg	Expulsion
1569 C.E.	Papal States	Expulsion
1571 C.E.	Brandenburg	Expulsion
1582 C.E.	Netherlands	Expulsion
1593 C.E.	Brunswick	Expulsion
1597 C.E.	Cremona, Pavia & Lodi	Expulsion
1614 C.E.	Frankfort	Expulsion
1615 C.E.	Worms	Expulsion
1619 C.E.	Kiev	Expulsion
1635 C.E.	Vilna	Mob Attack

1637 C.E.	Cracow	Public Torture & Execution
1647 C.E.	Lisbon	Jews Burned Alive
1648 C.E.	Poland	1/3 of Jewry Slaughtered. (Czhmelnicki) Khmelnytsky Uprising,– a Cossack rebel lion in Ukraine in 1648–1657
1649 C.E.	Ukraine	Expulsion
1649 C.E.	Hamburg	Expulsion
1652 C.E.	Lisbon	Stake Burnings
1654 C.E.	Little Russia	Expulsion
1656 C.E.	Lithuania	Expulsion
1660 C.E.	Seville	Jews Burned Alive
1663 C.E	Cracow	Public Torture &. Execution
1664 C.E.	Lemberg	Mob Attack
1669 C.E.	Oran (North Africa)	Expulsion
1670 C.E.	Vienna	Expulsion
1671 C.E.	Minsk	Mob Attacks
1681 C.E.	Vilna	Mob Attacks
1682 C.E.	Cracow	Mob Attacks
1687 C.E.	Posen	Mob Attacks
1712 C.E.	Sandomir	Expulsion
1727 C.E.	Russia	Expulsion
1738 C.E.	Wurtemburg	Expulsion
1740 C.E.	Liule Russia	Expulsion
1744 C.E	Bohemia	Expulsion
1744 C.E.	Livonia	Expulsion
1745 C.E.	Moravia	Expulsion
1753 C.E.	Kovad (Lithuania)	Expulsion
1757 C.E.	Kamenetz	Talmud Burning
1761 C.E.	Bordeaux	Expulsion
1768 C.E.	Kiev	3,000 Jews Slaughtered

1772 C.E.	Russia	Expulsion
1775 C.E.	Warsaw	Expulsion
1789 C.E.	Alsace	Expulsion
1801 C.E.	Bucharest	Mob Attack
1804 C.E.	Russian Villages	Expulsion
1808 C.E.	Russian Countryside	Expulsion
1815 C.E.	Lubeck & Bremen	Expulsion
1820 C.E.	Bremes	Expulsion
1843 C.E.	Austria & Prussia	Expulsion
1850 C.E.	New York City	500 People, Led by Police, Attacked & Wrecked Jewish Synagogue
1862 C.E.	Area under General Grant's Jurisdiction in the United States	Expulsion
1866 C.E	Galatz (Romania)	Expulsion
1871 C.E.	Odena	Mob Attack
1887 C.E.	Slovakia	Mob Attacks
1897 C.E.	Kantakuzenka (Russia)	Mob Attacks
1898 C.E.	Rennes (France)	Mob Attack
1899 C.E.	Nicholayev	Mob Attack
1900 C.E.	Konitz (Prussia)	Mob Attack
1902 C.E.	Poland	Widespread Pogroms
1904 C.E.	Manchuria, Kiev & Volhynia	Widespread Pogroms
1905 C.E.	Zhitomir (Yolhynia)	Mob Attacks 1919 C.E Bavaria Expulsion
1915 C.E.	Georgia (U.S.A.)	Leo Frank Lynched
1919 C.E.	Prague	Wide Spread Pogroms
1920 C.E.	Munich & Breslau	Mob Attacks
1922 C.E.	Boston, MA	Lawrence Lowell, President of Harvard, calls for Quota

		Restrictions on Jewish Admission
1926 C.E.	Uzbekistan	Pogrom
1928 C.E.	Hungary	Widespread Anti-Semitic Riots on University Campuses
1929 C.E.	Lemberg (Poland)	Mob Attacks
1930 C.E.	Berlin	Mob Attack
1933 C.E.	Bucharest	Mob Attacks
1938-45 C.E.	Europe	Holocaust

On July 4, 1946, in Polish town of Kiekce, mobs attacked Jews returning to the city after a false rumor spread that Jews had abducted a Christian child and intended to kill for ritual purposes. The rioters in this small town murdered at least 42 Jews and wounded approximately 50 more.

The Who's Who of Terrorism Against Israel.

1. HAMAS

Hamas was created shortly before the December 1987 Intifada as a more militant, Palestinian offshoot of the Muslim Brotherhood, a religious, political and social movement founded in Egypt and dedicated to the gradual victory of Islam. It is totally opposed to any agreement or arrangement that would recognize its right to exist. At the beginning of its charter there is a quotation attributed to Hassan Al-Bana, the Muslim Brotherhood's founder, that "Israel will arise and continue to exist until Islam wipes it out, as it wiped out what went before."

To achieve its goals: An uncompromising jihad must be waged against Israel. Jihad is the personal duty of every Muslim. Hamas founder Sheikh Ahmad Yassin stated in 1988: "We cannot separate the wing from the body. If we do so, the body will not be able to fly. Hamas is one body."

Hamas is designated as a terrorist organization by Israel, the United States, Canada, the European Union and Japan.

United States House of Representatives **Foreign Affairs Committee Chair Ileana Ros-Lehtinen** (R-FL) states: "Hamas is a Foreign Terrorist Organization that calls bin Laden a 'holy warrior,' remains determined to destroy Israel, and is responsible for the deaths of Israelis and Americans." Both the European Union and the U.S. deem Hamas a terror organization. The indoctrination of Palestinian youth into a culture of hate and the idolization of terrorists as martyrs are two points of contention that the U.S. Congress has with Hamas' leadership.

- 1988: Hamas publishes manifesto calling for 'holy war' to create an Islamic state from the Jordan River to the Mediterranean Sea, including Israel.
- 1989: Hamas militants kill Israelis in dozens of shooting attacks: Israel outlaws Hamas as a terrorist organization
- 1991: Hamas forms 'Izzedine al-Quassam Brigades," its military wing, for attacks against Israelis.
- 1994, April 6.: First Hamas car bombing kills eight in Israeli city of Afula.
- April 16, 1993 when a suicide bomber detonated the car in which he was driving at the Mehola Junction near the Jewish community, Beit El, in Israel.
- 1994, April 13.: First Hamas suicide bombing kills five in Israeli city of Hadera.
- 1994, Oct. 19.: Hamas suicide bomber blows up Tel Aviv bus, killing 22.
- 1996, Jan. 6.: Hamas master bomb maker Yehiyeh Ayyash killed in explosion, Israel held responsible.
- 1996, February to March : 47 Israelis killed in three suicide attacks in retaliation for killing Ayyash.
- 2000, September : Second Palestinian uprising begins
- April 16, 2001, Hamas launched its first rocket into Israel from Gaza.
- 2001, June 1, : Hamas suicide bomber blows up outside Tel Aviv disco, killing 21
- 2001, Aug. 9, : Hamas suicide bomber blows up Jerusalem restaurant, killing 15
- January 27, 2002, the first female Palestinian suicide bomber, Wafa

Idris, blew herself up on Jaffa Street in the heart of downtown Jerusalem, killing one person and injuring about 100 more.

- 2002, March 27. : Hamas bomber blows up Netanya hotel, killing 29.
- 2003, August-September: 39 killed in three Hamas suicide bombings) by Dr. Laurie Roth, CFP, 4-27-11 in Israpundit.
- June 2007, Hamas took control of the Gaza Strip through a violent coup, killing numerous Palestinians, some by pushing them off of tall buildings in Gaza. The Red Cross estimated that at least 118 people were killed and more than 550 wounded during the fighting in the week up to June 15.
- "Palestine from the river to the sea, north to south is our land. Not an inch can be conceded. The liberation of Palestine, all of Palestine is a duty, a right and a goal. Holy war and armed resistance are the real and right path to liberation and recovery of rights." – Khaled Meshal speaking at this week's Hamas 25 anniversary "celebrations." 12-11-2012 , by Simon Plosker , HonestReporting.Com

2. **HEZBOLLAH** also in South America
- 1992 March 17, the Israeli Embassy in Buenos Aires (Tehran orchestrated a Hezbollah bombing) terrorist bombing which killed 29 and wounded 242 people.
- 1994 July 18, a second bombing targeted the Jewish community center (AMIA) in the Capitol killing killing 85 and injuring hundreds.

This was a country known to harbor Nazis following WW II.

3. **"FATAH"** is a national, revolutionary movement and its membership is top confidential. It is the current dominant political party amongst the Arab-Palestinians, the PLO and the PA.

The Palestinian National Covenant is also the founding charter of the PLO, delineating the organization's stated aims and goals. Its tenets are echoed daily in the rhetoric of Palestinian leaders and media. Almost all of the articles in the Covenant explicitly or implicitly deny Israel's right to exist and reject any peaceful solution to the Arab-Israeli conflict.

The pivotal problem with the PNC resolution is that it did not change the Covenant. While the PNC declared its readiness in principle to change the document, the only practical step taken was the empowerment of a legal committee to draft a new Covenant for presentation at a future date. Since the Covenant is a legally binding document, declaring a willingness to alter it does not amount to amending it. No changes were adopted and implemented by the PNC, nor was there any specific mention of articles to be amended. The PLO's obligation to convene the PNC in order to amend the Covenant remains unfulfilled.

4. THE PLO

The PLO (an umbrella terrorist operation) can best be defined by their activities:

(1) The largest hijacking. September 1970, Popular Front for the Liberation of Palestine (PFLP) hijacked four aircraft in a single operation. A Pan American plane was blown up at Cairo while Swissair, BOAC and TWA aircraft were destroyed near Amman. A fifth plane, from El Al, evaded hijack.

(2) The largest number of hostages held at one time. Following the multiple hijack, 300 passengers were held hostage for political blackmail––the release of terrorists held by Britain, Switzerland and Germany. The blackmail was successful.

(3) The largest number of victims killed and wounded by a single booby-trap bomb. On July 4, 1975, 15 Israelis were killed and 87 wounded by a PLO bomb planted in a refrigerator in Zion Square, Jerusalem.

(4) The largest number of casualties in a terrorist raid. On March 11, 1978, Fatah terrorists killed 38 people and wounded 70 after seizing two buses of Israelis on a holiday outing. The operation was approved by Yasser Arafat.

(5) The worst mid-air explosion. On February 21, 1970, a Swiss airliner blew up and 38 passengers and nine crew members were killed. The PFLP-General Command claimed credit.

(6) The largest number of people shot at an airport. On December 17, 1973, Black September killed 31 people at Rome Airport; 29 were aboard a Pan Am plane.

(7) The most sustained terrorist campaign. Between September 1967 and December 1980, terrorists affiliated with the PLO carried out at least 300 attacks—bombings, shootings, hijackings rocket attacks, kidnappings —in 26 countries.   Total casualties: 813 killed, 1013 injured. More than 90 percent of the 2755 hostages were not Israelis.

(8) The largest ransoms. In February 1972, the PFLP hijacked a Lufthansa aircraft to Aden and held the passengers to ransom for five million dollars, which Lufthansa paid. In October 1977 another Lufthansa plane was hijacked by the PFLP on behalf of the German Baader-Meinhoff terrorists and a 15-million-dollar ransom was demanded. It was not paid because West German Special Forces freed the passengers at Mogadishu.

(9) The wealthiest terrorist organization. While it is impossible to give accurate figures, it is known that the PLO has an annual income of at least 800 million pounds sterling. In 1981 Saudi Arabia donated 30 million dollars.

(10) Greatest variety of targets. Between 1967 and 1980 the PLO committed over 200 major terrorist acts in or against countries other than Israel. They attacked 40 civilian passenger aircraft, five passenger ships, 30 embassies or diplomatic missions, and about the same number of economic targets, including fuel depots and factories.

We know this because of the unchanged PHASED PLAN in Cairo, June 9, 1974, The Palestinian National Council resolved:

On the basis of the Palestinian National Charter and the Political Programme drawn up at the eleventh session, held from January 6-12, 1973; and from its belief that it is impossible for a permanent and just peace to be established in the area unless our Palestinian people recover all their national rights and, first and foremost, their rights to return and to self-determination on the whole of the soil of their homeland; and in the light of a study of the new political circumstances that have come into existence in the period between the Council's last and present sessions, resolves the following:

The plan has three main articles:

"Through the "armed struggle" (i.e., terrorism), to establish an "independent combatant national authority" over any territory that is "liberated" from Israeli rule. (Article 2)

To continue the struggle against Israel, using the territory of the national authority as a base of operations. (Article 4)

To provoke an all-out war in which Israel's Arab neighbors destroy it entirely ("liberate all Palestinian territory").

The Phased Plan remains the basis of PLO actions, even in the era of the Oslo Accords. Speaking on September 1, 1993, just after the announcement of the 1993 Israel-PLO agreement, PLO Chairman **Yasser Arafat** announced on Radio Monte Carlo that the Oslo agreement: "…will be a basis for an independent Palestinian state in accordance with the Palestine National Council resolution issued in 1974 … The PNC resolution issued in 1974 calls for the establishment of a national authority on any part of Palestinian soil from which Israel withdraws or which is liberated."

Simon says:

It is clear that a people's own safety and existence depends primarily upon being alert to the reality, their belief in the justness of their cause, willing efforts for self-preservation and using the resources of their allies. There are too many examples to believe otherwise. Each one of the attacks on Jews, or on Israel, pogroms and farhuds started with propaganda.

We need to know how anyone can be fooled by this "science," called propaganda.

Countries first propagandize their own people to believe that there is an enemy lurking within and preparing "out there." This is the political propaganda at which TerVol has become most proficient and it needs to be understood if we are to resist its hypnotic powers.

Let's limit ourselves to two chapters exploring the enormous power of propaganda, particularly when it is the media or a government that has an agenda.

Perhaps we can overcome the propaganda with great effort because we have help from the access to the World Wide Web.

Let's start by defining propaganda and finding documentable examples so that we can be aware of when we are being manipulated. More work is ahead. Let's see how vulnerable our population can be. As we have encountered, even we are not immune. It seems we are up against a propaganda avalanche.

#6 The Invisible Avalanche of Political Propaganda

Are we wasting our time studying propaganda?

Everyone knows it exists. It is more than the elephant in the room. But did we recognize there is a herd in the room? We need to find out how this stands in the way of connecting the dots. TerVol has mastered this and maybe we are weaker than we think. If what I heard Salo mention, maybe we need to push through the fog.

At this point, Simon questioned that TerVol was the parent of propaganda and asked Salo for some help. Salo was prepared. He looked up from his laptop giving a silly, triumphant grin and slowly explained the key.

"Controlling people's minds is the first step in misleading people. If they have very limited sources of information they become like worker ants. History has shown that a country with weak propaganda (like reinforcing patriotism) was weak internally and internationally. Today powerful political propaganda invites economic, social, legal and literal war. That is why what Israel faces today is such a good example from which there is much we can learn."

"You see, Simon," Salo calmly replied like a cat with the mouse already in his mouth. "We are facing this today. In the real world there is something called "war propaganda" and it is very sophisticated, technologically enhanced and significant. And it is war by other means. It is even taught in universities! In many ways it is a weapon of bribery, mass distraction, disappearance, and distortion. It is controlled ambiguity," he smirked.

"Political propaganda is very similar to, but not identical to advertising or marketing as many might think. The main difficulty involved is in differ-

entiating propaganda from other types of persuasion, and avoiding a biased approach. Sure, it shares some techniques with advertising, public relations and even censorship. It is usually based in a one-sided viewpoint that is not open to contradiction even when it pretends that it is open. It is never information neutral and most often emotional.

Political propaganda takes so much money and creativity that it often originates from national or extra-national government resources or billionaires. Its intention is political, like terrorism is. Terrorism's political goals use fear of overwhelming surprise harm whereas good political propaganda can use fear, it is often also charming or enticing.

Political propaganda is the subtle first move that can lead to national cohesiveness or to divisiveness, mutual aid or violence, bloodshed or peaceful coexistence. It is started with repeated brainwashing by governments, religions, fifth columns, media bias and 'useful idiots.'

But for the existence of a truly independent media (not MSM) and web, this propaganda is almost impossible to resist. We have learned we must fact check. That is why we need to try to protect ourselves with knowledge of how it is done. If we only follow TV and main stream media, it is almost impossible to make correct decisions. False, contradicting or misleading assumptions lead to failures. Hear me out and I will share with all of you what I learned.

I have to give some credit to this report to Dr. Landmark and to Sophocles who said, 'What people believe prevails over truth'. We have many examples to share with you."

Before Before we start, let's ponder six thoughts.

1. As to the media, journalists, hired stringers, academics, elected officials, clergy, and big name artists, musicians and actors, that is those with the greatest mass attention, who are supposed to guard us, who

will guard the guards? - Quis Custodiet ipsos.

2. **Mark Twain** said "If you don't read the newspapers, you are uninformed, if you do read the papers, you are misinformed. ..."There are laws to protect the freedom of the press's speech, but none that are worth anything to protect the people from the press."

3. Experience demonstrates, time and again, that he who pays the piper (MSM) not only calls the tune, but often decides what cannot be played or when. It definitely sways elections.

4. **Niccolo Machiavelli** famously said in his book, The Prince: "Never attempt to win by force what can be won by deception."

5. **Language-corruption** (in tandem with moral relativism) has become THE weapon to dissolve our clarity on many subjects. For example, "Sodomy is an 'alternative life style," "cannibalism is nutrition by other means," "bestiality is just friendly pleasure", "jihad murder" is workplace-related violence,", "child pornography is just another art form", "Catholic institutions not providing contraception through their health insurance are part of a 'war on women', and Orwell's "Slavery is Freedom".

6. "The gallery in which the reporters sit has become a fourth estate of the realm." **Thomas Babington Macaulay**

We have seen the impact of propaganda. **Eleanor Roosevelt** noted in 1955 that "Arab propaganda on American college campuses across the country is beyond the wildest imagination," reported Kelsey. "It is a tool for controlling human thought and then behavior. I found that Roosevelt quote on page 5 of Israel and the Campus: The real Story, fall 2012 AICE (American-Israeli Cooperative Enterprise) cited from Near East Report, August 5, 1983.

Salo, not big on generalizations, sought to come back from philosophy to facts.

"With those thoughts under our belts as a basis for critique, we should now focus on more sophisticated political propaganda to which we are all subjected. I encourage you to put on your safety belts when you learn how you can be thrown around."

George Orwell presciently said, "Who controls the past controls the future. Who controls the present, controls the past."

Political Propaganda

It shrouds reality and (mis)directs the masses. It is about power and control. It is a repetitive (in volume, emotion, and form) communication aimed at influencing the attitude of a community toward some cause or political position so as to benefit the originator. It primarily relies on emotional triggers and factual disruption or factual deletion from a trusted source.

There are four modes of transmission, (much like diseases) with repetition as the common denominator.

1. **Electronic media** (TV, radio, Internet, Facebook, mobile phones, Twitter, Movies, the Web, transnational corporation computers, etc.).
2. **Print media** (government, newspapers, magazines, posters, wall paintings, books, graffiti, school books, etc.).
3. **Orally** on the street, meetings, university soap boxes, theaters and cafes.
4. **Fear** creating distress by through an image of power as in violent rallies, public shaming and punishing grades at Universities when students disagree with a professor: punitive, bullying p.c.

In the early 20th century, the term propaganda was used by the founders of the nascent public relations industry to describe their activities. At that time political propaganda was displayed in the form of party slogans.

This sales, marketing, advertising and messaging of "propaganda" usage died out after World War II, as the industry started to avoid the word, given the pejorative connotation it had acquired because it was representing the intentional dissemination of often false, but certainly "compelling" claims to support or justify political actions or ideologies of our enemies.

This redefinition arose because both the **Soviet Union** and **Germany's** government under **Hitler**, admitted explicitly to using glorious narratives favoring, respectively, **Communism** and **Nazism** in repeated forms of public expression. Yasser Arafat is a study in how to use propaganda ("Yasser Arafat, The Man and the Myth" by Thomas Kiernan, 1976) to gain power. As these ideologies were repugnant to liberal western societies, the negative feelings toward them came to be projected into the word "propaganda" itself.

Political propaganda is cognitive warfare. An example would be: We call our stuff "information" and the enemy's "propaganda." It is a war of information, disinformation, deleted information and misinformation, filling our eyes and ears so that nothing else can enter. It is taken to a new level called "War Propaganda." It is even offered as a university course because it is so sophisticated at the University of Kent, http://www.kent.ac.uk/history/centres /war-propaganda-and-society/. War colleges in every country engage in this educating, too.

To create the intended change, an effective political propaganda campaign takes creativity, aim, time, massive amounts of money and/or government support.

Stealth political propaganda is **censorship**. The same goal is achieved, not by filling people's minds with valid or unflattering information, but by preventing people from being confronted with opposing points of view from that particular propaganda source.

What sets political propaganda apart from other forms of advocacy is the willingness of the propagandist leadership to change people's understanding **through deception,** confrontation, emotional grabbers, withholding information, using fear and confusion rather than persuasion and understanding. It dramatically demonizes the "other."

Political propaganda is generally an appeal to emotion and incitement. It delegitimizes rather than criticizes. Beware as it is often in the form of attacking those in disagreement.

We can use again Israel as our canary. Israel is small and cannot financially compete against the multiple, hired professional PR campaigns from many countries to delegitimize it. This asymmetry with Israel becomes a good paradigm to demonstrate how propaganda works against someone small. And the U.N. has become a transmission belt to attack the exceptionalism of America and Israel.

Propaganda digs the graves and waits for them to be filled

Knowledgeable Jewish people are particularly aware of this. The war against the Jews has never been limited to bullets and swords; it has always been a war of ideas and words first. Today mobs become entranced by their leaders and chant "Death to the Jews" and "Death to America". Then bombs explode on buses, planes fly into buildings and rockets rain down on Israeli homes. The propaganda lies to cover up these crimes must be bold enough to misdirect the attention and importance not only of the victims, but the prospective massacre of millions. Iran races toward the construction of its genocidal nuclear bomb.

The goal of aggressive, accusatory political propaganda (such as hate) is to divert the attention from the substance of the discussion using gross generalizations defaming, denying, delegitimizing, dehumanizing and appealing to emotion rather than to fact. The intention of propaganda is to make the opponent submit, or the unwary act accordingly, perform poorly, or cower.

Included in propaganda is cunning journalism driven by an agenda, that expresses itself by what it says, what it doesn't say, how it says it, by who it quotes, who it does not quote, source credibility and the overall tone it attempts to create. This is journalism and speechmaking, not intended to report, but to undermine and confuse those who are not knowledgeable with that outlet's agenda.

Over 30 techniques of propaganda have been identified by universities in the area of social psychology.

Propagandists use messages that, while sometimes convincing, are not necessarily valid. As an example, **Peter Beinart** is saying that there is no difference between those who support Israel and decry its critics and those who oppose Israel and decry its supporters. This moral equivalence is absolutely necessary for propaganda. If you want to make a completely false argument sound reasonable, the first thing you have to do is erase all distinction between good and evil. In university type terms it is called casuistry.

To be better able to understand how all of us are influenced or mislead, researchers have categorized some of the techniques.

Propaganda techniques take many forms and were easily understood by Dr. Landmark. After all she was a forensic psychiatrist who had worked with CIA operatives and black ops people. A more complete rendering of these was found in her notebook at the end of this chapter. She then shared some of the more prominent techniques and over a hundred examples.

"Remember," she said, "that the abuse of a citizenry comes from repeating falsehoods, repeated denial of truths, claims of the sole source of truth, information overload, concealing information, and repeated appeals to emotions."

The first Ten Commandments of Propaganda

1. **Change the meaning.** That is to redefine or make up new words. *George Orwell* warned us of this. Often the propaganda is as simple as who gets to define the terms like "enemy" versus "ally"; "incitement" versus "advocacy"; "provocation" versus "response", "resistance" versus "aggressiveness", "victim" versus "perpetrator"; "terrorist" versus "freedom fighter", "murderer" versus "militant", and, of course, "Slavery is Freedom".

2. **Charges and Omissions. Saeb Erekat,** the chief Palestinian negotiator, claims that all the Palestinian "victims" since the beginning of the negotiations in August 2013 "were killed in cold blood" by Israel. A check of the names of those killed reveals a completely different picture and totally refutes Erekat's allegation. Almost all of those killed were combatants from radical and Islamic terrorist groups, including Hamas. Hamas has never renounced its Covenant and vows to destroy Israel. http://jcpa.org/article/cold-blooded-murder-or-a-war-on-terror/

3. **Change the Law: Use one religion's laws to displace the Constitution and then redefine international law.** This one is critical to understand in our time. **Andrew G. Bostom** wrote an eye-opening article, "Ten Key Points on Islamic Blasphemy Law". Let's just look at seven. Using religious law to supersede national or international laws creates control of national and international law, including penalties.

For over twenty years there has been an intensifying, global campaign through the U.N. to impose Islamic blasphemy law on non-Muslims in non-Muslim societies but including those living in of the House of Islam. What follows is a short version of the key points on the doctrinal origins and practical implications of this global campaign. The full article can be found in the annex:

1) According to the Sunna (the traditions of Muhammad and the early Muslim community), by using foul language against the Muslim prophet Muhammad, Allah, or Islam, the non-Muslim transgressors put themselves on a war footing against Muslims, and their lives became illicit (such as the poet Kaab b. al-Ashraf, who composed poems denigrating Muhammad, and was assassinated). This "offense" was then constructed and legitimated by Muslim jurists when Islam was politically, militarily, and economically dominant.

2) The jurists saw any such denigration as an unacceptable hostile act, punishable by death, automatically, as per Islamic Law (Sunni: Maliki, Shafii, Hanbali), and the major Shiite schools.

3) Two modern examples will illustrate the point. When Iranian theocrat Ayatollah Khomeini (February 19, 1989) issued a fatwa (rigid ruling) condemning author Salman Rushdie to death (along with those involved in the publication of Rushdie's book, "The Satanic Verses"), he promised eternal salvation to any Muslim "martyred" in this cause. No serious Muslim commentator has challenged the basic validity of the Ayatollah's fatwa. Additionally, this orthodox Islamic doctrine was incorporated, into the "modern" Pakistani legal code 295C

4) A report by the Pew Research Center's Forum on religion and public life issued August 9, 2011, called "Rising Restrictions on Religion" found that application of the Sharia (laws against blasphemy, apostasy or defamation of religion) at present resulted in a disproportionate number of Muslim countries, twenty-one — registering the highest (i.e., worst) persecution scores on their scale. These penalties are enforced in 60% of the countries in the region."

5) The 57-member Organization of the Islamic Cooperation has pushed for a UN resolution insisting that countries criminalize what it calls "defamation of religion" for over 20 years. It called for a specific ban on speech allegedly impugning the character of Islam's prophet, which the OIC terms "hate speech."

6) The Assembly of Muslim Jurists of America (AMJA), is well-accepted by the mainstream American Muslim community. The mainstream

AMJA goal is to implement Sharia in North America. One of their rulings sanctions the killing of non-Muslim "blasphemers". **AMJA Secretary General Salah al-Sawy**: (Dr. Salah Al-Sawy, 1/21/2009)

7) Blasphemy committed by a Muslim is considered apostasy. It is clear from the Muslim creed that apostasy requires severe, mandatory punishment, with a requisite death sentence since the advent of Islam. What is particularly frightening are the results of polling data collected by Wenzel Strategies during October 22 to 26, 2012, from 600 U.S. Muslims. It indicates widespread support (58%) among American votaries of Islam for this fundamental rejection of the basic freedoms of expression and conscience, as guaranteed under the First Amendment to the U.S. Constitution.

Fully 12% of this Muslim sample even admitted they believed in application of the draconian, Sharia-based punishment for crime of "blasphemy", answering affirmatively, "…that Americans who criticize or parody Islam should be put to death." http://www.americanthinker.com/blog/2013/03/ten_key_points_on_islamic_blasphemy_law.html#ixzz2NbJHCOqb

Politicians and journalists confuse us by interchangeably using these terms:

Reliable Ally ⟷ important ally ⟷ strategic ally (strategic partner) ⟷ conditional ally ⟷ "friend" ⟷ partner ⟷ core (vital, critical) interest ⟷ interest ⟷ asset ⟷ frienemy ⟷ resource piece ⟷ competitor ⟷ liability challenger ⟷ rival ⟷ adversary ⟷ enemy ⟷ **Mortal Enemy** (war).

"Interests" and "resources" are temporary.

"Assets" are expendable.

"Liabilities" detract from a country's well-being and security.

"Frienemies" is just a cutsie term. That was the only way Dr. Landmark could put it.

A special disingenuous, brand new invented propaganda term: "Islamophobia"

There is a new propaganda term thrown around that sounds like homophobia, an epithet thrown at those who they think do not accept the homosexual lifestyle.

It was invented as **"Islamophobia"** and the press bought into the word without meaning. "Islamophobia" was deliberately designed by a Muslim Brotherhood front organization, the **International Institute for Islamic Thought (IIIT)** to create the emotional response to "islamophobia" as already exists to "racism" and "bigotry."

Used effectively, those three terms can then be used to deride, derail and attack those who expose tragic events labeling them as hateful bigots, racists and "Islamophobes." Since it's not possible to prosecute these "Islamophobes" in current international law, those who are thus labeled are instead vilified in the media, mocked, socially isolated, economically harmed, deemed haters and marginalized as individuals who have no right to enter the conversation. "Islamophobe" can be used to drain a business or used against a politician to keep from getting support.

As a psychiatrist, Dr. Landmark spoke out, "Everyone knows that a phobia is an unreasonable fear of something that poses little or no danger or is non-existent.

So, the term, "Islamophobia," itself, has no value for dialogue. There are plenty of reasons for legitimate fear (international terrorism, Islamic laws against infidels), so that makes it a reality, not a phobia as anyone who follows the news knows. A more descriptive word could be **"Islamofauxbia."**

All mainstream Islamic sects and schools of Islamic jurisprudence teach that the Islamic umma (all Muslims) must wage war on unbelievers for all time or until they are subjugated to the rule of Islamic law (sharia) by conversion, dhimmitude or death. The codification of Sharia in Islam has the attribute of being immutable because it is Allah given and incompatible with man-made laws when there is a conflict. Violating Sharia is rebellion against Allah which is punishable. "Islamophobia," then, is used for silencing discussion or thought by asserting that it attacks/insults Islam or Mohammed. They declare themselves to be victims and now have a pretense to attack (in "defense").

"All in all," she concluded, "this is **Islamoreality**".

Abdur-Rahman Muhammad, a former member of the IIIT (International Institute of Islamic Thought) https://iiit.org/en/home/ who has renounced the group in disgust, was an eyewitness to the creation of the word. "This loathsome term," he writes, "is nothing more than a thought-terminating cliché' conceived in the bowels of Muslim think tanks for the purpose of beating down critics."

He said that the group was inspired by how the term "homophobe" had been used against critics of homosexuality, despite Islamic nation's punishment for homosexuals. Any confirmation of the veracity of the Jewish or Christian Bible is seen as an attack on the Islamic authenticity of the Koranic figures (taken from Jewish and Christian Bibles). **It becomes a reason to attack.** With the history of the Jews, its towns and stories, it resuscitates the Bible, the book that the Koran is supposed to supplant.

TerVol had to smile with this advance, initiating the divisiveness of humanity. As soon as TerVol can create ambiguity and divisiveness, the sooner the physical damage will occur.

The "Islamophobia" headline grabber should be debunked by reality.

In 2008, the FBI said 66.1 percent were anti-Jewish while 7.5 percent were anti-Muslim. This has been true of every year in the past decade, even in 2001 when anti-Muslim crime spiked in the wake of 9/11.

In 2010, only 13.2 percent of religion-based attacks were directed at Muslims. By comparison, 65.4 percent of such crimes were directed at Jews.

On November 20, 2011 the FBI released their annual crime statistics report which showed once again that hate crimes against Muslims remain relatively rare.

But, the 2013 FBI report demonstrated that threat facing Muslim Americans is not growing and remains dramatically lower than that facing black people, gays and Jews. In bias crimes involving religion, Jewish Americans were targeted in 674 incidents – 62 percent of all religiously-motivated crimes. That's five times more than Muslim Americans, fewer than 12 percent of all religiously-motivated crimes.

FBI reports do not come out until a year after their collection. https:/ /ucr.fbi.gov/hate-crime/2016/topic-pages/victims

Phillipe Asssouline's notebook at the end of this segment identifies many words that mean radically different things to the people in the West than that which the Arabs or Muslims accept. This makes the inherent faulty communication more than treacherous. Knowing this and not dealing with it makes one wonder how dumb can we be? Four fuzzy propaganda triggers repeatedly jump out from the press: "peace", "settler", "occupation" and "refugees".

Example: There is no real distinction, only a division of labor, when speaking about the "armed" wing, the "social welfare" wing, or "political" wing of groups like the Muslim Brotherhood (Ikwan), or Al Qaeda, or Hamas, or the PLO, or the Taliban, or Hezbollah, or Fatah. Many Arabs and Muslims use the term "settler" to mean "targets" in their minds. All Israelis are considered settlers by the P.A. and Hamas, not just those in land they do not control. There is no question on that.

Example: "Peace" in the West means respectful co-existence; people living sided by side without overt animosity. "Peace" in Islam can only occur when those in disagreement with Islam are eliminated or converted and the world is ruled by Islam. The is the official Islamic interpretation of history.

Example: The Associated Press has often white-washed what is happening: From the latest AP stylebook the definition of Islamism is so broad, so ambiguous, as to be uninformative, that it can hardly be considered a definition: "An advocate or supporter of a political movement that favors reordering government and society in accordance with laws prescribed by Islam. Do not use as a synonym for Islamic fighters, militants, extremists or radicals, who may or may not be Islamists. Where possible, be specific and use the name of militant affiliations: al-Qaida-linked, Hezbollah, Taliban, etc. Those who view the Quran as a political model encompass a wide range of Muslims, from mainstream politicians to militants known as jihadi."

When a popular military coup or "election" occurs with a victory by Islamists, the press chooses to no longer call them called 'Islamists", even though their protocols have not changed toward violence and intolerance. The critical deception is that in Western mindset, "popular elected officials" or "the government" is inversely proportionate to extremist. But in this case, they are two sides of the same counterfeit coin.

4. The Big Lie and then **double down-** the **Bigger Lie.**

Believing these outrageous tales begets the terms "dumb and dumber." This can be a repeated articulation of a complex of events or reversal of their order that justifies subsequent action. The descriptions of these events have some elements of truth that merge with the "Big Lie" generalizations to supplant the public's accurate perception of the underlying events. This is exactly how the enemies of Israel operate. Just as the Nazis posted outlandish fabrications about the Jews, the Arab/Muslims heavily and emotionally accuse the Jewish state of acting in an illegitimate and usually ugly fashion, thereby placing the burden of proof on those they defame. What happened to the concept, innocent until proven guilty?

> **Example:** Two Wikileaks cables from 2010 confirm the critique of Israel's foreign-funded NGO movement that many have been making for years — and they do so from the mouths of the NGO leaders themselves. The cables summarize meetings between U.S. officials and leaders of the, B'Tselem, and the Association for Civil Rights in Israel, called ACRI, a flagship NIF (New Israel Fund) project. They claim, because they have the external funding to investigating the Israeli military, that Israelis are not capable of an honest investigation. In fact, Israel's judiciary, both civil and military, is among the world's most independent. Yet advancing claims of judicial indifference to war crimes has become a central ambition of the anti-Israel NGO propaganda. The credible

prospect of such prosecutions would paralyze the IDF, which is exactly the point: They want to make the world believe that Israel is corrupt and its judiciary dishonest. These allegations are also made about America. http://cablesearch.org/cable/view.php?id=10TELAVIV184

Examples: We can learn more by remembering what Hitler achieved with his "double-down" propaganda: "All propaganda must be so popular and on such an intellectual level, that even the most stupid of those towards whom it is directed will understand it…. Through clever and constant application of propaganda, people can be made to see paradise as hell, and also the other way around, to consider the most wretched sort of life as paradise."— **Adolf Hitler**

"The size of the lie is a definite factor in causing it to be believed, for the vast masses of a nation are in the depths of their hearts more easily deceived than they are consciously bad. The primitive simplicity of their minds renders them a more easy prey to a big lie than to a small lie. For they themselves often tell little lies but would be ashamed to tell big lies."— **Adolf Hitler**

His propaganda success can be measured in millions of deaths.

Hitler, himself, makes two basic points in this connection: (1) "something of the most insolent lie will always remain and stick," and (2) the aim of propaganda is not to inform but to incite "wrathful hatred." Adolf Hitler, Mein Kampf, translated by Ralph Manheim (Boston: Houghton Mifflin, 1971), p. 232 a complex of events that justify subsequent action.

The descriptions of these events have elements of truth, and the "big lie" generalizations merge and eventually supplant the public's accurate perception of the underlying events.

After World War I the Germans were told that the cause of their defeat, a "stab in the back by the Jews,". This became a justification for Nazi re-militarization and revanchist aggression.

In our time, there has been wild unsupportable screaming that Israel is using disproportionate force defending itself against Arab attacks. The Arab-Israeli conflict is often said, not just by extremists, to be the world's most dangerous conflict – and, accordingly, Israel is judged the world's most belligerent country.

But is this true? It flies in the face of the well-known pattern that modern liberal democracies, historically, do not aggress; plus, it assumes, wrongly, that the Arab-Israeli conflict is among the costliest in terms of lives lost.

What are the measurable facts that disprove the Big Lie? To place the Arab-Israeli fatalities in their proper context, one of the two co-authors, **Gunnar Heinsohn**, has compiled statistics to rank conflicts since 1950 by the number of human deaths incurred. This grisly inventory finds the total number of perspective deaths in conflicts since 1950 numbering about 85,000,000. Some 11,000,000 Muslims have been violently killed since 1948, of which 35,000, or 0.3 percent, died during the sixty years of fighting Israel, or just 1 out of every 315 Muslim fatalities. In contrast, over 90 percent of the 11 million who perished were killed by fellow Muslims. *Sources: **Z. Brzezinski,** Out of Control: Global Turmoil on the Eve of the Twenty-first Century, 1993; **S. Courtois**, Le Livre Noir du Communism, 1997; **G. Heinsohn**, Lexikon der Völkermorde, 1999, 2nd ed.; G. Heinsohn, Söhne und Weltmacht, 2006, 8th ed.; **R. Rummel**, Death by Government, 1994; **M. Small and J.D. Singer**, Resort to Arms: International and Civil Wars 1816-1980, 1982; **M. White**, "Death Tolls for the Major Wars and Atrocities of the Twentieth Century," 2003. Arab-Israeli Fatalities Rank 49th by **Gunnar Heinsohn** and **Daniel Pipes** FrontPage-Magazine.com October 8, 2007

From the Official PA daily: "Palestinians [are] Jesus' descendants" and "Jesus' story is his [Palestinian] people's story" and "Jesus... the virtuous patriotic Palestinian forefather... brought forth his New Testament and spread it among mankind - which led the Jews to persecute him until they caught him, crucified him, and murdered him."

"The Zionist movement... wanted to falsify historical facts, to exile and crucify the Palestinian Arab nation and then murder it," revealed by Itamar Marcus and Nan Jacques Zilberdik May 17, 2013.

Having no ancient Palestinian history, the Palestinian Authority has tried for many years to convince its people that they have a history going back many thousands of years; that there was an ancient Palestinian nation, and that one of the great figures of history, Jesus, was their "forefather" and they are "Jesus' descendants." The fact that in Christian tradition Jesus is a Jew from the nation of Judea and that the historical record has no record of a Palestinian Arab people, is not taught by the PA.

The Palestinian Authority (PA) also ignores the fact that the Romans only changed the name of Jewish Judea to "Palestine" after the Judean Bar Kochba Rebellion in the year 136 AD and 400 years before Mohamed, centuries after the death of Jesus. Furthermore, according to Christian tradition, Jesus did not marry, had no children, and therefore Palestinians could not be "Jesus' descendants."

Another bit of propaganda is more typical than atypical. There was a disgusting, promoted exploitation of a disabled Arab-Palestinian child. Born with a rare genetic disease, leaving the child without full arms or legs a Gaza born child, **Mohammed al Farra** was treated by **Tel HaShomer Hospital** in Israel, but the parents and Hamas refused to pay or pick up the child. The Arab press and twitter pictured and reported that the child was a Gaza war victim.

http://honestreporting.com/disgusting-exploitation-of-a-disabled-palestinian-child/

Double down and repeat: Yearly at Christmas time, official PA daily papers, internet and TV messages present that "Palestinians [are] Jesus' descendants" and "Jesus' story is his [Palestinian] people's story".

"Jesus... the virtuous patriotic Palestinian forefather...brought forth his New Testament and spread it among mankind - which led the Jews to persecute him until they caught him, crucified him, and murdered him".

"The Zionist movement... wanted to falsify historical facts, to exile and crucify the Palestinian Arab nation and then murder it".

They know that they can have some success because there are enough anti-Semites and ignorant masses around to want to delegitimize Judaism and

Christianity in order to wrench Israel from them. http://palwatch.org/main.aspx?fi=157&doc_id=8979 by Itamar Marcus and Nan Jacques Zilberdik , May 17, 2013.

Supersized Lies

Ultra-malignant wild, anti-Israel propaganda and overt lies were expressed about fighting that occurred in Jenin, Israel in April 2002. The press and college campuses painted Israel as the world's pariah: "Nazis," "butchers," "conducting war crimes," "surrounding the infant Jesus with Israeli tanks," claims of 3,000 Palestinians being massacred, claims that Israelis poisoned the Palestinian water supply, and claims that Israel dumped Palestinian corpses into secret mass graves in Jenin. The media promoted that propaganda.

But, this supersize lie was exposed. No massacre occurred in Jenin! Less than one hundred armed terrorists were killed in "Operation Defensive Shield", and almost as many Israeli soldiers were killed because they were ordered to go from house-to-house to avoid civilian casualties wherever possible. But the lies and propaganda had spread around the world.

The BBC spread the claims of the PA that Israelis were stealing organs from dead terrorists, conducting experiments on prisoners which cause cancer, neglecting sick prisoners with a policy of slow death. The BBC never checked to see if there was any truth in these raging mendacious accusations. http://www.bbcwatch.org/20130/4/04/bbc-again-blindly-repeats-pa-accusations-regarding -dead-prisoner

There was another wide spread lie by the main stream media (msm) that has been exposed by **Daniel Greenfield,** "The Hard Life of Muslim Terrorists in Israeli Prison" on June 20, 2011 in the Daily Mailer, FrontPage.

"Six years ago, **Saeed Shalalde** stabbed an Israeli chocolate manufacturer named Sasson Nuriel to death. Today Shalalde lives a pretty good life in an Israeli prison. It is certainly safer, and sometimes they are more prosperous. There, terrorists actually mingle, throw parties, study for advanced degrees and stay in touch with their adoring fans on Facebook using their 3G mobile smartphones.

Other imprisoned terrorists use smartphone video to go shopping with their friends and pick out their own clothes, which are then brought to them in prison, and remotely attend family events. Sometimes it seems like they're not even in prison."

Muslim terrorists like Shalade, refuse to recognize the existence of Israel. They emphatically call Israel's birth a "catastrophe". Prisoners are not even forced to watch television programming from the Zionist entity. Instead they enjoy satellite Arab TV channels, courtesy of the Israeli prison system.

Greenfield continued with reports that every legally convicted Muslim terrorist receives a salary from the Fatah's Palestinian Authority, including members of Hamas. That money is provided by American and European taxpayers. As much as 10 percent of the Palestinian Authority's budget (growing yearly and reaching as much as $350,000,000 a year) is dedicated to paying the salaries of convicted, imprisoned terrorists. The benefits also go to their families and the families of terrorists who weren't lucky enough to end up in Israeli prisons but tried to shoot it out. This money does not necessarily go just to the people it was intended to help. https://www.jpost.com/Arab-Israeli-Conflict/Palestinian-Authority-paid-terrorists-nearly-350-million-in-2017-533227

Bigger lies…REFUTED such as "Jerusalem runs Washington"

Currently, there are five big propaganda lies about how "Jerusalem Runs Washington" exposed by **Aaron David Miller** March 21, 2012. Aaron David Miller is an American Middle East analyst, author, and negotiator. He is Vice President for New Initiatives at the Woodrow Wilson International Center for Scholars and has been an advisor to both Republican and Democratic secretaries of state.

1. **"The White House is Israeli-occupied territory".** Some spread the idea that American Jews, in collusion with the Israeli government hold U.S. foreign policy hostage. This is not only wrong and misleading, but a dangerous. It coexists with other hateful, anti-Semitic canards about how Jews control the media and the banks, and the world as well. It is reality distortion in the extreme, with scant basis in fact. The historical record just doesn't support it. Strong, willful presidents who have real opportunities (and smart strategies to exploit them) to

promote U.S. interests almost always win out and trump lobbies.

2. **"The U.S.-Israel relationship rests on shared values alone".** Israel's critics believe that without domestic politics, there would be little to the U.S.-Israel special relationship. Israel's supporters, meanwhile, like to believe that politics has little to do with it. Neither is totally right. The U.S.-Israel relationship is a curious marriage of shared values, national interests, and domestic politics.

3. **"The Jewish lobbies are evil".** The United States' Founding Fathers were very worried about factions with special interests. But lobbies and special interests advocating causes — from guns to tobacco to senior citizens to the spotted owl are special interests, too. They aren't some kind of dark cabal plotting in a cloakroom. They are a natural part of America's democratic political system and, yes, part of a culture that has many excesses that bend the system and often reflect the seamier aspects of U.S. politics. Citizens and groups organize to press their elected representatives to support an issue. The U.S. system, whatever the Founders intended, was a natural for lobbing and special pleading was a right reserved for their own citizens, not foreign entities.

4   **"His Jewish advisors made him do it."** This charge, which has been leveled at senior officials in Reagan's, Clinton's and George W. Bush's administrations — that presidents are controlled by a tiny group of American Jewish advisers. This borders on wacky conspiracy theorists. There's no question that all Presidents understand and appreciate the special relationship between Israel and the United States. Sure, these Presidents were frustrated by Israeli prime ministers too, but they also were moved and enamored by them (Clinton by Yitzhak Rabin, Bush by Ariel Sharon). They had instinctive, heartfelt empathy for the idea of Israel's story, and as a consequence they could make allowances at times for Israel's behavior even when it clashed with their own policy goals.

MORE PROPAGANDA TECHNIQUES

5. **Half-truth** A half-truth is a deceptive statement, which may come in several forms and includes some element of truth.

6. **Victimology** (a political jackhammer that penetrates people's brains without notice). One area that this is used against Israel is in property ownership. Victimology is often used by emotionally advocating individual claims (through the msm), often without any proof of stolen land or property or property ownership, or even displacement. They then go on the attack claiming colonization or occupation. This can only work with the press's aid.

Blame, then, alleviates feelings from the victim of shame and guilt for the responsibility of the problem or its amelioration or specific redress. It arouses an uneducated public's feelings to help the so-called underdog.

The victim demands that their problem needs solution by others.

Hence, the term "cry-bully" evolved. This is basic to Arab/PA propaganda. It ignores facts like whenever Arab-Palestinians have brought proof of ownership of contested territory to Israeli courts, including Israel's Supreme Court, the courts have at times issued decisions calling on the Israeli government to restore the property in question to its Palestinian claimant, even if that requires dismantling the private homes of Israeli citizens. The determination of territory as state land as opposed to private land is a necessary action which helps avert errors in the future when these areas are developed.

7. **Selective presentation of facts**. This is a diversion of attention by omission, denial or refocus to encourage a particular thesis.

    Example #1: In Pakistan, one human rights group estimates that 1,000 women are murdered in honor killings by their families every year.

In Nigeria, Islamic militants have killed more than 1,500 people in 2014, according to Amnesty International. And the death toll from the slaughter in

Syria—just spitting distance from Israel—adds up to a robust 191,000. But the world pays scant attention to these Muslim but non-Palestinian corpses. You've got to be a dead person in Gaza or Hebron for the media to grab the world's sympathy.

Merely being an Arab, or a Muslim, doesn't cut the mustard, because when Muslims are murdering other Muslims—like more than 2,400 Iraqis killed by other Iraqis in June of this year, the civilized world, or at least the chattering classes, does little more than shrug. https://www.google.com/?gws_rd=ssl#q=Dear+Fellow+Liberals%3A+I%E2%80%99m+Done+Apologizing+for+Israel

> **Example #2:** Israeli Children's Trauma Ignored by Washington Post by **Simon Plosker**, 6-6-13. The Washington Post has published a story examining the trauma suffered by Gazan children as a result of conflict. The scene is set with a vivid, graphic and emotive opening.

And herein lies the fundamental problem with the story – the description of an Israeli "invasion" paints a picture of Gazan children suffering as a result of Israeli malevolence. The article goes on with more vivid commentary: "Gaza was attacked, they say, for the same reason Israel struck in 2008 to kill Palestinians and seize more Palestinian land. (Israel says its warplanes carry out precision strikes on carefully identified terrorist targets.)"

A short sentence in parentheses is all that Israel's narrative warrants according to the Washington Post. Nowhere is there any reference to the thousands of rockets fired at Israeli civilians (itself a war crime) from Gaza. There is no mention about the Israeli town of Sderot and the surrounding areas of southern Israel that have experienced barely a day of quiet during the past decade. Israeli children have been brought up experiencing almost daily alerts that give them some 15 seconds to take cover or run for a bomb shelter.

While the trauma of Syrian children has featured in the Washington Post, they imply that Israeli children just don't suffer. Is this because fewer Israeli children have died than Palestinian children? This reduces the story to one based purely on unequal body counts and ignores the bigger picture.

Nobody disputes that Gaza's children have suffered as a result of conflict. But resorting to the knee-jerk "blame Israel" routine completely ignores reality. The reality is that Palestinian children are exposed to danger as a direct result of terrorists operating from within civilian areas turning children into human shields. It cannot ignore the measured facts that Israel makes supreme efforts to avoid causing harm to Palestinian civilians while Palestinian terrorists do their utmost to indiscriminately kill and maim innocent Israelis. Like much of the mainstream media around the world, the Washington Post exhibits the familiar tendency to imply that the Arab-Palestinians can only be victims and are never capable of affecting their own circumstances. The trauma of Israeli children doesn't even register on their pages.

> **Example #3:** Israel has been wildly accused of being brutal to civilians in war. Yet, in Afghanistan, the ratio of civilian to combatant deaths is 3:1 - three civilians killed for every one combatant. In Iraq and Kosovo, it was 4:1 - four civilians killed for every one combatant.

In Israel's "Operation Cast Lead" in Gaza in 2006, despite the repeated screams of 'Israeli war crimes', it was an astounding 1:1 - only one civilian killed every one combatant.

Current figures for "Operation Pillar of Defense", according to **Ha'aretz Newspaper,** of the earlier total of 95 Palestinians killed about half were "civilians", and according to the Israel Defense Forces, about one third were civilians. So, the civilian: combatant death ratio is currently either one civilian killed for every one combatant, or, even more astoundingly one civilian killed for every two combatants.

8. **Dualism** in propaganda can be disingenuously inverted (David and Goliath) by the media: By reducing the number of parties in a conflict to two (such as "Palestine" vs. Israel), it misleads everyone. Many countries, religious fanatics and terror groups have joined in attemps to destroy Israel. Stories that just focus on internal developments

often ignore such outside or "external" forces as foreign governments, transnational militaries, anti-Israel NGOs, mosques, some churches and transnational companies.

Example #1: The media often uses a David and Goliath analogy calling the Arabs the little David and calling Israel, the Goliath. Israel has been attacked by many Arab countries even before its foundation.

In factuality, Israel has always been the David and has the smaller population and tinier land mass. The Goliath is over a billion Arab/Muslims from many countries that want to see Israel destroyed.

Example #2: The press omits history to pretend that it is the Arab-Palestinians against the Jewish State of Israel when in fact the Goliath has always been the Arab/Muslim world of billions denying Israel's right to exist.

Cases abound, yet the press smothers the history, taking the story out of context. In December 1945, the Arab League launched a boycott of 'Zionist goods' that continues to this day

In November 1947, it rejected the UN "Partition Plan" for the British Mandate of Palestine adopted by the General Assembly in Resolution 181.

In June 1946, it established the Higher Arab Committee to "coordinate efforts with regard to Palestine," a radical body that led and coordinated attempts to wipe the Jews in the Mandated land off the map.

In December 1946, it rejected the first proposed Palestine partition plans, reaffirming "that Palestine is a part of the Arab motherland."

In October 1947, prior to the vote on Resolution 181 – the "Partition Plan" –the Arab Muslim world reasserted the necessity for military preparations along Arab borders to "defending Palestine."

In February 1948, it approved "a plan for political, military, and economic measures to be taken in response to the Palestine crisis."

In October 1949, the Arab League declared that negotiation with Israel by any Arab state would be in violation of Article 18 of the Arab League.

In April 1950, it called for severance of relations with any Arab state which engaged in relations or contacts with Israel and prohibited Member states from negotiating unilateral peace with Israel.

In March 1979, it suspended Egypt's membership in the League (retroactively) from the date of its signing a peace treaty with Israel. "http://www.bid-vertiser.com/bdv/BidVertiser/bdv_publisher_toolbar_creator.dbm">toolbar</a>

9. **Perpetuating perpetuation by repeatedly repeating** known falsehoods without allowing refutation or balance.

> **Example: #1** In 1969 a **Christian** from **Australia** started a fire in the Al-Aqsa Mosque in Jerusalem. He was arrested and tried in Israel. The Israeli court found him to be mentally ill and ordered him hospitalized. He was later sent back to Australia.As part of its promotion of religious hatred against Jews, the Palestinian Authority disseminated the libel that Israel and Jews were behind the 1969 arson.

Since the Al-Aqsa Mosque is an important holy site for Muslims, accusing "senior Jews of high position" of trying to destroy it is clearly an attempt by the PA to promote religious hatred against Jews. This particular accusation appeared in a documentary film about the arson and was shown at an event under the auspices of PA Chairman **Mahmoud Abbas.** "Those who planned the burning of Al-Aqsa were senior Jews of high position". A PA Minister: "Al-Aqsa was burnt 'by criminal hands... in collusion with the criminal occupation"; Israeli Arab MP: "Israel set fire to Al-Aqsa". http://palwatch.org/main.aspx?fi=157&doc_id=9627 Itamar Marcus and Nan Jacques Zilberdik

> **Example #2 Joseph Goebbels** exploited Theodore Kaufman's <u>Germany Must Perish!</u> to claim that the Allies sought the extermination of the German people over and over again.

Example #3 Yasser Arafat and Mahmoud Abbas adhered to the principals of Egyptian born, Muslim Brotherhood founder **Hassan al-Banna** (1906-49). Al-Banna called on Muslims to prepare for armed struggle against colonial rule; he warned Muslims against the "widespread belief" that "jihad of the heart" was more important than "jihad of the sword." He said he learned a great deal from the Nazis about the effectiveness of propaganda in spreading hatred of Jews. (Charles Wendell, Berkeley: University of California Press, 1978), pp. 45-6.) https://en.wikipedia.org/wiki/Hassan_al-Banna

Since few people actually double-check what they learn at school, such dis-information will often be repeated by journalists as well as parents, thus rein-forcing the idea that the disinformation item is really a "well-known fact", even though no one repeating the myth is able to point to an authoritative source. The disinformation is then recycled in the media and in the educational system (repetition). Such permeating propaganda may be used for political goals: by giving citizens a false impression of the quality or policies of their country, they may be incited to reject certain proposals or certain remarks or ignore the experience of others.

Example #4 Today, the most basic set of lies by the Iranian Mullahs is big enough to fill another 6 million graves. It de-mands that people believe that Israel is a conqueror, col-onizer and racist. In the hallways of the United Nations (192 desks) Israel is claimed to be an illegitimate entity. So, the outcomes of Israel's defensive wars make the atrocities of its enemies seem understandable and even justifiable.

"Huh," Tom blurted out. "Anyone, who has any sense knows that if Israel lost one of those wars, it would no longer exist. Today, all the losers from the Arab/Muslim countries still exist."

Example #5 The best place for organized hate propaganda to start is the schools where peer pressure and teacher's authority give clear pictures. It combines electronic, print and oral brainwashing. There was a study on the impact of the educational systems in Israel and the Palestinian Authority.

The Wexler Report (released after three years of study in 2012-3) found that 84 percent of characterizations of Jews in PA school books were very negative or negative, and likewise that 87 percent of descriptions of the actions of Jews were very negative or moderately negative. And the authors of this report consciously chose not to examine the sources for the hatred: the religious passages found in P.A. government distributed textbooks of Islam, whose foundations are in the religious books of the Koran, the Hadith and the Sunna. These religious texts provide strong support that Islam is totalitarian (controls the public education) and imperialistic. Leaving this out is an incomprehensible mistake!

Government run school systems and officially approved textbooks tell us something about the mindset of those who wrote and approved them. The report agrees that Israeli textbooks include many more positive references to the "other" (Arabs /Muslims or Arab/Christians); that peace is presented as the ultimate goal in Arab-Israeli relations; and that the books contain a more complex depiction of events regarding Israeli and Arab relations with some discussion of the Palestinian point of view. All of these are missing from the Palestinian textbooks, admits the report.

Example #6 After 9/11, 2001, certain radio presenters repeated, unchallenged, a report that Jews had been tipped off not to report to work at the World Trade Center that morning. Contributors running the clerical, jihadist, and guerrilla gamut blamed Jews for the attacks and urged the United States to "get rid" of its own.

The most effective propaganda comes about with a compilation of statistics or stories which must not only be difficult to quickly refute but must result in serious consequences for the target side.

10. APARTHEID ARSY-VARSY and ETHNIC CLEANSING ENEMAS to condemn Israel

Exactly what is apartheid and where did the term come from? It was an official, governmental system of racial segregation that existed in South Africa from 1948 until the early 1990s codified by racial stratification into one of four racial groups. It was illegal for most South African citizens to marry or pursue sexual relationships across racial lines. Apartheid forbade multiracial sport, which meant that overseas teams, by virtue of them having players of different races, could not play in South Africa. For instance, the Transvaal's constitution barred "Black and Coloured" participation in church and state. Nonwhites had separate amenities (i.e. beaches, buses, schools, benches, drinking fountains, restrooms). Nonwhites received inferior education, medical care, and other public services. Though they were the overwhelming majority of the population, nonwhites could not vote or become citizens. Nonwhites were prohibited from running businesses or professional practices in the white areas without permits. The South African government chose ten geographic locations of forced residence that were determined by racial classification designated as bantustans.

"That clears up what really apartheid is. I would gasp if this were Israeli policy, although I admit I heard of these things had happening from our government's policies in the past", announced Tom.

The volume of the lies creates propaganda with a maddening mendaciousness. Sometimes it is pure fabrication, sometimes by not reporting or inverting the time sequences of events. These lies, to be successful, require the MSM to propagate, repeat, and perpetuate these fantastical allegations.

To make the propaganda effective it requires the main stream medias to go out of their way to avoid sharing pictures like these:

Visible in the social order:

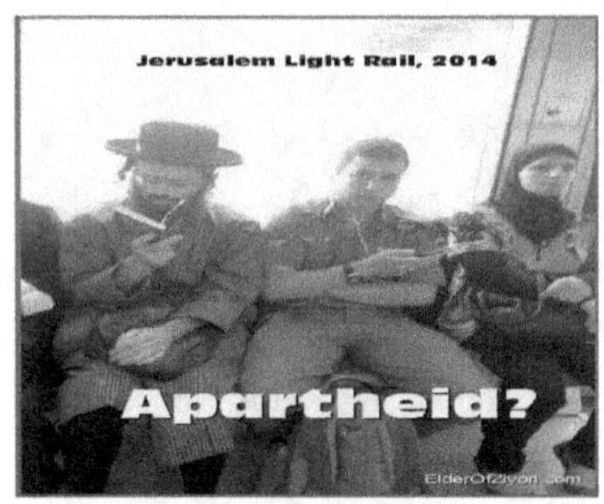

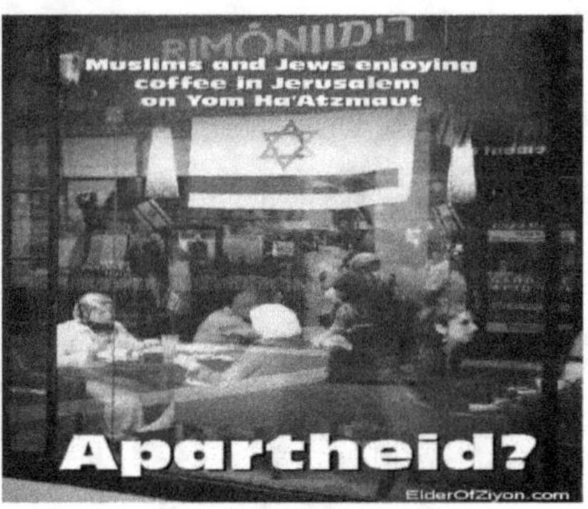

Some people are so filled with hate

they can't tell the difference.

Visible in the social order:

Visible in Academics and medicine:

Visible in the government and the military:

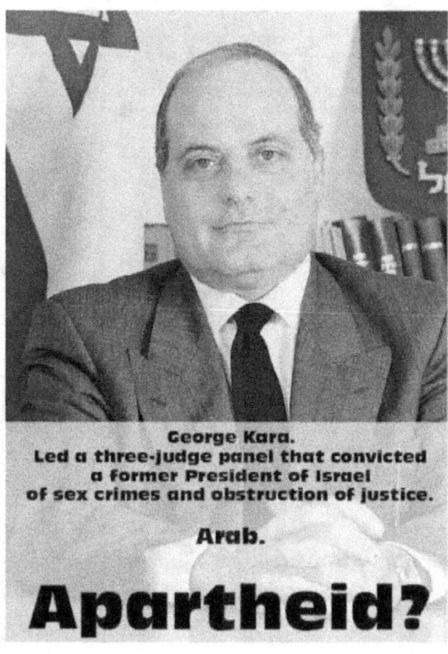

Visible in politics:

Visible in the entertainment, fashion and beauty industries:

Apartheid?
Lina Makhoul.
Chosen by Israeli
viewers as
2013 winner of
"The Voice."
Arab.
ElderOfZiyon.com

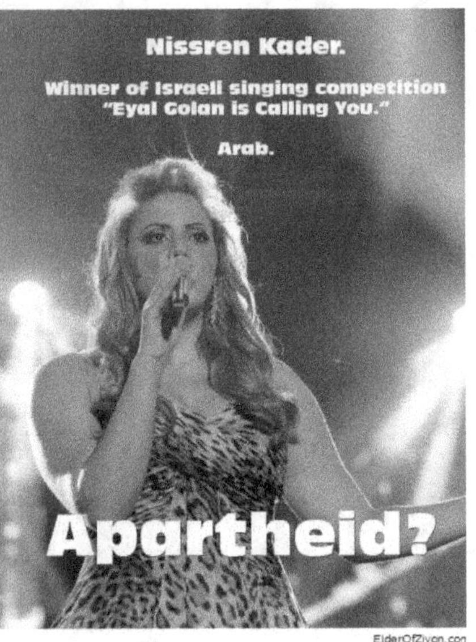

Nissren Kader.
Winner of Israeli singing competition
"Eyal Golan is Calling You."
Arab.
Apartheid?
ElderOfZiyon.con

Yiytish Aynaw.
Miss Israel 2013.
Apartheid?
ElderOfZiyon.com

Walid Badir.
Israeli football star.
Captain of
HaPoel Tel Aviv.
Arab.
Apartheid?
StandWithUs
ElderOfZiyon.com

Rana Raslan.
Former Miss Israel.
Arab.
Apartheid?
StandWithUs
ElderOfZiyon

Mira Awad.
Actress, singer, songwriter.
Represented Israel at the 2009
Eurovision Song Contest.
Arab.
Apartheid?
StandWithUs
ElderOfZiyon.com

Niral Karantinji.
Winner of Israel's Next Top Model.
Arab.
Apartheid?
ElderOfZiyon.com

"I will never allow a single Israeli to live among us on Palestinian land"
- Mahmoud Abbas, July 28 2010, speaking to Egyptian media
Now, that is Apartheid!
StandWithUs
Elder of Ziyon

Palestinian camp in Lebanon
Every Arab country has laws discriminating against Palestinians.
Now, that is apartheid!
StandWithUs
ElderofZiyon.com

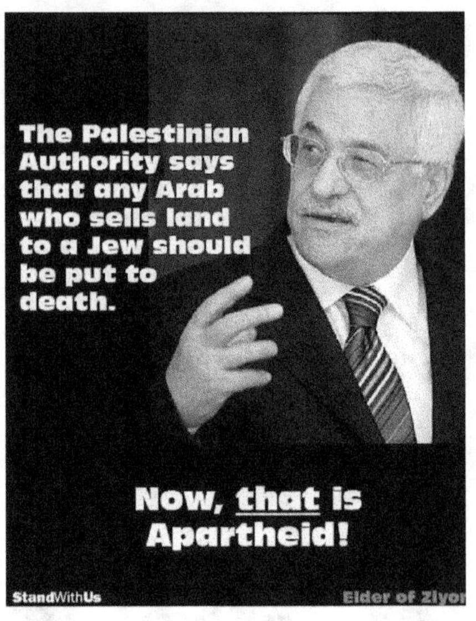
The Palestinian Authority says that any Arab who sells land to a Jew should be put to death.
Now, that is Apartheid!
StandWithUs
Elder of Ziyon

This Saudi stadium seats 68,000 men.
And no women.
King Fahd International Stadium
Riyadh, Saudi Arabia
Women are banned from attending games
When is Saudi Apartheid Week?
ElderOfZiyon.com

To remove any ambiguity and create some clarity, the term apartheid was first focused on South Africa. Accurate history is very important when exposing lies.

According to the **1998 Rome Statute**, the "crime of apartheid" is defined as "inhumane acts… committed in the context of an institutionalized regime of systematic oppression and domination by one racial group over any other racial group or groups and committed with the intention of maintaining that regime."

Libels about "Israeli Apartheid", despite proofs, are notoriously resistant to facts and truth, like mutant bacteria that resist antibiotics.

> **Anyone who knows anything at all about the Middle East understands that Zionism could never produce an apartheid regime. Zionism has been the opposite of racism in every way.**

The UNGA voted that Zionism is Racism. Racism claims superiority, while Zionism claims distinctiveness.

Racism seeks the persecution of powerless groups, while Zionism seeks to protect the members of a group long persecuted.

Racism seeks to degrade its victims, while Zionism seeks to protect those who have been victims of degradation.

Racism refers to beliefs and practices that assume inherent and significant differences exist between the genetics of various groups of human beings; that assume these differences can be measured on a scale of "superior" to "inferior"; and that result in the social, political and economic advantage of one group in relation to others.

Far from apartheid, Jews, Judaism, Jewish Law, and Jewish Zionists hold that any person may choose to become a Jew, via prescribed conversion procedures, and enjoy all the benefits and responsibilities of membership. Since anyone (i.e. regardless of race) can join the Jewish people with equality, we must conclude that Zionism is anti-racist. One of the benefits of Israel, according to the Zionists, is the right to live freely without fear of persecution, as a Jew, in the national homeland Israel.

Apartheid, which can be seen all through the Arab-Muslim world is based on the Islamic notion of inherent racial superiority.

An office holder in the **Palestinian Authority, Sari Nusseibeh**, threatens that a Jewish state must by definition be either a theocracy or an apartheid state, and that its Jewish nature opens the door to legally reducing its substantial non-Jewish minority "to second-class citizens (or perhaps even stripping them of their citizenship and other rights)."

But, Arabs have enjoyed full equality before the law since its founding. The designation of Arabic as an official language, the legal recognition of non-Jewish religious holidays, granting of educational, cultural, judicial, and religious autonomy, should be proof enough to thwart the lies. In Israel's entire history, Arabs in Israel have enjoyed more formal prerogatives than ethnic minorities anywhere in the Middle East or Africa.

Let's use some common sense. If the accusation of such racist policies were in fact true, why are the non-Jewish inhabitants of Israel not clamoring to emigrate to other countries, particularly the Arab countries?

Arabic is posted on all road signs.

Israel is the only country in the Middle East that has taken in Darfur refugees, the only country in the Middle East that gives refuge to gay men and women, the only country in the Middle East that protects the Bahia's.

In <u>The War Against the Jews</u>, **Efraim Karsh** (Israel Affairs(#8802) July 31, 2012) stated that while the affluent Arab classes left in the 1940's, those who were left were basically those who were impoverished. With Israel's help, by 2002, 86% of Arab households occupied dwellings of three or more rooms. Government allocations to Arab municipalities have grown steadily over the past forty years and are now on a par with the subsidies to the Jewish sector.

In 2005, **CAMERA** noted that "[t]hrough natural growth, and immigration (both legal and illegal) from the West Bank, Jerusalem's Arab population [grew] from 25.8 percent of the city in 1967, just after reunification, to more than 33 percent" at the end of 2003. Between 1967 and 2003, Jerusalem's Arab population increased by 233 percent, while its Jewish population increased by just 129 percent. So much for the propaganda that the government won't let the Arabs can't live where they want.

With facts like these, how can this be considered apartheid or ethnic cleansing? Let's look at a map of real ethnic cleansing of the Jewish People from Arab countries. Compare it with Arab growth in Israel

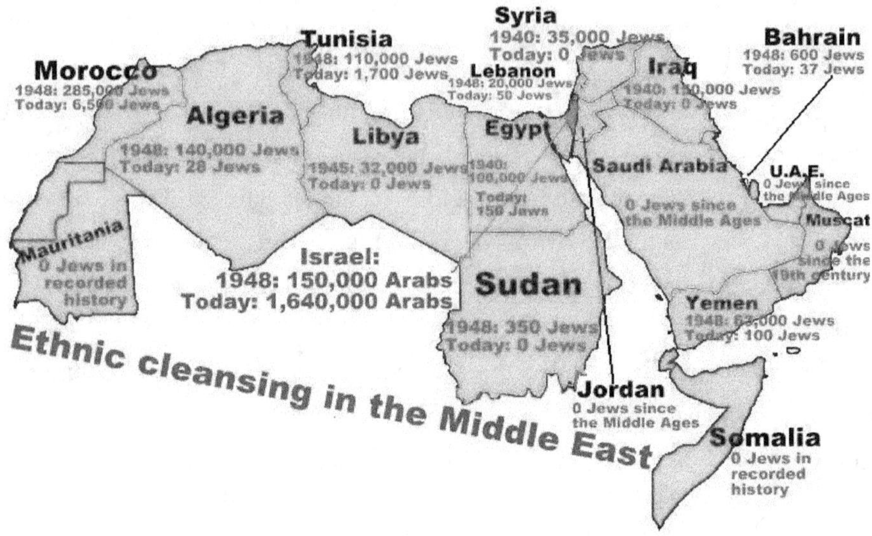

Jerusalem, 2012, has 800,000 residents, including 268,000 Arabs. In the nearly 45 years since the 1967 Six Day War, the Arab population has grown by 200,000, and many Arabs today covet their Israeli rights and services. The number of Arab Jerusalemites granted Israeli citizenship quadrupled from 2006 to 2010. If Israel is engaged in ethnic cleansing how is it that Israel has seen an Arab population increase due to higher quality of life including more freedoms?

WHAT FREEDOMS DO MUSLIM COUNTRIES DO COMPARED TO ISRAEL?

Example #1: The **Bahai**'s are severely persecuted in Iran, flourish in Israel, where they have their world center. In Iran, the Bahai's (the largest religious minority) are forbidden to study in any university or to run their own universities.

Example #2: Ahmadi Muslims, severely persecuted in Pakistan and elsewhere, are kept safe by Israel; the holy places of all religions are protected under a specific Israeli law. Arabs in Israel can go anywhere they want, unlike blacks in apartheid South Africa. They use public transport, they eat in restaurants, they go to swimming pools, they use libraries, they go to cinemas alongside Jews - something no blacks were able to do in South Africa. Is this apartheid?

Example #3: After the annexation of 1967, 70,000 Palestinians lived in the annexed territory in 1967, and found themselves under Israeli rule. Israel offered these residents citizenship, which was rejected collectively on the grounds that accepting Israeli citizenship would legitimize the annexation and obliterate the residents' Palestinian identity. Therefore, the residents of eastern Jerusalem received the status of permanent residents of Israel. After the annexation of 1967, 70,000 Palestinians held blue identity cards; at the beginning of 2010 the number was estimated at 300,000. In 1967 they constituted 25% of the total population of the "united" Jerusalem, now they constitute more than 35%.

Why? Because it is better than living under a brutal and corrupt P.A.

According to face-to-face surveys conducted according to the highest international standards, more Palestinians in east Jerusalem would prefer to become citizens of Israel rather than citizens of a new Palestinian state.

In addition, 40% said they would probably or definitely move in order to live under Israeli rather than Palestinian rule. "What Do the Arabs of East Jerusalem Really Want" - **David Pollock** (Institute for Contemporary Affairs-Jerusalem Center for Public Affairs)

That is certainly not Apartheid, yet the media unthinkingly continue to pass around this distortion. Propaganda tries to make Israeli hospital's medical care for Arab-Palestinian children and training of doctors appear second rate.

The official PA daily reported on a visit by the PA Minister of Health, **Hani Abdeen**, to Israel's Hadassah Hospital in Jerusalem. The daily noted "that 30% of the child patients in Hadassah are Arab-Palestinians and that the

Israeli hospital is training "… sixty Palestinian medical interns and specialist physicians who will be returning to the [Palestinian] Authority areas to carry out their work. The hospital has a special program to train Palestinian doctors to treat cancer among children", reported the PA daily. Who would condemn Israel for "apartheid"?

http://www.palwatch.org/main.aspx?fi=157&doc_id=9049 by Itamar Marcus and Nan Jacques Zilberman 5-22-13

> **Example #4:** Israeli hospitals not only treat Jews and Arabs, they also treat Arab-Palestinians from Gaza or the West Bank on the same wards, in the same operating theaters.

There are EIGHT "West Bank" offices open 24 hours a day for health care of the citizens there.

In Israel, women have the same rights as men: there is no gender apartheid. Gay men and women face no restrictions, and Palestinian gays often escape into Israel, knowing they may be killed at home.

The **Circassians** (about 4,000 Sunni Muslims) in Israel refers to the **Adyghe** community who live in Israel. They tend to put an emphasis on the separation between their religion and their nationality. Most other Muslims do not.

As is the case with the Israeli Jews and the **Israeli Druze** population groups living in the state of Israel (except for the Israeli Druze population living on the Golan Heights) must complete the Israeli mandatory military service since 1958. This includes all male Circassians (at their leader's request) upon reaching the age of majority, while females do not. The percentage of the army recruits among the Circassian community in Israel is particularly high.

> **Example #5** At **Shaare Zedek Hospital** in Jerusalem, "coexistence is not a dream; it is a normal reality," says **Dr. Eli Picard,** Director of the Pediatric Pulmonary Unit. Rather than ignore religious and ethnic differences, Shaare Zedek

respects them. This credo is most vividly displayed in our Pediatric Dialysis Unit. More than 70% of the Unit's patients are Arab children. Friendships often develop between the Arab and Jewish families, as they discover over a cup of coffee that there is much more that unites them – particularly the challenges of coping with an ill child – than that which divides them.

Shaare Zedek Medical Center also believes that one of the key components of treating patients is being able to speak to them in their own language, in a voice that they can understand. It is to be expected that the Hospital would have its share of Russian, Yiddish, and Arabic speakers, but there are also Norwegian, Filipino, Ladino, Croatian and Chinese speakers on staff. At last count, more than 40 languages are spoken at Shaare Zedek!

A report published recently by Israel's Coordinator of Government Activities in the Territories Unit (COGAT) shows that 219,464 Arab-Palestinian patients received medical treatment in Israeli hospitals during 2012–21,270 of them children. These numbers include companions accompanying the patients to Israel.

The numbers show a dramatic increase in Arab-Palestinians receiving treatment from Israeli medical professionals. 197,713 Arab-Palestinians received medical treatment in Israel in 2011, and 144,838 in 2008. "Increase in Palestinians Treated in Israeli Hospitals" By **Aryeh Savir** Tazpit News Agency http://www.algemeiner.com/2013/08/02/increase-in-palestinians-treated-in-israeli-hospitals/ August 2, 2013

Simon says:

From our research it is clear that we are not finished with this topic. Professional propagandists can be convincing and very, very good when well-funded. We better get more supplies and more information on how this has blanketed so many cloistered academic thinking individuals because we are going to be here a lot longer.

We must respect how powerful propaganda can fool even the smartest. We need to be able to identify when something is propaganda so that we can resist and expose it.

It shakes me that so many people fall for propaganda or do not have the interest to have independent sources of information.

But I admit that I was once that way, too. I bet you were, too.

Kelsey and Salo, have discovered even more proof in five additional major propaganda techniques and themes.

One of the cute ones is the "They claim" technique which she will share with us in the next chapter.

#7 The Mysterious Kidnapping of the Fourth Estate

"The ultimate result of shielding men from the effects of folly is to fill the world with fools." Herbert Spencer, English Philosopher

Simon Says:

I thought we'd be finished with this propaganda avalanche by now, but I was fooled. Weren't you?

Now we learn that there are more ways we can be duped. I didn't realize the jeopardy in which it places the average person who reads one newspaper or watches only a favorite news channel, or one radio station without getting other coverage. It turns discourse into rants, emotional posturing, blame games, misdirection, and the name calling creates bitterness and divisiveness. At the end of this chapter, I found five more major divisions and too many examples to consider these merely coincidence, so I put them in a ten-page annex for the more curious. We can be fooled more by the media than anywhere else. It is time to expose more tricks of TerVol.

Media Bias is a ravenous termite form of propaganda and ultimately more damaging to people's understanding of events. What you don't know can hurt you. Public opinion is largely shaped through the mainstream media (MSM), whether news or entertainment. They reach the largest audiences. To be professional and ethical, the media must follow certain rules. If they do not, they are biased. If it's repetitive and emotion-based, it's propaganda.

Next to truly free democratic elections, the most essential pillar of a functioning democracy is the mainstream news media's integrity. It is supposed to be an antidote and vaccine when government power is excessive, irresponsible, lacks transparency, or is not held accountable. It is supposed to let us know where crime is being committed here and internationally. It is supposed to expose corruption and greed in business, lies and thefts by government employees so that the public is aware of what is happening. The media has the power to be like a 5th column. This incredible power is exposed in "Red Lines: HonestReporting.com's 8 Categories of Media Bias" Kindle Edition by Pesach Benson (Editor)

"There are laws to protect the freedom of the press's speech, but none that are worth anything to protect the people from the press." **Mark Twain**

We found several relevant examples of media partiality, favoritism and bias

The media (who get much of the information from the government) loses its credibility when they lack aggressive, balanced and fact-checked reporting with verifiable sources.

The Main Stream Media (MSM) must be a source of unbiased coverage placed in context; appropriate, honest photos with accurate captions, equal space given to credible sources of both sides of a dispute or event; giving appropriate prominence to an event, page placement in the paper (front or back), article placed next to a photo of another article and opinion conclusions based on facts.

"Above the line" is a term used by the printed press that is used for what the editor thinks is most important as it appears above the fold on the front page. Any failure of the media steals the citizen's rights in a constitutional democracy. At that point, the main stream media has become a mouthpiece of propaganda for an oligarchy from which they reap rewards. http://www.americanthinker.com/2011/11/palestinian_identity_theft.html by **Jerold S. Auerbach,** professor emeritus of history at Wellesley College, blogs at www.jacobsvoice.tumblr.com.

Most of the American and European public is aware they must depend on the "independent" MSM for information, and movies/plays/books to get an emotional understanding. The majority of Americans still lack confidence in the mass media to report the news in context, balanced, accurately and fairly.

Gallup has measured the power of headlines, based on over 1,000 telephone interviews conducted Sept. 8-11, 2011. The 44% of Americans who have a great deal or fair amount of trust and the 55% who have little or no trust remain among the most negative views. On the average, five times as many people read headlines as the body of the article, yet a Majority in U.S. Continues to Distrust the Media, Perceive Bias September 22, 2011 by **Lymari Morales** WASHINGTON, D.C

"Here are just a few of literally hundreds of examples that we found by ourselves. We tried not to overwhelm you with the full list because you would fall asleep because of its length," added Simon.

> **Example #1:** Journalist, **Matti Friedman,** has shared extremely valuable and revealing observations about press coverage of Israel, in an article entitled, "An Insider's Guide to the Most Important Story on Earth that the foreign media and its coverage is against Israel."

"As a former insider, and as an Israeli with left-wing opinions that are not radical, I think the decisions that the bureaus of the large global media outlets in Israel make are politically motivated and disguised as motivated by journalistic considerations…"

"The people who make the decisions at the newspapers – I speak from direct experience – are hostile toward Israel. They see themselves as part of an ideological alliance that includes NGOs and UN agencies.

"…They move in social circles that are pro-Palestinian and hostile toward Israel and, and they see journalism not as a way to explain the complex story to people but as a political weapon with which they arm one side in the conflict."

According to Friedman, activism has trickled into the profession. "It's political activism disguised as journalism. If you don't agree to run the most important story of the year because it will make Israel look good, then you are an activist. You are here not to explain, but to use your influence for the benefit of your own side." http://www.haaretz.com/news/features/.premium-1.615621 http://www.tabletmag.com/jewish-news-and-politics/183033/israel-insider-guide. 9-14-14

Even the **Wall Street Journal** had to correct its brethren MSM on the identity of the thugs who stormed the British embassy in Tehran — breaking windows, burning the British flag, ransacking offices, trashing a portrait of the Queen, and terrorizing the staff. The Journal notes the attack was not impromptu. "Police stood by, and Iranian state television broadcast events live."

But, continues the editorial, "By some strange reflex, Western media insisted the attackers were 'students.'" To Iranians who know better, they were the **basij** militia, the regime's first line of defense. These are thugs who were called out to brutally put down the 2009 Green Revolution—a genuine student-led uprising.

International demagogues use propaganda to demonize those who they would destroy by appealing to emotions, particularly fear. Propaganda energy is first focused internally on the people of that country. It is directed against those they chose to oppose.

The media is sometimes the tool and sometimes the source of war propaganda. Since sloppy journalism is always looking for fresh news, it quickly loses interest in past events and even history. With no past, there is no future. With no context, there is no clarity.

Propaganda is a way of creating allies and enemies. It relies on the media to spread its distortions. Israel, from its inception, has been reluctant to fight for its recognition as a legitimate state in the eyes of the media. This lack of enthusiasm to respond encouraged the enemy to increase Israel's delegitimization in the eyes of the free world. The wealthy Arab/Muslim world can successfully limit the IDF's freedom of action by propaganda claiming the most horrid of stories, controlling the media.

The MSM and Israeli leadership are guilty in three ways for not exposing the pervasiveness of this hatred behind the terror attacks on civilians in Israel.

First, they relayed, as authoritative news, unsubstantiated Palestinian lethal narratives of blood libels.

Second, they did **not** report the hate in the Arab media, their mosques and their schools that inspired such narratives.

In the summer of 2000, the PA/Arab World machine was hurricane blasting hatred of Israel. If the MSM was surprised by Arafat's "no" at Camp David, it's because they ignored what he and his compatriots were saying in Arabic when they actually had access to that information. Those worshipping at Camp David alter were driven by a fanatical belief that peace was around the corner. They felt that dwelling on such bad news would dump the process they had labeled the answer to "peace."

And third, those responsible for the safety of the Israeli citizens did not respond in an adequate way or any way at all to the provocations and multiple individual attacks.

They are many examples proving a media bias against Israel with the tacit support of the current government. It seems there is a group of ideological journalists whose job is to catalogue Jewish /Israeli moral failings. They are often rewarded by their editors with better assignments, more publications, getting invited to dinner parties or getting promoted. People need examples to understand some things.

Simon had to interrupt with this wise warning by **Cicero**: "A nation can survive its fools, and even the ambitious. But it cannot survive treason from within. An enemy at the gates is less formidable, for he is known and carries his banner openly. But the traitor moves amongst those within the gate freely, his sly whispers rustling through all the alleys, heard in the very halls of government itself. For the traitor appears not a traitor; he speaks in accents familiar to his victims, and he wears their face and their arguments, he appeals to the baseness that lies deep in the hearts of all men. He rots the soul of a nation, he works secretly and unknown in the night to undermine the pillars of the city, he infects the body politic so that it can no longer resist. A murderer is less to fear."

> **Example #2:** The Oslo propaganda war was supported by the press's religion of "peace around the corner" that virtually completely ignored **Sheikh Halabiya**'s sermon calling on Muslims to slaughter the Jews (not just Israelis) everywhere. **William Orme** wrote a piece on Palestinian incitement in which he quoted Halabiya saying: "Labor, Likud, they're all Jews." The press mostly ignored this, too.

Example #3: Propaganda acts by way of hiding information. **Haj Amin al Husseini**, the **Muslim Mufti of Jerusalem** spent months with Hitler in Berlin over 70 years ago. Editors spiked most of the reports and minimized that history from us.

The Mufti's contribution to the "final solution" was pumped into the Arab world with Nazi propaganda. The mufti spent time recruiting 20,000 Muslim volunteers for the SS, who participated in the killing of Jews in Croatia and Hungary.

Historical research, not the MSM, indicated there were many Nazis who escaped justice and fled to Egypt, Syria and Iraq to continue their work. Burying this is not a quirk of journalism, but a widespread practice of a "post-colonial" mind set of Middle East studies in the wake of **Edward Said**'s guilt trip masterpiece of cognitive warfare forbidding Westerners from "othering" Muslims.

Example #4: The "First Lebanon War": Israel fought to protect its civilians from relentless rockets, but the outcome wasn't decided in the battlefield. It was the media pressure, which became unbearable for the Israeli leaders. That determined the date and method at which the Israeli military evacuated Lebanon. This meant that Hezbollah could celebrate the expulsion of the IDF. That is propaganda. They used that to gain unprecedented strength in Lebanese politics.

In addition, with the MSM and their fauxtography, terrorist groups can expect enthusiastic recruiting of fighters and money for their causes. Its "truth" is projected in the media and it is this "truth" that forms the trusting public opinion. The IDF has caused stunningly minimal "collateral damage" to innocent civilians, despite Arab Hezbollah and Hamas fighters using human shields in every conceivable way.

Any fighting force in densely populated areas, particularly cities, has increased collateral damage because civilians are in harm's way. Israel's image was defamed in the media when the facts were reported later. Reporters, commentators and headlines must be brief. Without positive media coverage, there is no chance to win the media war. The media war then politicizes the war. Often, like in Vietnam for the Americans, or in Lebanon for Israel, this means winning the war, full speed ahead or not at all. http://www.israeldefense.com/? CategoryID=483&ArticleID=1626&print=1 Israel Resource Review Israeldefense.com, Sept. 7, 2011.

> **Example #5:** The UNGA "partition' Resolution #181 in 1947 referred to "the Jewish State" and "the Arab State," and expressed hope for cooperation "between the two Palestinian peoples." This means that "Palestinian" does not refer only to Arabs, yet the press continued on that distortion.

> **Example #6:** It the UN's 1947 partition resolution referenced "the hill country of **Samaria and Judea."** That is a term that is almost 3,000 years old. UNGA #181 never mentioned a "West Bank", yet journalists repeat the **newly minted 1950 Jordanian designation** as though it always existed. For Israel or the U.S., it is in the east and should be called the "East Bank."

> **Example #7:** The wild accusation of the death of little Mohammed al Dura by Israeli troops was proven a sensationally mendacious accusation, yet it throbbed through the media for years, with the purpose of defaming Israel.

In the tactical media war theater, Israel's enemies have shown exceptional creativity, unlimited fabrications, money and talent to capture and select the most "incriminating" pictures and videos against the Israeli Defense Forces and give them excitable captions. This has happened even when the picture had nothing to do with the event or even took place in the same country.

As in the Mahmoud al-Dura canard, many in the media have not shied away from staging incidents for the purpose of filming "brutal Israeli Defense Forces (IDF) behavior."

Wounded children, ambulances, schools and mosques are among the favorite "decorations" for the fabrication of such movies. Sure, the IDF has caused "collateral damage" to civilians, as would any fighting force in densely populated areas, but its image has been defamed in the media, far out of proportion to the real events or compared to other fighting forces.

The enemy's success in this arena is such that the IDF and U.S. military are forced to limit their actions to a fraction of their capabilities. This becomes government policy—tactical maneuvers designed to avoid incidents rather than achieve a self-protective goal. This failure of goals is called "incidentism." It is to put avoiding an incident above winning. The U.S. has also fallen into this trap, but its enemies have not.

General Douglas MacArthur warned that "It is fatal to enter any war without the will to win it." **British Admiral John Fisher** was clearer, "Moderation in war is imbecility."

Salo had to interrupt, "I even saw an independent video of an Arab funeral for one of their martyrs. Hundreds of people cried, screamed, pushed and shoved as the body was being taken for burial. The pall bearers accidentally tilted the open coffin, and the body fell off its stage. To everyone's surprise, the corpse got up and climbed on to continue the televised show."

> **Example #8:** In the summer of 2014, the New Yorker magazine described the summer's events by dedicating one sentence each to the momentous horrors in Nigeria and the Ukraine, four sentences of the bloody ISIS massacres and thirty sentences to Israel and Gaza. The imbalance exposes the bias.

> **Example #9:** In 2008, when **PM Ehud Olmert** made an extremely generous offer to the P.A. leader **Mahmoud Abbas**, he replied that it was not good enough. The Associated Press chose not to report that Israel made a desperate peace offer which was rebuffed. The average citizen never knew.

The Associated Press had more staffers in Israel than all the "Arab Spring" countries combined and where the action was. Why? Yet, at the same time, the murderous Hamas charter was never mentioned. That technique is called "whitewashing.". One thousand and six hundred women were murdered in **Pakistan** in 2013, 193 of which were burned alive; the Mexican drug wars showed a death toll from 2006 to 2012 of 60,000; 5 million humans died (as of 2012) in the Congo, yet the press continued to act like Israel was the most important story on the planet. That is more than bias. It borders on Nazi propaganda. They have kept the world ignorant of major tragedies.

Example #10: The impact of media bias and propaganda in Europe is evidenced from a huge study by the **German Friedrich Ebert Foundation**: 63% of Poles and 48% of Germans think "Israel is conducting a war of extermination against the Palestinians." Meanwhile, 41% of the British and 42% of the Hungarians think the same thing, as well as 38% of Italians. In the survey, 55% of Poles and 36% of Germans responded: "Considering Israel's policy, I can understand why people do not like Israel." This is from a 2013 article. https://www.gatestoneinstitute.org/4100/israelophobia www.fes-gegen-rechtsextremismus.de ISBN 978-3-86872-653-4

Example #11: The MSM showed Israel uprooting more than 8,000 of its citizens, and generations of Israelis from their homes in the Gaza District. Some had lived there for three decades. Israel withdrew every soldier, evacuated every Jew, dug up bodies from graves, and left nothing behind except the valuable greenhouses in which the Israelis had grown fruit and flowers for profitable export in hopes of improving the Gaza economy. Those hi-tech greenhouses were trashed within two days following the Arab takeover. That part of the tragedy barely got media coverage. The unbalanced MSM regurgitated Hamas propaganda following this enormous and painful deracination, that the thousands and thousands of rockets that they shot at Israeli civilian homes and schools after removal of the Israelis, were "resistance to the occupation". The MSM never reported it for what it clearly was, a "crime against humanity". The Hamas narrative considers all of Israel occupied, illegitimate, a cancer, and a crime against humanity. Hamas's objective, openly declared, is to "liberate", that is destroy Tel Aviv and the rest of pre-1967 Israel. The Muslim Brotherhood founded Hamas, and elimination of Israel is their constitutional 'raison d'être. Should not the MSM cover this boldly?

If the League of nations was silent, why not the MSM? The **League of Nations** was mostly silent as Muslims slaughtered Jews in Israel in 1920, 1921,1929,1936,1937 and 1938. To the average person, this means the carnage did not happen.

Why doesn't the MSM educate us to the facts: the sniping, rocket firefighting, attacks, marauding or battles predated the Jewish State. **On-going attacks from 1900 to the 1940's proves that "occupation" could not have had anything to do with causing war.**

All the defensive fighting Israel had to do before 1967 had nothing to do with presumption of "occupation." Yet the MSM spreads the idea that the hatred and murder is due to "occupation."

Example #11: "Dutch orchestra attacked": At the end of July the Palestinian News Network published an article widely distributed among international media outlets. It covered a story about a Dutch orchestra that was supposedly attacked by the IDF during a performance in the Palestinian village Kfar Qadum. However, a member of the orchestra wrote a detailed account about the actual events. The orchestra was not playing, but participating in the weekly, often-violent demonstrations against an IDF checkpoint in the vicinity of the village. The missing piece in the accounts was that Arabs started throwing stones at the soldiers, precipitating the whole incident. There was no performance and no peaceful demonstration.

Example #12: "Olive trees destroyed" is another claim that originated from an Arab-Palestinian source, involved the alleged destruction of 200 olive trees in the village Al Walaja near Bethlehem. There was no investigation or supporting information before the MSM had disseminated it all over the world.

The media also covered a story that an Arab would lose his land to Givat Ya'el - a planned Jewish community adjacent to Al Walaja. The truth was "In accordance with Israeli Supreme Court rulings regarding the rerouting of Israel's security fence, the Israel Defense Forces (IDF) transplanted trees from Mr. Na'el Khalil's property to an adjacent plot, ensuring that he was able to continue working his land. The Israeli court authorities have previously denied several petitions seeking ownership of the land adjacent to the Palestinian village Al-Walajah by the Givat Ya'el community, a private building project in Judea." The Arab newspaper Al Ahram reported it one sided.

Example #13: The Arab newspaper, Al Ahram and The Economist "Bemoan Fate of Stone Throwers". According to The Economist, Israel routinely arrests Palestinian minors at night, some as young as eleven, and "shows no mercy" when they stand trial.

Contrary to what was written in The Economist's article, there are almost no cases where Palestinian minors under the age of 14 have been convicted for stone throwing. Trials are quick, defendants have legal representation, and most minors are released.

The Economist also quoted, actually misquoted Israeli, **Eran Segal**, from Halamish, allegedly saying that "Israeli soldiers don't maim enough

Palestinians". Segal denied he ever said a thing like that. In fact, he had told The Economist: "If the IDF would have taken the incidents more seriously and had acted in a different way, the stone throwing would have been a thing of the past".

> **Example #14:** The **Egyptian paper, Al Ahram** charged "Israel's most aggressively racist government ever with prosecuting and imprisoning Palestinian children at will on bogus charges such as throwing stones". These were lies disseminated to the ignorant masses.

The Israeli Military Prosecutor's Office pointed out that "stone" throwing is a criminal offense in Israel (and in the U.S.). Often these are very large stones, pieces of concrete and bricks. This is done by crowds of 10-30 people. Throwing a barrage of stones can cause severe injuries and even - as has happened in the past - death. Israeli law calls for the punishment of stone throwers, just like laws in the United States, even if they are minors and regardless of their nationality or religion.

> **Example #15:** Blatant lies are propaganda, too. In an e-mail to Missing Peace, **UNRWA's Gunnes** wrote the following: "127 people expelled in Ma'ale Nikhmas - displaced for settlement in the last few weeks. Is that enough?" Yet, the 127 Palestinians expelled from Maaleh Michmas 'displaced for settlement' were in fact Bedouins who decided to leave, as UNWRA's own press release states. There is no evidence that Ma'aleh Michmas residents took their place.

However, 16 Bedouin were evicted in the Maaleh Michnas area at the end of July after they illegally camped within a closed military zone and after they had received eviction orders two years previously. The MSM chose to bury this history from the public.

> **Example #16:** Some may have been fooled by the news from Al Jazeera. They carry the same event in two different languages for two different groups with different narratives poisoning people's minds: "Two Faces of Al Jazeera" by **Oren Kessler** Middle East Quarterly Winter 2012 http://www.me-forum.org/3147/al-jazeera

One of the principal beneficiaries of the Arab uprisings has been Al Jazeera television. Viewers are praising the English and Arabic channels' comprehensive coverage of the revolts while the Obama administration continues to court the network as part of its signature foreign policy goal of improving ties with the Arab and Muslim worlds. The fact that a vast gulf still separates the channel's English iteration from the original Arabic, which fifteen years after its birth continues to inflame Arab resentments in its promotion of anti-Americanism, Sunni sectarianism and, in recent years, Islamism.

On August 1, 2011, **Al Jazeera English** (AJE) began broadcasting to two million cable subscribers in New York, the third major U.S. city to carry the station after Houston and Washington, D.C. To appreciate what Al Jazeera English is, it's critical to remember it isn't remotely like its Arabic-speaking progenitor.

In the aftermath of the 9/11 terrorist attacks, **Fouad Ajami** traveled to Qatar to write a profile on **Al Jazeera Arabic** (AJA) for The New York Times Magazine. "Although Al Jazeera has sometimes been hailed in the West for being an autonomous, Arabic news outlet, it would be a mistake to call it a fair or responsible one," he wrote. "Day in and day out, Al Jazeera deliberately fans the flames of Muslim outrage."

In 2006, months before going on air, Al Jazeera English (AJE) hired **Dave Marash**, a former anchor for NBC Nightline. He cited a series called "Poverty in America" to illustrate what he described as AJE's underlying anti-Americanism. "This series reported nothing beyond the stereotype and the mere fact that there were homeless people living on the street in Baltimore ... It was enough for them to show poor people living in wretched conditions in a prosperous American city and decry it."

Judea Pearl expressed hope that Al Jazeera might "learn to harness its popularity in the service of humanity." "Today, we have much deeper concerns with Al Jazeera. It is no longer a clash with journalistic standards but a clash with the norms of civilized society," Pearl wrote. "Our charming infant is smashing windows now and poisoning pets in the neighborhood. A slap on the wrist is perhaps way overdue."

A correspondent of the Al Jazeera network in Cairo resigned from the Qatari broadcaster, accusing it of airing lies and misleading viewers. "Unfortunately, I was working in a place which I thought it had credibility, but it is credibility based on a despicable political position," said **Wessam Fadel.**

Al Jazeera is closely linked to the Muslim Brotherhood to which Egyptian ex-president, Mursi, belonged. Qatar, from which Al Jazeera originates, is a gas-rich Gulf emirate and staunch backer and financier of the Mursi regime http://gulfnews.com/news/region/egypt/al-jazeera-correspondent-in-cairo-quits1206719.

Propaganda using Spin

It started with an enlarging guerrilla war in 1947. After the Arab countries rejected the United Nations Partition Plan and many of the Arabs living on the land, became full belligerents in the conflict. Rather than accept a Jewish state in 1948, after five-and-a-half months of low level warfare, Palestinian Arabs called upon their brethren from six surrounding countries to invade and crush the nascent Jewish state. Five actually sent troops.

Academically only, the term "Nakba" first entered the language in 1920, to describe the calamity in Arab eyes who saw themselves as Syrians and were enraged by being cut off from their homeland when the victorious Allies divided the land cutting off "northern" Syrians from "southern" Syrians. There was no Zionist state then. That Nakba had nothing to do with the Jews. (from "the Arab Awakening", page 312 by **George Antonious**). The Arab's media kept repeating that the birth of the Jewish State of Israel was their "Nakba", holding the state as being illegitimate. This is powerful propaganda to their children who now believe that the land was theirs (as a people), it was stolen from them and that they had the right to take it by any means possible. It is also an Islamic precept that any land whenever and wherever conquered is theirs in perpetuity.

The **Alliance of Civilizations**, formed by the Organization of the Islamic Conference (OIC) in the UN in 2005, actually used the Nakba politically to be a propaganda counterweight to the Holocaust and thereby impose their "narrative" on the West.

Palestinian Authority President, **Mahmoud Abbas,** also tried to establish as a fact for media preservation, that Arab armies "intervened" to stop the alleged efforts to expel Arabs and create a Jewish majority. Virtually every history book, outside the Arab world, notes that Arab terrorists had attacked Jews for decades, most overtly in the 1929 pogrom in Hevron, where Arabs slaughtered 67 Jews, burning many alive. Mahmoud Abbas wrote that "war and further expulsions" ensued but omitted reminding readers that every war against Israel was launched by Arabs. He did not mention the war drums that seven Arab nations kept beating until the beginning of the Six Day War in 1967.

Propaganda can make up new words that piggy back on the emotional resonance of like "racism". **Nonie Darwish** lived half her life in the Middle East, specifically Egypt. She became especially sensitive to recognizing fake outrage and shaming forced upon ordinary people by the social system. She says that this intentional shaming, often fake and bogus, is done to claim moral superiority for the purpose of manipulating and controlling others. In America, expressions like "racist", and in the Muslim world expressions like "apostate", can do the trick of silencing citizens and keeping them muzzled and beaten down. Sometimes the labels can be legitimate and that is why it works. She continues that the Muslim world is at the top of the list of cultures that perfected the art of fake and exhibitionist. It is a term used to imply that someone is a bigot and racist, morally degenerate and whose discourse is unacceptable. When done on the internet it is now called cyber-bullying.

"Islamophobia" is about what isn't; and "Islamoreality" is about what is "It seems we have all been taken in. I am embarrassed. I will share part of what I learned", lamented Tom.

1   **Example**: In 1830 at **NYU Prof. Bush's** book stated what Islamoreality is prepared to offer, "[Mohammed] promised robes of silks, marble palaces, groves and fountains and beautiful virgins to those who fought for the faith…offering his enemies the alternative; the Koran or the sword…. It was inflamed by zeal for a totalitarian religion which assured the soldier of victory now and paradise hereafter. The permanence of this religion is now apparently secured by education…in regions where freedom of thought is unknown (p. 155-6)."

…"O prophet of God, I will beat out the teeth, pull out the eyes, rip open the bellies and cut off the legs of all who shall dare to oppose thee" (pp. 36-37) … [Muhammed] was cruel on principle. He did deliberately what other men do from impulse…. The ambition which tramples on the right of men to think or to live is the greatest of human crimes…. The sword is the key of heaven and hell. A drop of blood shed in the cause of God is of more avail than two months of fast and prayers. Whosoever falls in the battle his sins are forgiven… and the loss of his limbs shall be replaced by the wing of angels (103-4) …Hatred of Christians and Jews is rooted in their hearts from childhood (p. 137)"

2.   **Example:** Some allege that **Thomas Jefferson** used to keep a Koran by his bed. It was purely political and military for him to understand his adversaires. He did study the Koran, but to become more knowledgeable about a chief enemy, the Muslim Barbary Pirates, who plundered American ships, enslaved Americans, demanded protection money and ransom for their release. During 1784-1789, while Jefferson (the 3rd US President) was ambassador to France and John Adams (the 2nd US President) was ambassador to England, they met with the Barbary Ambassador to London, in an attempt to stop the anti-US piracy. **Ambassador Sidi Haji Abdrahaman** told them: "[Piracy] was founded on the laws of the Prophet, as it was written in the Quran; that all nations which had not acknowledged [Islam's] authority were sinners; that it was [the Moslem's] right and duty to make

war upon them and enslave them as prisoners, and that every Muslim slain in battle was sure to go to Paradise."

3. **Example:** Some talking heads have said that Islam is a "religion of peace". This fable is not even new. **John Quincy Adams**, sixth US President (1825-1829), thought otherwise a long time ago. He wrote after his presidency and before his election to Congress in 1830:

"The precept of the Koran is perpetual war against all who deny that Mahomet is the prophet of God. The vanquished may purchase their lives, by the payment of tribute; the victorious may be appeased by a false and delusive promise of peace; and the faithful follower of the prophet, may submit to the imperious necessities of defeat: but the command to propagate the Moslem creed by the sword is always obligatory, when it can be made effective. [Mohamet] declared undistinguishing and exterminating war, as a part of his religion, against all the rest of mankind…. Between [Christianity and Islam], thus contrasted in their characters, a war of twelve hundred years has already raged. The war is yet flagrant…." (Blunt, 29:274).

4. **Example**: In 1916, **Teddy Roosevelt** observed: "Wherever the Mohammedans have had a complete sway, wherever the Christians have been unable to resist them by the sword, Christianity disappeared."

5. **Example: Ali Gomaa,** the grand mufti of Egypt, **the highest Muslim religious authority in the Sunni world,** supports murdering non-Muslims. In the daily Al Ahram (April 7, 2008), he said, "Muslims must kill non-believers wherever they are unless they convert to Islam." He also compares non-Muslims to apes and pigs.

6. **Example: PM Erdogan** of Turkey, speaking at the "Fifth Alliance of Civilizations Forum" in Vienna's Hofburg Palace bellowed, "Just like Zionism, anti-Semitism and fascism, it becomes unavoidable that Islamophobia must be regarded as a crime against humanity…" February/28/2013 VIENNA - Anatolia News Agency.

7. **Example**: When we hear that Islam does "council against war," does that mean that Muslims should surrender [to the enemy]? Islam states:

"Whatever good there is exists thanks to the sword and in the shadow of the sword! People cannot be made obedient except with the sword! The sword is the key to Paradise, which can be opened only for the Holy Warriors! There are hundreds of other (Qur'anic) psalms and Hadiths (sayings of the Prophet) urging Muslims to value war and to fight." O.K., this is "Islamoreality".

8. **Example:** The blueprint for American Sharia Courts, instead of American Courts and Constitution, was created as early as 1993 by TAM, **The American Muslims.**

9. **Example:** With but a smattering knowledge of history, it should be clear that the Jews are indigenous to the Holy Land. Alone among other nations, Jews' language, history, culture and folklore were born and forged in the Holy Land. There is no statute of limitations on being indigenous as long as a people continue to exist with the same identity and roots. Archeological discoveries continue to support that. The Jews are the oldest of any people on earth who have kept their national identity and cultural heritage intact.

Anti-Zionists repeatedly and dishonestly caterwaul that the Jews are colonizers in the Holy Land and the Arabs are victims. Their goal is delegitimizing the unbreakable, maternal ties to the land that make the Jews indigenous.

The repeated propaganda spread round the world by wealthy Arab/Muslim countries causes many countries and people to forget that Zionists did not steal Israel, nor did they conquer it. Jews had the right to return to the only place on the planet where they would be accepted as a nation in a world of massacres and persecutions.

10. **Example:** The claim is often made that in 1948 a Jewish minority owning only 5 per cent of the land of Palestine made itself master of the Arab majority, which owned 95 per cent of the land. In May of 1948 the State of Israel was established in only a small part of the area allotted by the original League of Nations Mandate and San Remo International Law. Over 8 per cent of the land was owned by Jews and

3.3 per cent by Arabs living in Israel. Sixteen and nine tenths percent of the land had been abandoned by Turkish and Arab owners who imprudently heeded the call from neighboring countries to "get out of the way" while the invading Arab armies made short shrift of Israel. The rest of the land, over seventy per cent, had been vested (Appendix 2 127) in the Mandatory Power, and accordingly reverted to the State of Israel as its legal heir. The greater part of this 70 per cent consisted of the Negev (desert). From the "Government of Palestine, Survey of Palestine, 1946, British Government Printer, p. 257.)" http://word-fromjerusalem.com/wp-content/uploads/2008/11/the-case-for-israel-appendix2.pdf

Moral Equivalence = Moral Relativism; No Truth and No lies = No good and no Evil

This is one of the most potent ways to destroy history, reality, human dignity and peace. Under moral relativism, only force can dominate. Now there is the force created by the media.

TerVol was in grandeur over this one as he set termite colonies loose. Nothing can create ambiguity in a people as well as this bias. The propaganda is rapidly spread by creating a myth with a technique called "moral equivalence" or the "cycle of violence." It is also known as moral relativism—an easy out for those without facts or taking the time to view history.

A cycle means symmetry, automatic tit-for-tat, absolutely mindless action and reaction, in which all sides, and none, can be held morally responsible. Was the American Revolution a cycle of violence? Were the Americans morally equivalent to the King of England? Was world War II a "cycle of violence"? Were the Democracies morally equivalent to the Nazis?

But attack and defense, terror and counter-terror, incitement and fear are neither symmetric nor morally equivalent. This moral equivalence is a form of perfected circularity, a dishonest solipsism of how things work.

A clearer understanding of a society (all societies have criminals) is not judged by crimes of a few, but on the basis of how that society deals with its criminals and what heroes it celebrates.

Israeli thugs and murderers are denounced roundly and emphatically by Israeli society, caught quickly, and jailed fast by the government. Nor are they released five minutes later. They are skunks, not heroes of the Zionist movement and the Jewish people.

In contrast, Arab thugs and murderers of Israelis are celebrated and feted widely by the entire Arab world society, in their media, by their leaders. Terrorists are sheltered methodically from justice and rewarded generously. The Arab terrorists are released from Arab prisons just as quickly as international attentions turn elsewhere – there is an infamous "revolving door" record of the P.A.

Israel has sought conflict resolution, not jihad. Israel wants to resolve the conflict through compromise, not end the conflict by annihilation of the enemy. Israel wishes to live at peace and cooperate with its Arab neighbors and has no desire to conquer the Arab and Islamic nations from Tunisia to Indonesia.

For journalists or politicians to equate those two societies as morally equivalent is disturbingly shallow, possibly mendacious, probably meretricious, and abusive of their bully pulpits.

Creating this symmetry provides false hope for peace by way of creating a mirror image of the democratic society with Judeo-Christian values and the Islamic concept of supremacy and goal of subjugating the world under Sharia.

The press and some politicians often portray Arabs as unwillingly locked into a vicious tit-for-tat loop. The MSM by in large, minimize coverage of the murderous attacks on innocent Israeli civilians and ignore the continuous incitement that fills PA school books, mosques and media. They lapse into a repetitive stupor that all that is needed is to break this unrighteous cycle is to recognize the narrative and fears of "the other." With this imagined symmetry, they have convinced themselves, there is a basis for peace.

Jeanne Kirkpatrick wrote a brilliant essay on "The Myth of Moral Equivalence," asserting that *when there is a society with no right and no wrong, no victim and no villain, no distinction between a friend and an enemy, that society is frozen from moving forward and defending itself.*

Philosopher, **Sir Dr. Rabbi Jonathan Sacks** was clear that, logically, it is impossible to defend Western freedoms with a basis in moral relativisms. If everything is relatively equal, why defend one set of values which can claim no moral superiority? What would inspire people to make sacrifice for the "common good" or the freedoms we should hold dear?

Tervol's termite propaganda dissolves a democratic society's cohesiveness and its resolve in the justness of its cause for existence. What cause could be better than another if one side boldly declares the narratives are relative and equal?

This is well expressed, particularly regarding our exceptionalism, in an article by **Daniel Greenfield,** "Better Than Them" in October 18, 2011.

He exposes a thinking that produces a suicidal urge not to fight back from any aggressive behavior. Greenfield explains that self-destructive Jews, in particular rationalize when all other arguments for why we can't fight back have been exhausted. It is the way of the termite: "We are better than them." "Fight back? But then we'd be no better than them."

"We are better than they are!" is the argument put forward so often by those aware that our society is better off for not being like movements committing crimes against humanity. This implies that we should not behave like them. We should, however, strive to retain all the freedoms around us, the accomplishments, the achievements, the knowledge we have gained and the society we have built.

Our laws were crafted to protect these achievements, the opportunities, the exceptionalism of the individual from the government, and that of the nation from internal and external enemies. The laws have no individual life apart from the culture of the nation that created them and maintains them. No mere document can safeguard rights and freedoms that a culture has been persuaded not to value, and no culture that does not value them is deserving of their protection if such protection has the cumulative effect of destroying those same rights and freedoms.

Against external enemies there is the war of armed conflict, technological conflict, economic competition and geographic positioning.

Freedom isn't just defended on the battlefield. By the time things get that bad, the damage will be so much costlier to contain. We defend our culture internally every day by defending the culture that makes it possible.

Against the internal enemy there is the termite culture war, the war of ideas, people connectedness and institutions. It is the task of the culture warriors (termite inspectors) to rebuild those connections so that the culture understands itself. People are not some random mass defined only by passports or identity cards or place of birth— the people are the keepers of the flame of their culture. This need not be a matter of birth. Immigrants can be among the greatest heroes and natives among the greatest traitors.

Anyone committed to complete control or the total destruction of the culture, in concrete or abstract terms, in the immediate present or the indefinite future, by definition, is treasonous.

Ideas are sterile without a culture and media to propagate them. If the termites weaken the structure of a culture and infect the media, the ideas become orphans and the structure collapses.

We, as a free people, rely on a free press to vet our candidates and balance the issues. In totalitarian societies, whether communist or Islamic, the people know their media is state run, but Americans think we have a free media.

It has been suggested that our media is state manipulated, sometimes voluntarily. Those who toe the party line get access to government briefings, stories, promotions, scoops, private interviews, jobs, and get invited to dinners, asked to be on TV and get to write guest columns in prestigious papers.

Tolerance and civil rights need to be defended. Any form of tolerance which leads to its own destruction is not tolerance. Tolerance of intolerance is morally repugnant as well as stupid. It is psychopathically self-destructive. All healthy entities, whether biological, organizational or intellectual contain the means for their own continuance and self-perpetuation. Any entity which does not support its perpetuation, is terminally termite infested and must be treated as such. Not to do so is political suicide.

Another way moral equivalence weakens us is explained by **Rabbi Shraga** Silverstein who postulated, "To tolerate everything is to respect nothing."

Lawfare. This is "Legal" Propaganda and War

The legal arguments of the PLO have been removed one after another, but the victimization propaganda and the repetition by the media assures it will stick in the minds of many.

In a lengthy trial that ended before the **Court of Appeal of Versailles**, March 13, 2013. The Court of Appeal stated Israel was within its rights because "Neither the Palestinian Authority nor the PLO are States, therefore international laws applied to sovereign states who signed on to these laws do not apply to them." The Geneva Conventions and the Hague Convention of 1907 simply, are not applicable. http://feedburner.google.com/fb/a/mailverify?uri=drzz/Pxvu&loc=fr_FR

Tom lamented, "International courts are not above suspicion for following law objectively. Often there is a conflict between an international law and sovereign law or is not signed on to by all countries. At the outset, lawsuits are often big news. Results of rulings are time-distant from accusations and the world public has dropped interest. But the media has repeatedly imbedded the indictments into the public consciousness. Additionally, not all international coverage through different countries has the same values that the West does and can be parsed for propaganda. Lawfare is intended to be very expensive and smaller countries often cannot sustain those expenses. On the other hand, it becomes free propaganda for the powerful."

How the media sullies its own reputation to knowledgeable people

Electronic and print media can repeat or proffer a slant or a blame or an accusation with the result of molding public opinion. This is propaganda.

Instead of P.P.C. (poisonously politically correct), this is the **"They claim"** = T.C. technique. This rarely gives credible attribution, balance or sources.

1. They claim (T.C.) that Israel is the core of the conflict in the ME and to be rid of Israel is to be rid of war.
2. T.C. that the creation of another Arab state will stabilize the region and the EU will have better access to the Arab world.

3. T.C. the West must be convinced that another Arab State with Jerusalem as its capital and full return of refugees and abandonment of Israel's Zionist character will bring peace.

4. T.C. that Zionism and the Israeli's government is making a Jewish State (Judaizing) out of the Jewish State, as though that was something bad.

5. T.C. that democracy cannot coexist with Judaism but can with Christianity or Islam.

6. T.C. that any critique of Islam, its history or Mohammed is blasphemy and hate speech that must be punished in law.

7. T.C. that laws against anti-Semitism are not in the West's interests and that these laws were to create guilt that keeps the governments subservient to Zionist interests.

8. T.C. that the Israeli government is provoking Islamic terrorism.

9. T.C. it would be a better world with no borders.

10. T.C. rock throwing, arson and hand grenades are "peaceful protest".

Ad Nauseum.

There is more.

APPENDIX I - A Palestinese Lexicon

A Palestinese Lexicon by Philippe Assouline

timgoz.blogspot.com/2012/09/a-palestinese-lexicon.html Sep 24, 2012

This describes the use of words to color a position. Often when Arabs say one thing, we don't get that it means something different to them than to us. That is called either poor communication on one side or deceptive, emotional language jiu-jitsu. People reading these words are placed off balance because they do not know that we use those words to mean something very different. Here are some of the Arab/Muslim declarations and distortions of our reality, as Mr. Assouline cutely sees them. See how many you can identify in daily press releases:

1. **Aboriginal/Native**: Any non-Jew, preferably Arab, who has immigrated to Israel/Palestine within the last 150 years or is a remnant of Arab colonial conquests. For example, Yasser Arafat and Edward Said who were lamented in Egypt call themselves "Native" Palestinians.

2. **Apartheid Wall**: A separation fence erected in response to countless terror attacks in order to protect both Jews and Muslims from suicide bombings as a manifestation of "Zionist Aggression."

3. **Checkpoint**: A cruel and malicious security measure erected in the West Bank in response to years of deadly suicide bombings, to be equated with the worst forms of human torture. Not to be confused with security checkpoints at airports and international borders which, though identical in the inconveniences they cause, are perfectly acceptable.

4. **Civilian**: An armed Palestinian terrorist in the act of planning or staging a terror attack who is targeted or killed by Israel.

5. **Demonstration**: The violent rioting by Palestinian mobs including the throwing of stones and Molotov cocktails at soldiers and civilians and the firing of machine guns granted to Palestinians pursuant to "Peace" accords. In any other context, the peaceful distribution by vegans of leaflets printed on hemp paper.

7. **Fascist:** Anyone who questions the Palestinians' exclusive historical claims. Interchangeable with the term Orientalist.

8. **Frustration**: Murderous anti-Semitism that directly precedes "Resistance."

9. **Genocide**: The deliberate campaign by "Zionists" to exterminate Palestinian Arabs which has resulted in the explosion of the Arab-Palestinian population from just 6-700,000 in 1948 to over 6 million around the Middle East today, including over one million Israeli Palestinians represented in the Israeli parliament.

10. **Jerusalem**: An Occupied Arab capital and central focal point of Arab culture and aspirations for 3000 years, despite the fact that — unlike Cordoba, Baghdad, Damascus, Mecca, Cairo, Timbuktu or Dearborn Michigan — it was never an Arab capital or central focal point of Arab culture. Also, an area bereft of any significance to Jewish people or Jewish history. See also Bethlehem, Rachel's Tomb, Hebron, Shiloh and the Brown Derby Deli.

11. **Jews:** People who descend from Khazzar Turkic peoples and have no connection whatsoever to ancient Judeans or Israelites who were in fact "Palestinians." Also, Jews are the group of people that supplies Palestinian propaganda with its theories, mouthpieces and arguments. E.g. **Norman Finkelstein** is a "Jew"; **Ehud Barak** is not a "Jew".

12. **Judaism:** An abstract concept of liberal, pro-Palestinian ethics that is no way tied to 3,500 years of Jewish history on the land of Israel. Not to be confused with the religion of Jesus or the Prophets who were, of course, "Palestinian."

13. **Judea:** A made up political term for the territory known since classical antiquity… as in "the West Bank."

14. **Land for Peace**: The process by Israel is deprived of both land and peace.

15. **Martyr**: Any person who dies while killing or attempting to kill "Zionist" civilians having a picnic.

16. **Massacre**: Any imagined or real, accidental or deliberately caused death of one or more Arabs in an armed fight usually started by said terrorists. Also, the Arabs use this term for every act of Jewish self-defense, ever.

17. **Occupation**: The perpetual state of Palestinian politics, regardless of the absence of Israeli soldiers in certain Arab areas, and an excuse for every Arab excess including public domestic violence. It hides the fact that 96-98% of Arabs calling themselves Palestinians are governed by their own sort of elected leaders.

18. **Oppression**: Jewish self-determination and any reminders thereof. E.g. a border control between Gaza and Israel is "Oppression." Also, anything that a Arab activist doesn't like. E.g., that Hamas lost the war it caused in 2009 is a form of "Oppression."

19. **Palestinian State**: A geographic and political entity that is to live side by side as well as over and instead of the "Zionist Entity."

20. **Peace**: The process by which Israel voluntarily ethnically cleanses every last Jewish person from territory won in a defensive war in exchange for increased terrorism, demonization, European and Turkish meddling and summits at the White House.

21. **Peoplehood**: The state of every grouping of individuals that share a history, language, culture and geographic origin, except when they are Jewish.

22. **Racism**: Any expression of Jewish will that is not a parroting of Arab claims. For example, it is racism to insist on teaching the Holocaust.

23. **Racist**: The state of any act, event, person or thing that accepts in any way, tacit or explicit, the existence of Israel or interrupts albeit temporarily the world's obsessive preoccupation with Palestinians' claims. Also, an adjective which is always appropriate before any word, whether referring to an object, abstract concept or person related to "Zionists," e.g., the racist pill-cam that saved my mother in law's life was made in the "Zionist Entity" by "War Criminals."

24. **Refugee**: Any Arab anywhere in the world who claims that one of his relatives was forced to leave Israel as a result of a war started by Arabs despite pleas to the contrary from the nascent State of Israel in 1948. Jews expelled from Arab states in 1948 as a result of the same war are not to be included in this term.

25. **Resistance**: The act of deliberately murdering Israeli school children or other innocents in restaurants, buses, nurseries or other areas, or the firing of rockets without provocation. E.g., massacring 11 Israeli athletes who were napping in their rooms at the Munich Olympics was called "Resistance."

26. **Zionism**: The inchoate and indefinable global movement for evil that is the cause of all ills plaguing the Arab world since 1300 AD including Mauritania, Southern Yemen and Malmo, Sweden, and, conveniently, also the cause of the meltdown of the Western financial system. Expressed by such pernicious phenomena as the credit crisis of 2008, slow Syrian internet connections and trained sharks operating as spies off of the Egyptian coast.

27. **Zionist Aggression**: The response, after ample warning, to unprovoked "Resistance" against unarmed women and children and/or any act of self-defense when carried out by Jews. E.g., it is "Zionist Aggression" that the Israel police officer shot a Palestinian terrorist attempting to run over carpooling Israelis with his bulldozer.

28. **Zionist Entity**: A colonial, illegitimate and evil collection of people which, as a form of "Propaganda" and "Racism," regularly produces scientific breakthroughs that alleviate human suffering and improve life everywhere.

Now that we have learned terms used to deceive by Anti-Israel propaganda, we can get back to the formal propaganda techniques.

APPENDIX II

These additional, certified **PROPAGANDA TECHNIQUES** should remind us how easily we can be fooled.

1. Ad nauseam: Using tireless repetition of an idea. An idea, especially a simple slogan, that is repeated enough times, may begin to be taken as the truth. This approach works best when media sources are limited or controlled by the propagator.

2. Appeal to prejudice: Using loaded or emotive terms to attach value or moral goodness to believing the proposition. Used in biased or misleading ways.

3. Bandwagon and "inevitable-victory": appeals attempt to persuade the target audience to join in and take the course of action that "everyone else is taking".

4. Inevitable victory: invites those not already on the bandwagon to join those already on the road to certain victory. Those already or at least partially on the bandwagon are reassured that staying aboard is their best course of action.

5. Join the crowd: This technique reinforces people's natural desire to be on the winning side. This technique is used to convince the audience that a program is an expression of an irresistible mass movement and that it is in their best interest to join.

6. Beautiful people: The type of propaganda that deals with famous

people or depicts attractive, happy people. This makes other people think that if they buy a product or follow a certain ideology, they too will be happy or successful.

7. A Cult of personality: arises when an individual uses mass media to create an idealized and heroic public image, often through unquestioning flattery and praise. The hero personality then advocates the positions the propagandist desires to promote. For example, modern propagandists hire popular personalities to promote their ideas and/or products.

8. Demonizing the enemy: Making individuals from the opposing nation or from a different ethnic group, or those who support the opposing viewpoint appear to be subhuman (e.g., the Vietnam War-era term "gooks" for National Front for the Liberation of South Vietnam aka Viet Cong, or "VC", soldiers), worthless or immoral, through suggestion or false accusations. Dehumanizing is also a term used almost synonymously with demonizing, the latter usually serves as an aspect of the former, leading to delegitmization.

9. Disinformation: The creation or deletion of information from public records for the purpose of making a false record of an event or the actions of a person or organization, including outright forgery of photographs, motion pictures, broadcasts and sound recordings as well as printed documents. A powerful approach is to invert the timeline of events.

10. Euphoria: The use of an event that generates happiness, or using an appealing event to boost morale. Euphoria can be created by declaring a holiday, making luxury items available, or mounting a military parade with marching bands, big concerts, with select messages.

11. Fear, uncertainty and doubt: An attempt to influence public perception by disseminating negative and dubious/false information designed to undermine the credibility of their beliefs.

12. Flag-waving: making an approach patriotic as opposed to any other approach.

13. Glittering generalities Emotionally appealing words applied to a pro-

duct or idea, but that present no concrete argument or analysis. Also known as PT Barnum effect.

14. Half-truth: A deceptive statement, which may come in several forms. The statement might be partly true, the statement may be totally true but only part of the whole truth, or it may utilize a deceptive element, such as improper punctuation, or double meaning, especially if the intent is to evade, blame or misrepresent the truth.

15. Silky deception: If a reader believes that a paid advertisement is in fact a news item, the message the advertiser is trying to communicate will be more easily "believed" or "internalized".

16. Labeling: By creating a "label" or "category" or "faction" of a population, it is much easier to make an example of these larger bodies, because they can uplift or defame the mark without incurring legal-defamation. "Liberal" is a dysphemism intended to diminish or enhance the perceived credibility of a particular mark. By taking a displeasing argument presented by a mark, the propagandist can quote that person and then attack (all) "liberals" in an attempt to both (1) create a political battle-ax of unaccountable aggression and (2) diminish the quality of the mark. Labeling can be thought of as a sub-set of Guilt by association, another potentially logical fallacy.

17. Love bombing: Often used to recruit members to a cult or ideology by having a group of individuals cut off a person from their existing social support and replace it with members of the group who bombard the person with affection in an attempt to isolate the person from their prior beliefs and value system.

18. Creating Disapproval: Many politicians frequently stretch or break the truth. This technique is used to persuade a target audience to disapprove of an action or idea by suggesting the idea is popular with groups hated, feared, or held in contempt by the target audience. Thus, if a group that supports a certain policy is led to believe that subversive people support the same policy, then the members of the group may decide to change their original position. This is a form of bad logic, where a is said to include X, and b is

said to include X, therefore, a = b. This technique is used to persuade a target audience to disapprove of an action or idea by suggesting the idea is popular with groups hated, feared, or held in contempt by the target audience. Favorable generalities are used to provide simple answers to complex social, political, economic or military problems.

19. Straw Man: An informal fallacy based on misrepresentation of an opponent's position.

20. Testimonials: are quotations, in or out of context, cited to support or reject a given policy, action, program or personality. The reputation or the role (expert, respected individual) is what is most important.

21. Irrelevance: Presenting data or issues that, while compelling, are irrelevant to the argument at hand, and then claiming it validates and stereotypes. Although slogans may be enlisted to support reasoned ideas, in practice they tend to act only as emotional appeals. Opponents of the US's invasion and occupation of Iraq use the slogan "blood for oil" to suggest the invasion and its human losses was done to access Iraq's oil riches. On the other hand, supporters who argue the U.S. should continue to fight in Iraq use the slogan "cut and run" to suggest withdrawal is cowardly or weak.

22. Graphic propaganda: This includes war posters and faux-tography. This might include portraying enemies with stereotyped racial features. This technique attempts to arouse prejudices in an audience by labeling the object of the propaganda campaign as something the target audience fears, hates, loathes, or finds undesirable. For instance, reporting on a foreign country or social group may focus on stereotypical traits the reader expects, even though they are far from being representative. This technique is used when the idea the propagandist wants to plant would seem less credible if explicitly stated. The concept is instead repeatedly assumed or implied. Frequently Astroturf groups or front groups are used to deliver the message.

23. Association: This is a technique that involves projecting the positive or negative qualities of one person, entity, object, or value onto

another. Often highly visual, this technique utilizes symbols (e.g. swastikas, hijabs or kaffiyahs) superimposed over other visual images (e.g. logos).

24. Virtue words: Words in the value system of the target audience that produce a positive image when attached to a person or issue. Peace, happiness, security, wise leadership, freedom, jihad, martyrdom, "The Truth", etc.

25. Selective presentation of facts: This is bias by omission to encourage a particular synthesis, or using loaded messages to produce an emotional rather than rational response to the information presented. The desired result is a change of the attitude toward the subject in the target audience.

26. Narrowing the sources: Done by omitting credible, opposing points of view. Often using the military perspective, prevents using experts to provide insights into the situation from another perspective.

27. Perpetuating known falsehoods with no proof or refutation.

Simon says:

About now we can believe how vulnerable we can be.

But even political propaganda can only succeed with the support of the media and a susceptible audience. Søren Kierkegaard, the great Danish philosopher had remarked that there are two ways to allow yourself to be fooled. One is to believe what isn't true; the other is to refuse to believe what is true.

The words of politicians and journalists have been twisted from their understood meaning to control the uninformed. Propaganda twists history, inverts time sequences and unhinges facts. When an enemy wants to destroy a country or group they first delegitimize them by stealing their identity and then claim that no legitimate identity, the don't have a right to self-defense. For instance, the concept of "Self-determination" cannot be realized by rejecting all offers of peace and deliberately robbing the Jewish people of its history instead. Even the legal concept of self-determination does not trump sovereignty or peace.

As Demosthenes asked, why is it that a sane man would let another man's words rather than his deeds tell him who is at peace and who is at war with him?"

Propaganda can become libel in the United States. This libel is what the KKK did to blacks in America. This is what the Nazis did. This is what Lenin did in Russia. This is what Mao did in China. This is what the Japanese did to the Chinese. They steal legitimacy and identity.

This was the first step that enemies of democracy took against the tiny democracy of Israel, to steal identity and legitimacy. It is critical for us to know how this has been attempted. It is critical because lies that happened first to the Jews never stops with the Jews. No wonder there's been such a problem in uncovering this part of the mystery: They lie, we don't deny, innocent civilians die.

What else could the public know without taking the time and effort to go to reliable alternative sources of information like a fact checked internet? Without reliable sources, how does one find out that their identity is being stolen?

Jewish identity has been locked into Zionism for 3,000 years. We must find out what our canary in the mine, "Zionism", is. How has Zionism's public identity been skewed and perverted?

If U.S. exceptionalism, our identity, is perverted to the public as something bad, we could lose our constitutional democracy. Here is where it has hit home. We have to be aware.

"If a nation thinks of its past with contempt, it may well contemplate its future with despair; it perishes through moral suicide." Rabbi J.H. Hertz.

We must dig in and learn how Israel and Zionism can be our working model. First, of how our identities can be stolen and secondly the rational duty we have to preserve them. The fate of the USA depends on this clarity.

We can do this!